For a Radical
Higher Education

SRHE and Open University Press Imprint
General Editor: Heather Eggins

Current titles include:

Catherine Bargh *et al.*: *University Leadership*
Ronald Barnett: *Higher Education*
Ronald Barnett: *The Idea of Higher Education*
Ronald Barnett: *The Limits of Competence*
Ronald Barnett: *Realizing the University in an age of supercomplexity*
Tony Becher and Paul R. Trowler: *Academic Tribes and Territories (2nd edn)*
Neville Bennett *et al.*: *Skills Development in Higher Education and Employment*
John Biggs: *Teaching for Quality Learning at University*
David Boud *et al.* (eds): *Using Experience for Learning*
David Boud and Nicky Solomon (eds): *Work-based Learning*
Tom Bourner *et al.* (eds): *New Directions in Professional Higher Education*
Anne Brockbank and Ian McGill: *Facilitating Reflective Learning in Higher Education*
Ann Brooks and Alison Mackinnon (eds): *Gender and the Restructured University*
Sally Brown and Angela Glasner (eds): *Assessment Matters in Higher Education*
John Cowan: *On Becoming an Innovative University Teacher*
Gerard Delanty: *Challenging Knowledge*
Chris Duke: *Managing the Learning University*
Gillian Evans: *Academics and the Real World*
Andrew Hannan and Harold Silver: *Innovating in Higher Education*
David Istance *et al.*: *International Perspectives on Lifelong Learning*
Norman Jackson and Helen Lund (eds): *Benchmarking for Higher Education*
Merle Jacob and Tomas Hellström (eds): *The Future of Knowledge Production in the Academy*
Peter Knight: *Being a Teacher in Higher Education*
Peter Knight and Paul Trowler: *Departmental Leadership in Higher Education*
Mary Lea and Barry Stierer (eds): *Student Writing in Higher Education*
Ian McNay (ed.): *Higher Education and its Communities*
Moira Peelo and Terry Wareham (eds): *Failing Students in Higher Education*
Craig Prichard: *Making Managers in Universities and Colleges*
Michael Prosser and Keith Trigwell: *Understanding Learning and Teaching*
John Richardson: *Researching Student Learning*
Stephen Rowland: *The Enquiring University Teacher*
Maggi Savin-Baden: *Problem-based Learning in Higher Education*
Peter Scott (ed.): *The Globalization of Higher Education*
Peter Scott: *The Meanings of Mass Higher Education*
Anthony Smith and Frank Webster (eds): *The Postmodern University?*
Colin Symes and John McIntyre (eds): *Working Knowledge*
Peter G. Taylor: *Making Sense of Academic Life*
Richard Taylor *et al.*: *For a Radical Higher Education: After Postmodernism*
Susan Toohey: *Designing Courses for Higher Education*
Paul R. Trowler (ed.): *Higher Education Policy and Institutional Change*
Melanie Walker (ed.): *Reconstructing Professionalism in University Teaching*
David Warner and David Palfreyman (eds): *The State of UK Higher Education*
Diana Woodward and Karen Ross: *Managing Equal Opportunities in Higher Education*

For a Radical Higher Education

After Postmodernism

Richard Taylor,
Jean Barr and
Tom Steele

The Society for Research into Higher Education
& Open University Press

Published by SRHE and
Open University Press
Celtic Court
22 Ballmoor
Buckingham
MK18 1XW

email: enquiries@openup.co.uk
world wide web: www.openup.co.uk

and

325 Chestnut Street
Philadelphia, PA 19106, USA

First Published 2002

A catalogue record of this book is available from the British Library

ISBN 0 335 20868 1 (pb)   0 335 20869 X (hb)

Library of Congress Cataloging-in-Publication Data
Taylor, R.K.S. (Richard K.S.)
    For a radical higher education after postmodernism / Richard Taylor,
Jean Barr, and Tom Steele.
        p. cm.
    Includes bibliographical references and index.
    ISBN 0-335-20869-X – ISBN 0-335-20868-1 (pbk.)
    1. Education, Higher – Social aspects – Great Britain.   2. Postmodernism
and higher education – Great Britain.   I. Barr, Jean, 1944–   II. Steele, Tom,
1946–   III. Title.

LC191.8.G7 T39   2002
378.41–dc21   2001059326

Typeset by Graphicraft Limited, Hong Kong
Printed by St Edmundsbury Press, Bury St Edmunds, Suffolk

Contents

Preface

The idea for this book came originally from our increasing unease and dissatisfaction with accounts of and prescriptions for higher education policy in the United Kingdom, and in other comparable developed societies, which were, broadly speaking, postmodernist in their approach. When we began to talk seriously about this we also agreed that this was, for us, one manifestation of a much broader perspective on contemporary society, which we believed to be largely mistaken and frequently reactionary, although often unintentionally so.

Elizabeth Wilson has referred to the 'promiscuity' of the term 'postmodern', which has led to 'an endless debate as to what it means, and a persistent doubt as to its value, combined with a refusal to leave it alone'.[1] At the risk of being accused of flogging a dead horse (after all, as Mike Featherstone[2] pointed out in 1988, postmodernism had already been pronounced dead as early as 1975), we make no apologies for engaging with it in this book. For what is remarkable about postmodernism is that despite intimations of its demise, it simply will not lie down. Taken up by journalists and advertisers as well as academics, it has become the fashionable term for the *Zeitgeist* or mood of the time. This indeed may be the most useful way to view it, says Wilson; that is, as a style, mood or sensibility, but 'relatively lacking in explanatory power and certainly in moral or political values'. Moreover, '[i]ts very widespread usage and the definitional discourse that it has generated may also have obscured trends and events that could not be successfully linked to it, so that it has occluded as much as it has illuminated'.[3] That is our standpoint in this book: we seek to illuminate these trends and events obscured by postmodernist analyses of higher education and to propose a future for higher education after postmodernism that is ethically, epistemologically and politically defensible.

This book is written from a 'committed' perspective. We believe there is a paradox in the increasingly consensual and uncritical culture and politics of contemporary society, and the simultaneous deepening of social and economic inequalities and intensification of the control of corporate capital on a global scale. Higher education, although of course a micro-cosm in the wider scheme of things, occupies a pivotal position at the centre of the so-called 'knowledge society'.[4] Our argument here is that the epistemological, cultural and fiscal crisis of higher education is already leading to the effective incorporation of the academy into the world of cor-porate capital and its accompanying ideology. Much policy analysis of higher education falls within a proclaimed postmodernist frame of reference and, often by default, facilitates this process.

We argue in this book that the fundamental tasks of radical educators in higher education must be to counter these arguments, expose the fallacies of such analyses and reassert a progressive and revitalized commitment to a higher education that is, in outlook, critical, sceptical and concerned with 'really useful knowledge' addressed to the lived realities of contemporary late capitalist society. The university should retain and extend its role as a site for the open and vigorous contestation of knowledge and values.

All of us have backgrounds in adult and higher education and have been active in a variety of social movements concerned with education and social change. We also have different but we hope complementary disciplinary perspectives. The book thus attempts to address the issues from several disciplinary standpoints: political and social theory, philosophy, cultural studies and contemporary history. At a different level, we have tried too to draw on socialist, feminist and libertarian theoretical perspectives to inform the discussion.

The scope of the book is thus wide and the approach both analytical and polemical. We hope that it contributes both to discussions of policy orienta-tion in higher education and to the analysis of the relationship between higher education and the wider society.

Although Richard Taylor has undertaken the bulk of the writing, this has been a genuinely collaborative venture and, in that sense, is collect-ively owned. However, the structure and authorship responsibility require clarification.

Part 1 provides an introductory overview. Part 2, which comprises Chapters 2, 3 and 4, is an analytical and contextual framework for Part 3 (Chapters 5, 6, 7 and 8), which concentrates more specifically on policy and practice issues in higher education. Part 4, the concluding chapter on radical perspectives for the new higher education, draws the arguments together and focuses on some of the positive aspects of the contemporary context.

Chapter 1 is written by Richard Taylor. In Chapter 2, Richard Taylor and Jean Barr discuss the *political* context, with a special emphasis on the feminist contribution to the debate. Chapter 3, by Tom Steele and Jean Barr, analyses the evolution of the Enlightenment perspective, the pre-vailing contemporary critiques of this tradition, and argues the case for a *revaluation* and reassertion of some of its core values and approaches in the current policy context. In Chapter 4, Jean Barr, drawing on philosophical ideas and feminist theory, argues for the importance of ontology, and the essential connections between the academy and lived experience in the outside world.

In Chapters 5, 6 and 7, Richard Taylor focuses more specifically on the policy debate in higher education. Chapter 5, which has some input from Jean Barr, provides an analytical overview of the evolution of higher education policy since the 1960s. Chapter 6 discusses the contested concepts of 'lifelong learning' and Chapter 7 three of the key areas in this contestation. These chapters detail the ideological terrain on which policy formulation and its implementation take place. The persistent themes running through all these debates are ideological contestation and contradiction and the fallacies inherent in much consensual contemporary analysis. Chapter 8, also by Richard Taylor, looks critically at one important aspect of recent university expansion: professional and vocational education.

Chapter 9, written collectively and following on from the foregoing analysis, summarizes the radical reorientation of higher education policy we advocate and focuses on some of the areas for the positive development of an open and plural concept of the university.

We hope that this book contributes to the ongoing debate about these policy and political questions. Despite all the problems, this is a good time to be involved in lifelong learning and higher education, not least because of the potential for change. We believe that there are real possibilities for developing the current agenda along progressive lines but, equally, if these are to be realized, a reassertion and rearticulation of socialist values is necessary.

We are grateful to several colleagues at the Universities of Leeds and Glasgow for advice and sometimes quite critical comments; in particular, we would like to thank Denise Johnson of the University of Leeds, who produced the manuscript, working from some untidy drafts, with efficiency and good humour.

Richard Taylor, Jean Barr and Tom Steele
Pooley Bridge, Cumbria

Notes

1. Elizabeth Wilson (2001) *The Contradictions of Culture: Cities, Culture, Women*. London: Sage, p. 2.
2. Mike Featherstone (1988) In pursuit of the postmodern: introduction, *Theory, Culture and Society*, 5(2–3): 195–216.
3. Wilson, op. cit., p. 13.
4. In the text, we refer both to 'higher education' and 'universities'. The focus of our attention is the overall system of higher education within which, in our view, universities in the United Kingdom as elsewhere are normally culturally dominant. There are exceptions, however, as exemplified in the influence of the polytechnic institutions, structures and values in many societies in the years since the 1980s.

Part 1

Introduction

1

The Postmodernist Position on Higher Education

Postmodernism is held, by its advocates, to be the pervasive spirit of our age. It is not, in the words of one authority, 'an ideology or position we can choose to subscribe to or not, post-modernity is precisely our condition: it is our historical fate to be living now . . . [and the pervasiveness of post-modernity is due to] the overall failure of that experiment in social living we can term "modernity"'.[1] Despite its claims to pervasiveness, there is a coyness about attempting to define its exact nature. 'To be consistently post-modern', as Usher and Edwards point out, 'one should never call oneself a postmodern. There is a self-referential irony about this which we find ludically apt'.[2]

Despite their reluctance to engage in any potentially 'totalizing' delineation of postmodernism, its advocates are insistent that it has its focal point in the perceived failure of modernism, particularly as characterized by and through the Enlightenment, rationalist project. Whatever intellectual slipperiness there may be in the wider terrain of postmodernist thinking, the perceived inadequacy of modernism and its 'grand narratives' are at the core of what postmodernists term their discourse (although normally, as we go on to argue, we prefer to see this as their *ideology*).

The aim of this book is to examine critically this postmodern intellectual edifice as it applies, or is held to apply, in one specific context in one specific society: higher education in the United Kingdom in the last half of the twentieth century, particularly in the period from around 1980 to the early years of the twenty-first century. It is our contention, as the title of this book implies, that postmodern analysis and mindset – while seductive and in some respects innovative and salutary – is, at base, intellectually deficient, and that its adoption leads in our view to ultimately reactionary consequences. We shall argue for a 'return to reason', for an alternative, radical reassessment of the roles and purposes of the university in the twenty-first century. We maintain that the postmodern perspective is inadequate in two fundamental, separate but related respects. First, postmodernism is a flawed social analysis, which leads to a series of intellectual and political fallacies.

This analysis is applied, among many other things, to higher education in terms of its present configuration and likely development, and the resultant diagnosis is, predictably, analytically flawed. It is an inadequate and largely unhelpful characterization of the (very real) dilemmas of higher education. Secondly, despite the protestations of its advocates to the contrary, postmodernism implicitly embodies a clear series of value judgements, even though many of them are couched in the sterility of moral relativism and a reactive 'anything goes' attitude. We shall argue that this is, again, an untenable stance in general – in moral, political and social terms – and, in the particular context of higher education, it is especially, almost ludicrously (rather than ludically) inapt.

The aims of this introductory chapter are, first, to summarize, albeit somewhat schematically, postmodern views of higher education, and then to put forward the broad hypotheses that map the main inadequacies, as we perceive them, of the postmodern position.

Our approach is thus both analytical and polemical. We do not maintain that postmodernism is wholly misguided, that it is without intellectual appeal or foundation. On the contrary, like all significant ideological formations – indeed, like almost all 'grand narratives' – it has many salient criticisms to make of the established orthodoxies, both political and intellectual. It offers many necessary correctives to what has all too often been an overly deterministic and oppressive socialist tradition. Moreover, as any honest observer of the contemporary scene would acknowledge, socialism as it has been known and practised in all its forms is now, in Terry Eagleton's words, 'probably more plagued and notional an idea than at any stage in its turbulent career'.[3] However, we believe that postmodernism represents essentially a counsel of despair, based upon a flawed analysis. There are alternative analyses which this book attempts to delineate and which we believe offer not only a more intellectually rigorous perspective, but also a politics that will avoid relinquishing 'the vision of a just society, and (acquiescing) in the appalling mess which is the contemporary world'.[4]

Before launching into this analysis, however, we wish to summarize briefly the main elements of the postmodern perspective on higher education, within the overall context of postmodern thinking generally.

Postmodernism has many roots and many disciplinary and intellectual articulations.[5] In philosophy, history and the social sciences – the areas which relate most closely to our concerns over higher education – the starting points are, arguably, two-fold. First, an analysis of the social and, in particular, economic context of the last two decades of the twentieth century, encapsulated under the label of post-Fordism. And, second, a rejection, through the bruising experience of a violent and disillusioning century, of all the 'big ideas', the totalizing explanations stemming from the Enlightenment and the rise of industrial society: liberalism and, in particular, socialism.

Both of these factors, as depicted by postmodernist analysts of higher education, have a direct and shattering effect on any of the traditional

notions of the university, leading more than one commentator, for example, to observe that 'we have to recognise that the university is a *ruined
institution*'[6] and that 'the Western university is at an end. But a new university can arise'.[7] Why are these analyses held to have such profound impacts
upon the university, both conceptually and in practice? Universities, after
all, have an almost unprecedented longevity in Western societies. Why should
the merchants of doom, so to speak, have become suddenly so prominent
and vociferous? This is especially ironic, given that, by common consent,
we live in a society increasingly dominated by knowledge, where education
and training are assuming unparalleled importance, and the numbers of
learners engaged in university study have increased exponentially in recent
years. The dimensions of this expansion and its policy ramifications are
discussed in detail in Chapters 5 and 6. Here, the intention is to explore
postmodernist explanations and analyses of this phenomenon.

We should begin, as noted, with post-Fordism. Post-Fordism is both a
sociological and an economic analysis of contemporary trends in Western
society. It is not, however, in any sense an innocent analysis: no analysis is
ever value-free, but this has particular ideological antecedents and overtones. At one level, it is clearly drawing reasonable conclusions from incon-
trovertible empirical data. It *is* the case that 'the class formations produced
by the industrial revolution, radically . . . modified by the rise of a post-war
consumer society',[8] have been changed, if not transformed, by the restructuring of capitalist economic processes in Western societies. New, fragmented
patterns of work organization, the virtual demise of mass manufacturing
and heavy industry and the manual working-class occupations that went
with this formation, and the growth of service sector occupations, all these
have contributed to a new socio-economic foundation. (However, it should
be noted that, in the British context at least, the destruction in the 1980s of
the mining industry and the manufacturing base by the neo-liberal ideologues
of Thatcherism was more a political than an economic project.)

There has been, as Peter Scott has noted, a change of emphasis in the
analysis 'from technological and economic change to wider social and institutional transformations . . . not just an economic system derived from particular technologies but an entire social system . . . is being transformed'.[9]
There may be a degree of hyperbole here: how often have intellectuals
heralded a cataclysmic change – Daniel Bell's end of ideology in the 1950s,
Fukuyama's end of history in the 1990s, just to choose two almost at random. Subsequently, in Chapter 5, we discuss in more detail the evidence
for and against this claim of social transformation. In this context, though,
the salient point is to note the degree to which post-Fordism identifies not
merely an *economic*, structural change (as did the earlier, more restricted,
ideology of post-industrialism), but a change in the nature of the social
system. The antecedents of this contention are rarely mentioned by postmodernists. However, post-Fordist perspectives are in fact a re-articulation
of the old embourgeoisement thesis of the 1960s and 1970s: 'we are all
middle-class now'. This, in turn, is related to James Burnham's 'Managerial

Revolution' thesis from the 1940s, and the subsequent sophistication of this claimed division between ownership and control and its heralding of the end of social class, in the social democratic formulations of Anthony Crosland and the revisionist right of the Labour Party from the 1950s through to the Social Democratic Party (SDP) of the 1980s.[10] This is not the context to discuss these antecedents in any detail, but it is important to note that postmodernism's and post-Fordism's claims of social transformation are not new. As we discuss in more detail in Chapter 2, the end of social class, the consequent proclamation of the irrelevance of socialism and, above all, the claim that capitalism and the systems of inequality and exploitation that it produces have somehow been transcended, are familiar tunes, even if post-modernism's orchestration and arrangement has repackaged them rather attractively.

None of this is to decry the importance of post-Fordist changes. The accelerating pace of technological change, in particular the pervasive importance of computer-based organizations, goes hand-in-hand with globalization to produce a very different pattern of both employment and organizational structures and the skills required in the labour market. This has important consequences for higher education and for the needs and desires of its learners and, consequently, for curriculum and academic objectives. As Peter Scott has argued, it is incorrect to attribute the moves to vocationalism, instrumentalism and performativity in higher education entirely to the ideology of Thatcherism: there is clear evidence of structural change in both the British and other Western economies which predates the rise of the crude market ideology of the 1980s.[11]

There are other important features of post-Fordist change, in addition to these structural changes, however. Globalization is a key feature of con-temporary Western society, in part because of the rapid growth of elec-tronic communication, much celebrated by postmoderns. But it is also due to the growth of multinational capital, now more dominant than ever before, a factor which neo-Marxists rather than postmodernists tend to emphasize.[12] This is combined with the increasing emphases on decentral-ization, regionalism and small-scale production to produce what Peter Scott terms 'glocalization'.[13] As Scott notes, 'the key to globalization . . . is the velocity of advanced capitalism which trades not only goods but also symbols (including, of course, that most powerful symbol, money, but also events, lifestyles and experiences), enabled by the new information tech-nologies . . . The flows of foreign exchange trading are many hundreds of times larger than the flows of traded goods'.[14]

The other key feature of post-Fordism, according to postmodernism, is the shift from an economy and society founded primarily upon pro-duction and producers to one centred on consumption and consuming. Postmodernism places great emphasis on lifestyle, individual difference and choice as defining characteristics for contemporary society. 'Lifestyles, as realised through personal participation in consumption, are now perhaps more fundamental determinants of personal identity and social hierarchy than life chances, as determined by one's place in the division of labour or conventional social hierarchy'.[15] In its more extreme articulations, this emphasis on lifestyle becomes somewhat risible: 'the consumer and consumerism increasingly reign supreme ... the goal of life [is] an endless pursuit of new experiences, values and vocabularies ... the ludic is a form of resistance'.[16] Nevertheless, there is a serious point to be made here. There has undoubtedly been a weakening of the ties of social class and of the pull of family, community and fixed geographical location. Taken with the growth of youth culture and consumer power in music, fashion, sport and leisure pursuits generally, this heralds a significant change in patterns of social living – if not necessarily in patterns of social, economic and political *inequality*, an issue to which we return in Chapters 2, 5 and 9.

Stuart Hall has commented that contemporary society is characterized by 'greater fragmentation and pluralism, the weakening of older collective solidarities and block identities and the emergence of new identities associated with greater work flexibility, the maximisation of individual choices through personal consumption'.[17] This applies not only to consumerism and lifestyle, of course, but also to the increasing importance of arguably older factors in determining individual and collective identity: gender, ethnicity, nationalism and religious fundamentalism. Postmodernism celebrates at least the first of these two: the emphasis upon, and appreciation of, difference, and of a genuine equality of regard for such difference is one of the keynotes of postmodernism (as, it must be noted, it has been of the progressive Left since at least the 1970s).

The implications of this post-Fordist analysis for higher education are significant. The wider world in which the university's graduates seek employment is a far more complex environment than hitherto. Moreover, given both the pace of change and the fragmentation of organizational structure, long-term employment prospects for graduates are far from guaranteed; this, of course, is exacerbated by the large increase in the numbers graduating and in employer perceptions of institutional reputation. There has also been an impact on curriculum and the criteria for assessment of 'quality' and 'standards'. Issues of 'excellence', 'performativity' and so on are all raised starkly in the higher education context by the post-Fordist aspects of the postmodern analysis. All these issues are returned to in some detail in later chapters. The point here is to note the *profundity* of the challenge to established university assumptions that is posed by postmodernism.

These observations lead to the second key feature of the postmodern analysis, in the context of higher education, that was noted at the outset of this section: the assertion that the big ideas, the grand narratives of the Enlightenment project must be rejected. This assertion rests essentially on two contentions. The first is that, in the light of the almost unbelievable horrors of the twentieth century (and, indeed, in many respects of the nineteenth century too), the inherent optimism of the social Darwinism of the two great secular projects, liberalism and socialism, has been shown to be illusory. The notions of progress, albeit involving struggle, sacrifice and suffering, which are so central to Marxism in particular, resulted in the bestiality of Stalinism, the Gulag, the Show Trials and all the rest. Western European liberalism and social democracy, despite the depth of its societies' civilization, the long centuries of high culture and its 'maturity', ended up by producing Hitler and the Holocaust. If proof were needed, postmodernists argue, of the dangerous fallacies inherent in totalizing ideologies, it is here in all its stark enormity. Even worse than this, in one sense, it is argued that 'the Holocaust, rather than denying, actually represents the triumph of rationality and the application of scientific principles and knowledge to the efficient conduct of human affairs'.[18] Reason, in other words – the bedrock of Western civilization and, quintessentially, the defining cultural and methodological characteristic of the university, encompassing the disinterested pursuit of knowledge and truth through scientific method – is actually the root *cause*, in one sense, of the catastrophic failures of the grand narratives in their social and political application in the real world.

These are large questions – none larger. In the relative microcosm of higher education, however, postmodernism applies, with some force, this root and branch rejection of the grand narratives to the university itself. Postmodernists deny that scientific method (in the generic sense of rationalist analysis), organized according to the methodologies thought to be (or developed through long experience to be 'proved' to be) appropriate to particular disciplines, represents the key, the way to knowledge and truth. Similarly, postmodernists deny that this approach, and the knowledge and perceived truth it produces, are in any way value-free or objective. There is a certain degree of setting up straw men here. Both advocates and critics of any ideological position are prone to this, as Terry Eagleton has noted.[19] In this particular context, though, it is worth noting that many of these strictures have been directed against university orthodoxy – again with some force – by radical critics from within the social purpose, liberal tradition of education.[20]

Postmodernism, according to Usher and Edwards, 'describes a world where people have to make their way without fixed referents and traditional anchoring points . . . But the significant thing is that in postmodernity uncertainty, the lack of a centre and the floating of meaning are understood as phenomena to be celebrated rather than regretted. In postmodernity, it is complexity, a myriad of meanings, rather than profundity, the one deep meaning, which is the norm'.[21] There is thus not one knowledge, actual or potential, and one methodology (or rather variants on positivist scientific rationalism, dependent upon the precise disciplinary context); rather, there is an infinite number of *knowledges*, endlessly interweaving and cross-fertilizing.

All these arguments have a direct bearing on the conceptualization of the idea of the university *qua* university. The three most prevalent traditional models of the university – Kant's central concern with reason; Newman's, with its emphasis upon the disinterested pursuit of knowledge and wisdom for their own sake; and Humboldt's, focusing upon research, predominantly scientific enquiry – had in common their strong belief in the university remaining separate from the world and its more immediate and practical concerns, although rather less so in the development of the Humboldtian tradition. As Michael Peters and Simon Marginson have noted, 'the thread that has held these Ideas of the University together is the role of the University as the central knowledge institution of the modern state ... [this] has its fullest flowering in the national system building period between the 1950s and 1970s'.[22] However, as Peters and Marginson also note, the British tradition in particular has consistently emphasized Newman's belief in the 'non-utilitarian notion of teaching as personal formation, and for a vision of the University as a place apart from the day-to-day turmoils of life'.[23]

For the university to fulfil its proper functions, it was argued, it was essential that it operated, if not autonomously, then certainly at a remove from worldly pressures. One of the undoubted characteristics of the mass higher education system now pertaining in the United Kingdom, as elsewhere in the developed world, is the marked change in this context. The university is very clearly, and increasingly, in and of the world. For many in the academy this is a cause of deep concern – not least because of the strident dominance of the ideology of market capitalism – whether in its pure Thatcherite form, or more nuanced in New Labour, or similar, softer tones. These issues are again discussed in more depth in Chapters 5 and 6 (in relation, among other things, to the virtual collapse of welfare state perspectives as a core element of the social democratic project). For postmodernists, however, this deep involvement of the university in the wider community is not only of significance, it is a cause for celebration and another reason for arguing that the concept of the university has to be reconfigured.

It is true that universities have always, in one sense, been in part vocational in orientation – the *raison d'être* of the ancient universities in Britain, for example, lay to a large extent in their vocational training, as we might now term it, of clergy. And this was soon followed by medicine and law. However, the growth of vocationalism in the twentieth century, and in particular since the 1980s, has been unprecedented. The dimensions and detailed implications of these changes are discussed in Chapter 5 and, in particular, Chapter 8. However, in terms of postmodern perspectives, the importance of these factors is linked to several other features of the contemporary higher education context, which, together it is argued, call for a wholesale redefinition of 'the university'.

First, there is the rapid growth of technology, enabling learning to take place, through computerized open and distance learning techniques, on a global scale, not related necessarily to any physical presence on campus; or, indeed, in principle, to the existence of a physical campus at all. Thus, Ronald Barnett can observe that 'the postmodern university ... has no centre, no boundaries and no obvious moral order. Both *in extenso* and virtually, it is located globally. Its research, its activities and its conversations are conducted across the world, aided by the Internet. But it also retains local interest and networks'.[24]

Secondly, there is the complex of knowledge, referred to earlier, and the changed criteria by which learning in higher education is to be evaluated. The world of education, postmodernists argue, 'functions more and more like a marketplace. The question . . . now asked by the professionalist student, the State, or institutions of higher education is no longer "Is it true?" but "What use is it?" In the context of the mercantilisation of knowledge, more often than not this question is equivalent to "Is it saleable?" '[25] Market criteria are thus increasingly prominent in higher education, as they are in the wider society. For some commentators, critical of postmodernist perspectives, this process of involvement with the world has gone beyond all tenable limits. For Bill Readings, for example, the current context has produced a culture where 'excellence', without referent content, is the key criterion, but a wholly empty one. This rush to the market, Readings claims, means that 'the university is not just *like* a corporation; it *is* a corporation. Students in the University of Excellence are not *like* customers; they *are* customers'.[26] For postmodernists, though, the involvement of the university in the fragmented, diffused knowledge society, suffused with difference, is to be welcomed. Individuals operating freely in a free and global environment are much better served by the postmodern university – or, rather, their perspectives are more congruent with a more deconstructed and involved university. Rather than being inducted and socialized into a unilinear, totalizing epistemology and cultural process through the grand narrative of the rationalist project, the postmodern university offers complexity, difference and a stimulation to our understanding of the world. The old, rigid and now anachronistic disciplines, which corresponded in no meaningful way to external reality, have been deconstructed and made more flexible, interactive and responsive. Here, as elsewhere, the postmodern icons of difference and complexity are writ large.

Finally, and related to the preceding factors, we would draw attention to the prominence of the idea of performativity in the postmodern perspective. In response to a range of socio-economic changes (discussed in detail in Chapter 5), universities have become much more *functional* during the twentieth century. And by functional is usually meant more geared to skills enhancement and training, in relation to perceived labour market needs. 'Rather than being governed by some vision of a just society, the activities of professionals are increasingly governed by the criteria of efficiency'.[27] This is, of course, the underpinning of the competence-based qualifications orientation of successive British governments and their quangos.

For postmodernists, this criterion of performativity is linked closely to the assertion that we live in an increasingly uncertain world (although a fascinating and dynamic one, because of the complexity, diversity and celebration of difference that are inherent within it). No longer is the notion of the grand narrative relevant: 'the university has the responsibility to inject further uncertainty into an already uncertain world; and it has itself to comprehend that role and itself to take on the conditions of uncertainty of the wider world'.[28]

Whether this celebratory, positive view of the contemporary world in general, and in our context of higher education in particular, is a correct perspective, is one of the main focuses of this book. The remainder of this introductory chapter is devoted to an exposition of the main hypotheses on which we base our critique of the postmodern position. At a level of generality, we, like postmodernists in many ways, take the contemporary social and political environment as our yardstick. However, rather than focusing on the grand narratives and their inadequacy or worse, we begin with material reality. We contend that there is a material world beyond intellectual theorization, that such theorization only has relevance and meaning if it is related to this material reality, and that for radicals in education an essential objective has always to be the relationship between education and its potential for contributing to progressive change. The task is thus to link theory and practice, learning and experience, within a properly coherent radical framework of intellectual analysis. This is, in effect, a rearticulation of the old idea of *praxis*.

We are at one with postmodernism in acknowledging the dramatic failure of any of the grand narratives to deliver their grandiose objectives. The history of the twentieth century has certainly been a dire and salutary correction to any Darwinian, let alone idealistic, view of human society and the nature of the individuals and collectivities of which it is composed.

The solutions, if such there be, do not lie, in our view, in postmodern analysis and formulations. As Ralph Miliband has noted, 'the contemptuous formulation' of one of the high priests of postmodernism, J.F. Lyotard, which decries 'all large schemes of social renewal, however cautious and qualified – as a dangerous illusion' is not new: such sentiments have always been 'an intrinsic part of conservative thought'. What is startlingly new about the postmodern movement is that it 'has also now become part of the thinking of a substantial part of the intellectual Left'.[29] As Terry Eagleton has observed, perhaps rather mildly in this particular passage (although his work as a whole is very critical of postmodernism), it is not that socialist critics are 'proposing that we have some fully-fledged alternative to postmodernism at our fingertips, just that we can do rather better'.[30] At one level, this book is an attempt to see whether we 'can do rather better' in analysing higher education and suggesting future priorities in the context of this debate.

It may be otiose, but it still needs emphasis perhaps, that on every level the contemporary socio-economic system is, to put it mildly, far from perfect. For anyone with a lingering, residual belief in the good intentions and effects of Western liberal democracy, a brief scan of, say, John Pilger's 1998 book *Hidden Agendas* will be sufficient: it catalogues, in relentless detail, the duplicity, cynicism, deliberate subjugation and torture of millions of people across the world, in the name of democracy, but in fact in the interests of an ever more powerful international capital.[31] To quote from Ralph Miliband again:

It is quite obvious that the 'new world order' [following the disintegration of the Communist world] is in fact immense disorder . . . Far from being in the least attenuated, the woes of the world grow ever more pronounced and painful. The threat of nuclear annihilation by war between the 'super-powers' has gone, but nuclear proliferation makes a 'local' nuclear war more rather than less likely in the years ahead. To this must now be added such issues as ecological disaster, the population explosion, the growth of mega-cities in which a decent life for the majority cannot be had, and the perpetuation and growth of poverty, deprivation and destitution on a global scale.[32]

We are faced, therefore, with the question of why so many formerly socialist intellectuals have embraced the conservative perspectives of postmodernism. Indeed, the aforementioned Lyotard, probably the single most influential figure in postmodernism, has a past history not just of socialism, but of intensely Leftist, activist Marxism, tinged with syndicalism:

A militant in the far-left group *Socialisme ou Barbarie* [linked to *Solidarity* in the United Kingdom][33] for a decade (1954–64) during which he was an outstandingly lucid commentator on the Algerian War, Lyotard remained active in its split-off *Pouvoir Ouvrier* for another two years . . . He was active in the university ferment at Nanterre in 1968 and still reinterpreting Marx for contemporary rebels as late as 1969.[34]

Our first hypothesis relates to this conundrum. Our view is that the appeal of postmodernism to many intellectuals, some socialists among them, lies in its providing a comfortable and suitably subtle ideological shelter for the refugees of failed modernism. Writing in the early years of the Cold War, Richard Crossman gathered together somewhat agonized apologias for *The God that Failed*.[35] But these were sturdier, more pragmatic individuals, largely committed to political action in the mainstream rather than purely intellectual theorizing. Others in the British context who rejected Communist orthodoxy, but espoused other varieties of socialist praxis, include pre-eminently E.P. Thompson, John Saville, Raymond Williams and Ralph Miliband.[36] The list could be extended almost indefinitely: the point here is to emphasize that these and other more internationalist socialist intellectuals found politico-intellectual outlets of varying degrees of socialist identity.

However, as Perry Anderson argued persuasively in 1976 in his *Considerations on Western Marxism*,[37] the preponderant history of Marxist intellectuals in the West, as the twentieth century wore on, has been one of considerable philosophical development and sophistication, but of retreat from 'real world' politics. Real politics, so to speak, become almost impossible as the twin reference points – of radical social democracy and Marxist-Leninist Communism – became increasingly discredited. We should add that, in common with postmodernist critics, we would emphasize that 'real world' politics includes a rich diversity of social movement theorization and activism, in addition, complementary, to *class* politics. These include, for example, gender and ethnic political movements and peace and ecological movements.

This separation of intellectual theorization from engagement with social and political issues in the real world was, of course, hugely exacerbated with the fall of Communism and the collapse, or serious undermining, of the whole socialist project. As active political engagement outside the academy thus became so difficult, intellectuals tend to have taken what for them has been the easy escape route: into self-referential, esoteric, often obscurantist debate. As Frank Webster has observed, despite their profound radicalism, many of these intellectuals are ensconced in 'safe' theoretical debate, with each other, in often tenured, sometimes prestigious academic posts.[38] There has been an associated decline in 'public intellectuals', those who addressed and wrote for the intelligent public; for example, in Britain, among many others, H.G. Wells, Marghanita Laski, Arthur Koestler, George Orwell, Bernard Shaw and A.J.P. Taylor.[39] (These issues are discussed further in Chapters 3 and 9.)

Thus our first hypothesis is that postmodernism represents a bolt hole, both culturally and politically, for intellectuals who find modernism's perceived failures too much to cope with, too difficult politically. Just as Anderson argued that Western Marxism has retreated, on the whole and with honourable exceptions, into a somewhat rarefied intellectual world of its own, so have postmodern intellectuals escaped into a cosier, abstract world, where lifestyle pursuits and the enjoyment of stimulating difference can be applauded, rather than having to be justified against the criteria of the hard real world of inequality, exploitation and capitalist domination. This is escapism, it could be argued, on an impressively grand scale.

Our second hypothesis lies at the heart of the whole argument and, at one level, the whole of the rest of this book is an attempt to argue through and justify its assertion. We believe, as we noted at the outset, that the postmodern perspective has two fundamental flaws. First, it is so partial and, ironically, so ideologically rooted in its analyses that it leads to seriously misleading theorizations of contemporary society. Thus, at the purely intellectual level, we find postmodernism to be a deeply unsatisfactory position, or series of positions. As noted earlier, this is not to deny postmodernism's appeal, nor indeed to gainsay its many insights and necessary correctives to established ideas and assumptions. Still less is it to imply that we support the maintenance of the *status quo* or a straightforward allegiance to any of the old grand narratives.[40]

The second fundamental flaw, in our view, is related to but separate from the first. We hold that, despite its protestations of rather chic radicalism – whether in the tones of Islington New Labour or Santa Barbara marginality – postmodernism is predominantly and dangerously reactionary and negative in its consequences. Ralph Miliband articulates this with his customary force:

> The many defeats and disappointments which the Left has suffered in recent decades ... [have] greatly encouraged the many currents of

thought which have helped to subvert any belief that a comprehensive alternative to capitalist society was possible or even desirable . . . The accent is now [in postmodernism] on partial, localized, fragmented, specific goals and against universal, 'totalising' perspectives . . . In suggesting that there is no real alternative to the capitalist society of today, it plays its own part in creating a climate of thought which contributes to the flowering of poisonous weeds in the capitalist jungle . . . racism, sexism, xenophobia, anti-Semitism, ethnic hatreds, fundamentalism, intolerance. The absence from the political culture of the rational alternative which socialism represents helps the growth of reactionary movements which encompass and live off these pathologies and which manipulate them for their own purposes.[41]

This is a harsh judgement and many espousing postmodernism have, of course, been vigorous proponents of egalitarian and non-discriminatory practice, most notably on feminist and ethnicity issues. And we would agree that, on many occasions, the almost exclusive concentration by socialists upon social class analysis and consequent prescriptions have obscured and marginalized key constituencies and perspectives. However, it is our contention that the overall burden of postmodern analysis and, consequently, attitude and influence, has been such as to encourage the 'poisonous weeds' to which Miliband refers. Thus, it is postmodern*ism* as a perspective, a mode of analysis, that tends to lead to such negative conclusions: some of those proclaiming themselves to be postmodernists have progressive inclinations.

Our third hypothesis, again related to and stemming from the two preceding hypotheses, can be briefly stated. In the relative microcosm of higher education in Britain, we believe that postmodern analysis and prescription undermine a series of potentially positive developments. These arguments are explored in detail in subsequent chapters. However, it is important to emphasize here that the context is one of extreme volatility and rapid change. There are contradictory tendencies in higher education, as there are in education as a whole. There is, for example, the tension between widening participation, equality of opportunity and education for social purpose ('citizenship' as the current jargon would have it) on the one hand, and the pressure towards skills training and employer involvement (based largely on implicit capitalist assumptions of the nature and purpose of education) on the other. These objectives are not wholly incompatible, of course, but they *are* in tension – for larger ideological reasons. Another example is the pressure within the system for extending and, indeed, formalizing the undoubted hierarchy of higher education institutions. There is clearly a political danger that the self-styled elite institutions will effectively separate themselves from the rest, leaving a (perceived) second-class higher education for a (perceived) second-class student body.

These are familiar arguments and, as noted, will be returned to in Chapters 5, 6, 7 and 9. The point here is two-fold: to note the volatility and unpredictable nature of the policy debate and subsequent implementation since the 1990s, and to emphasize that the postmodern take on these issues has at best diverted attention from the very real possibilities for radical change and at worst has presented an analysis that actually militates against progressive change and, by default, buttresses the forces of reaction. In this context, these contentions are merely asserted: subsequent chapters argue through these positions, and address related questions, in more detail.

Notes

1. Keith Jenkins (1997) Introduction, in Keith Jenkins (ed.), *The Postmodern History Reader*. London: Routledge, pp. 3–4.
2. Robin Usher and Richards Edwards (1994) *Postmodernism and Education*. London: Routledge, p. 3.
3. Terry Eagleton (1996) *The Illusions of Postmodernism*. Oxford: Blackwell, p. ix.
4. Ibid., p. 3.
5. Perry Anderson (1998) *The Origins of Postmodernity*. London: Verso.
6. Bill Readings (1996) *The University in Ruins*. Cambridge, MA: Harvard University Press, p. 169.
7. Ronald Barnett (2000) *Realizing the University in an age of supercomplexity*. Buckingham: SRHE and Open University Press, p. 11.
8. Peter Scott (1995) *The Meanings of Mass Higher Education*. Buckingham: SRHE and Open University Press, p. 90.
9. Ibid., p. 91.
10. See Anthony Crosland (1956) *The Future of Socialism*. London: Cape.
11. Scott, op. cit., note 8, p. 91ff.
12. In the context of 'lifelong learning', see, for example, Griff Foley (1999) Back to basics: a political economy of workplace change and learning, *Studies in the Education of Adults*, 31(2): 181–96. For a more detailed discussion of globalization in the context of lifelong learning, see pp. 114–19, this volume.
13. Scott, op. cit., note 8, p. 94.
14. Ibid.
15. Peter Scott (1997) The postmodern university?, in Anthony Smith and Frank Webster (eds) *The Postmodern University? Contested Visions of Higher Education in Society*. Buckingham: SRHE and Open University Press, p. 44.
16. Usher and Edwards, op. cit., note 2, pp. 11–16.
17. Stuart Hall (1988) Brave new world, *Marxism Today*, October, p. 24, cited in Scott, op. cit., note 8, p. 103.
18. Usher and Edwards, op. cit., note 2, p. 10, summarizing the views of Bauman and Lyotard.
19. See Eagleton, op. cit., note 3, p. viii.
20. See, for example, Richard Taylor, Kathleen Rockhill and Roger Fieldhouse (1985) *University Adult Education in England and the USA: A Reappraisal of the Liberal Tradition*. Beckenham: Croom Helm.
21. Usher and Edwards, op. cit., note 2, p. 10.
22. Michael Peters and Simon Marginson (1999) Introduction, *Access: Critical Perspectives on Cultural and Policy Studies in Education*, 18(2): ii.
23. Ibid.

24. Barnett, op. cit., note 7, p. 17.
25. Usher and Edwards, op. cit., note 2, p. 175, citing J.F. Lyotard (1984) *The Postmodern Condition: A Report on Knowledge.* Manchester: Manchester University Press, p. 5.
26. Bill Readings, op. cit., note 6, p. 22.
27. Usher and Edwards, op. cit., note 2, p. 176.
28. Ronald Barnett (2000) Reconfiguring the university, in Peter Scott (ed.), *Higher Education Re-formed.* Brighton: Falmer Press, p. 128.
29. Ralph Miliband (1994) *Socialism for a Sceptical Age.* Cambridge: Polity Press, p. 69.
30. Eagleton, op. cit., note 3, p. ix.
31. John Pilger (1998) *Hidden Agendas.* London: Vintage.
32. Miliband, op. cit., note 29, p. 191; see also Cynthia Cockburn (1999) *The Space Between Us.* London: Zed Books.
33. For a discussion of the ideology and actions of *Solidarity* in the context of the British Peace Movement of 1958 to 1965, see Richard Taylor (1983) The British Nuclear Disarmament Movement of 1958 to 1965 and its legacy to the Left, unpublished PhD thesis, University of Leeds, pp. 795–807.
34. Anderson, op. cit., note 5, p. 27.
35. Richard Crossman (ed.) (1950) *The God that Failed: Six Studies in Communism.* London: Hamilton.
36. See, for example, E.P. Thompson (ed.) (1960) *Out of Apathy.* London: A.&C. Black; E.P. Thompson (1978) *The Poverty of Theory and Other Essays.* London: Merlin Press.
37. Perry Anderson (1976) *Considerations on Western Marxism.* London: Verso and New Left Books.
38. Frank Webster (1998) The postmodern university? The loss of purpose of British universities, presented to the Annual Conference of the Society for Research into Higher Education (SRHE), Lancaster University, December.
39. Ibid.
40. See, for example, Taylor *et al.*, op. cit., note 20; Kevin Ward and Richard Taylor (eds) (1986) *Adult Education and the Working Class: Education for the Missing Millions.* Beckenham: Croom Helm.
41. Miliband, op. cit., note 29, pp. 69–70.

Part 2

Contexts

2

Postmodernism and Politics

Introduction

Postmodernism claims to be both accurate in its characterization of the nature of contemporary society and progressive but realistic in its political stance. 'Politically, postmodernism entails engaging in multiple, local autonomous struggles for liberation, rejecting the imperialism of an enlightened modernity that presumed to speak for others (colonized peoples, blacks and ethnic groups, religious minorities, women, and the working class) with a unified voice.'[1] What is asserted, therefore, is certainly not an *end* to politics – analogous to Fukuyama's 'end of history' – but rather a rejection of socialism's totalizing insistence, following Marx, that social class is the key factor, within a contradictory socio-economic system of capitalism.

Not only, it is argued, has social pluralism in the latter decades of the twentieth century created 'a whole range of small-group, non-class political practices – micropolitics',[2] it is also that 'there is not a single enemy group against which they can struggle. Late capitalism has become such an impersonal system that it is difficult to develop convincing representations of a "ruling class" as an identifiable group'.[3] Politics thus becomes global *and* local, complex *and* personal (in the sense of being located in struggles and issues that relate directly to individuals' and groups' immediate concerns, rather than to broad, teleological goals) and pervasive but not dominant.

This sense of the amorphous complexity of the postmodern world is exacerbated by other contextual socio-economic factors:

> In a society where information mattered more than production 'there is no longer an artistic *avant-garde*', since 'there is no enemy to conquer' in the global electronic network ... rather there are countless individuals ... communicating and competing with each other ... [so that there might emerge] a shared symbolic order of the kind that religion provides – the ultimate agenda of postmodernism.[4]

As we noted in Chapter 1, from a politically progressive perspective there have been many positive aspects of postmodernists' foregrounding of the previously marginalized – including specific groups such as ethnic minorities of various sorts in different societies and principled opposition to deep-seated discrimination and inequalities based on gender and other grounds. But the preponderant political import of postmodernist perspectives is, from a progressive point of view, negative. The most conspicuous feature of contemporary politics, Zygmunt Bauman argues, 'is its insignificance . . . This politics lauds conformity and promotes conformity'.[5] There is an ideological juxtaposition of huge, global forces beyond the control, even the full comprehension, of both individuals and any explanatory framework, and an insistence that the only politics possible (and desirable) in postmodernity is focused on local, micro concerns. At its worst, this concentration upon the intensely local and the particular is a symptom of withdrawal, escapism and alienation. Zygmunt Bauman illustrates this graphically:

> There is a story of a drunken man who searched for a banknote under a lamp-post – not because he lost it there, but because the part of the pavement underneath was better lit. Transferring anxiety from global insecurity and uncertainty, its genuine causes, into the field of private safety, follows, roughly, the same logic.[6]

This has been an intellectual conviction, as discussed in Chapter 1, and a morally neutral, political *fact*. Political activity, at the micro level, thus takes place on the (highly ideological) assumption that there is no alternative to market capitalism. 'There could be nothing but capitalism. The postmodern was a sentence on alternative illusions.'[7] This fundamental ideological stance has had a profound impact upon the ethos, policy parameters and curricular structures and approaches of the academy.

Postmodernists have celebrated difference. As we note throughout this study, the foregrounding by postmodernism of issues of gender, ecology and ethnicity has been and remains a valuable corrective to some traditional, monolithic, often hierarchical perceptions of progressive politics; although it should be noted that these dimensions of radical politics pre-date postmodernism *per se*. On the libertarian left, in some Trotskyist movements, in Eurocommunism and, in particular, in social movements, these have been familiar themes.

The problems with postmodernists' political perspectives do not relate to the prominence given to issues of gender, ethnicity and so on. These are crucial dimensions of the global system of increasingly irrational and anarchic capitalism. The problems are, rather, two-fold. First, struggles over gender, ethnicity or whatever are seen as discrete phenomena, in a context of complexity, variety and differentiation. They are not related, ideologically or theoretically by postmodernists, either with each other or more importantly with overall frameworks of exploitation. After all, to do so would be to resurrect one or other of the 'grand narratives': a bridge too far. The second problem is the persistent distancing within postmodernism of theory and practice. Issue politics are concerned essentially with social movements as well as ideological (or moral) commitments. As with all progressive political activity, they are dynamic and effective only when operating through *praxis*, bringing the two elements together. Postmodernism sits uncomfortably with the notion of social movements, which are by definition based upon political and moral precepts related to material reality – and, more often than not, one or other of the grand narratives.

Postmodernism, then, analyses from a distance, removed from the messy real-world politics of the social movement. Postmodernism also rejects any overarching conception of politics and power relations. In one sense, it thus finds its most natural, comfortable home in the removed abstraction of the academy.

Yet politics is essentially concerned with power: how, why and by whom and to what effects power in society is exercised. If the overall context of power relations – in economic, social and cultural terms – is an immutable given, then ameliorative, progressive political activity has by definition a modest agenda and is played in a minor key.

The view of Marxist and other socialist critics is that such postmodernist perspectives on politics lead to 'liberal complacency or (worse still) to ultra-conservative nihilism'.[8]

The main aim of this chapter is to examine the bases of the postmodernist political perspective and to justify the assertions of its critics that, despite genuinely progressive elements in its politics, the postmodern position is essentially reactive and conservative. Later chapters then relate these broad arguments to the specific concerns of higher education.

A secondary aim is to analyse the nature of feminist politics, in part because of its inherent political importance, in part because of the representative nature of its relationship with postmodernist thinking in the context of social movements, and in part to provide some specificity to the general arguments outlined in the earlier section of this chapter.

Postmodernism: a political critique

The starting point for the analysis of the first of the questions is the postmodernist critique of the 'Enlightenment project', articulated in its fullest form through the socialist and, in particular, the Marxist tradition. This has been well summarized by Gregor McLennan. Most of the basic tenets of Enlightenment thought are held by postmodernists to be fallacious. Thus, just as knowledge, like society, is neither holistic nor cumulative, so rationality itself, as the basis of methodological analysis, is discredited. Nor is knowledge universal or objective. Furthermore, postmodernism maintains that it is both naïve and fallacious to hold 'that scientific knowledge, once validated and acted upon, can lead to mental liberation and social betterment amongst humanity generally'.[9] In summary, the postmodernist thesis claims that both the structures of society and the 'foundations of modern social *thought* have become obsolete and dogmatic'.[10] This contention strikes at the very foundation of the academy's epistemology and culture.

Within the Marxist tradition, there are two broad frameworks of response to these assertions. One, represented for example by Alex Callinicos, refutes the postmodernist perspective root and branch: 'I deny the main theses of poststructuralism, which seems to me in substance false. I doubt very much that Postmodern Art represents a qualitative break from the Modernism of the early twentieth century. Moreover, much of what is written in support of the idea that we live in a postmodern epoch seems to me of small calibre intellectually, usually superficial, often ignorant, sometimes incoherent.'[11] The second perspective, exemplified particularly in the work of Frederic Jameson,[12] argues that, while the socio-economic and political system remains incontrovertibly capitalist, the late twentieth century *is* significantly changed in a number of ways, which can be generally characterized as postmodern. For Jameson, 'postmodernism [is] the cultural logic of late capitalism';[13] and for him, 'the temptation to be avoided, above all, [is] moralism. The complicity of postmodernism with the logic of the market and of the spectacle [is] unmistakeable. But simple condemnation of it as a culture [is] sterile'.[14]

Much in this debate turns upon social class as an analytical category, rather than a sociological phenomenon (in relation to concepts such as working-class culture or working-class movements). Postmodernists see social class in two ways. First, social class, it is held, is essentially a modernist category, in the sense of being the key characteristic of industrial capitalist systems and thus of the ideological frameworks that arose from these societies – principally, liberalism and socialism.[15] Secondly, as Terry Eagleton has commented, 'social class tends to crop up in postmodern theory as one item in the triptych of class, race and gender, a formula which has rapidly assumed for the left the kind of authority which the Holy Trinity occasionally exerts for the right'.[16] As he goes on to point out, in one sense this is wholly unexceptionable: just as sexism and racism are bad things, so too is, ostensibly, 'classism'. That is, it is, for anyone of progressive principle, unacceptable to discriminate against people because of their class (or caste) origins. Moreover, we should not imply that gender and race issues should be seen exclusively in descriptive, superstructural terms. They, too, have structural dimensions, albeit in rather different ways.

Marxists, however, conceive of class in a wholly different way.

what was original about [Marx] and Engels's thought was not the discovery of social class, which had been as obvious as Mont Blanc long before they came to write. It was the more controversial claim that the birth, flourishing and demise of social classes, along with the struggles between them, are bound up with the development of historical modes of material production . . . Marxism is not just a high-sounding way of finding it distasteful or 'privileged' that some people belong to one social class and some to another, as it might be thought objectionable that some get to attend cocktail parties while others have to make do with a can of beer from the icebox. Marxism is a theory of the role played by the conflict between social classes . . . or it is nothing.[17]

It is not necessary here to enter into Marx's intellectual framework, centring on historical materialism and the role of class, class conflict and class domination; or on the pivotal role – held by Marx, Engels and virtually all later Marxists (although with a few notable exceptions[18]) – of class *consciousness* in the revolutionary transformation of capitalism to socialism. In the classic texts of Marxism, and in many commentaries and developments of Marxian theory since, these ideas have been articulated exhaustively.[19] This body of thought *was* familiar, at least in outline and with a greater or lesser degree of sophistication, both to those involved with virtually any radical movement *and* to all those educated to higher education level in the social sciences (and most of the arts). Now, however, not only is Marxism (understandably if perhaps temporarily) a discredited ideology in the former Eastern bloc societies, the West is also 'now bulging at the seams with political radicals whose ignorance of socialist traditions, not least their own, is certainly among other things the effect of post-modernist amnesia'.[20] Eagleton may go a little far in his polemic when he caricatures postmodernists as believing that 'a long time ago we fell into an obscure disaster known as the Enlightenment, to be rescued around 1972 by the first lucky reader of Ferdinand de Saussure'![21] Nevertheless, the point is well made. As Ralph Miliband has noted, 'This Marxism [that is, class analysis] remains of incomparable value for the understanding of class societies and their conflicts . . . [Those who] deprive themselves of its help are thereby greatly impoverished.'[22]

The argument, therefore, turns upon whether or not, in broad terms, the Marxian conception of class analysis is applicable to late capitalist societies. There is little if any dispute – how could there be? – that capital remains dominant. It is rather that 'the power of capital is now so drearily familiar . . . that even large sections of the left have succeeded in naturalizing it, taking it for granted as such an unbridgable structure that it is as though they hardly have the heart to speak of it'.[23]

This, in turn, raises the question of the validity of the post-industrial thesis. This is one key area in which the two perspectives noted earlier – represented by Callinicos and Jameson – part company. (Although, as discussed below, 'belief in the existence of a postmodern era does not necessarily depend upon the bankrupt idea of post industrial society'.[24]) Callinicos has no doubts about this issue. The opening sentence of the relevant chapter of his main work on postmodernism declares: 'the idea of post industrial society is, of course, nonsense'.[25] For Jameson, on the other hand, 'this new postmodern global form of capitalism will now have a class logic about it, but it has not yet reconstituted itself on a global scale, and so there is a crisis in what classes and class consciousness are'.[26]

So, from within a Marxist frame of reference, is the post-industrial thesis really 'nonsense'? It has certainly been an influential thesis in terms of the epistemological and programmatic development of the contemporary academy.

Undoubtedly, it is the case that very significant changes in the economy and, by extension, the workforce and the class structure, have taken place in all developed societies since, roughly, the 1970s. Among these are:

the growth of service jobs and the decline of manufacturing employ-ment; the introduction of new technologies based upon the microchip; the shift in the structure and composition of labour markets, from a male, full-time workforce towards a female, part-time workforce; a change in consumption practices, with a greater emphasis placed upon choice and specialization.[27]

More contentiously, perhaps, some analysts have argued that 'the transforma-tion of office work by information-process technology . . . [is] equivalent to the radical shift in industrial society from craft-based, factory production to a system of mass manufacture'.[28]

Some of the original theorists of post-industrialism went a lot further than this. Alan Touraine, for example, argued, as long ago as the early 1970s, that social divisions were no longer the result of social class, which has become a largely redundant concept; rather, the new social divide stemmed from access to information.[29] Daniel Bell, a more conservative figure in this debate, developed from this position a theory of the knowledge society where information is 'more than a resource . . . it is also regarded as a commodity which can be bought and sold in the marketplace'.[30] Manuel Castells has elaborated, from a perspective more sympathetic to Marxism, the nature of the information society.[31] Reiterating that knowledge is a com-modity in its own right, he places particular emphasis upon the centrality of information technology in transforming the ways in which multinational capital operates.[32] For Andre Gorz, social divisions resulting from this phe-nomenon produce 'an "aristocracy" of secure, well-paid workers, on the one hand, and a growing mass of unemployed, on the other'.[33]

There are, then, several radically differing interpretations of post-industrialism. No analysts deny that significant changes have taken place since around 1970 in the economic, organizational structure of developed societies, which in turn have resulted in shifts in employment patterns and class composition. This is clearly not a unique period in the evolution of capitalism, however. Capitalism has been characterized among other things by change – and the pace of this change, and the pervasiveness of the accom-panying volatility, has increased markedly through the twentieth century. The key issue, in the context of this discussion, is not whether significant changes have taken place but whether these changes constitute an *end* to social class and to the inequalities, exploitation and inherent structures of conflict that are endemic to class societies.

The assertion by post-industrial analysts that the service sector has be-come dominant at the expense of manufacturing must be heavily qualified. Undoubtedly, the role of the service sector has increased markedly but, taking the twentieth century as a whole, this 'has taken place primarily at the expense of agriculture rather than manufacturing industry'.[34] Indeed, as Ernest Mandel has noted, agriculture itself 'is step by step becoming just as industrialised as industry'.[35] The point is, simply, that capitalism changes in response to technological advance, as it always has. Thus, what were specialist quasi-artistic areas – fashion, entertainment, even sport – have now become industrialized and subject to the process of marketization. As Mark Murphy has argued, 'post-industrial society, rather than delivering some utopian world based on theoretical knowledge, is instead a speeded up process of capitalist modernisation . . . the latest example of capitalism trying to manage its contradictions . . . what is occurring is the internationalisation of economics'.[36]

Callinicos goes on to argue that technological advance has a much greater impact on manufacturing: productivity has increased much more in the manufacturing sector than in services.[37] More importantly in this context, it is erroneous to equate white-collar workers with the service sector: 'White-collar employment embraces at least three distinct class positions – "managerial capitalists" who are, in effect, salaried members of the bourgeoisie, the "new middle class" of upper-echelon professional, managerial and administrative employees, and routine white-collar workers whose insecurity, relatively low earnings, and lack of job control place them in the same fundamental position as manual workers'.[38] Moreover, although there has been large and undoubted growth in employment related to information technology, the growth in fast food and other restaurant and leisure services has been even greater: and the workers in these service industries are predominantly low paid with little job security and no union representation.[39]

Finally, in this economic context, *internationally* industrialization has increased hugely. Most third world countries have seen the proportion of their populations engaged in manufacturing rise dramatically. Clearly, the globalization of the economy entails the internationalization of class divisions – and the global extension of industrial manufacturing.[40] For Callinicos, although the power of global capital has increased markedly and information technology has been a major force in enabling financial and manufacturing companies to transcend nation-state boundaries and governmental control, 'the nation-state retains considerable economic strength'.[41] The point is not to deny globalization *per se* (see Chapter 6), but to stress the exaggeration of postmodernism's claims: the state 'was neither omnipotent before 1970 nor impotent thereafter'.[42]

For orthodox Marxists, therefore, new patterns of economic and employment organization signify changing social class composition, but not a change in capitalist social relations. Inequalities both nationally and internationally have widened, in relative terms,[43] and the structural conflicts inherent in capitalism have been exacerbated, in objective terms.

The glaring problem with this position, politically, is all too clear. Until the end of the 1980s, although the Left was always a minority force, 'it was still a significant presence in most of the leading capitalist states';[44]

subsequently, there has been not only an economic but a political 'neo-liberal grand slam',[45] although this may of course be short-lived, particularly given the volatility of capital in its enhanced global phase. One of the leading theorists on the intellectual Left, Perry Anderson, puts this argument starkly, maybe overly so:

> For the first time since the Reformation, there are no longer any significant oppositions . . . within the thought-world of the West; and scarcely any on a world scale either . . . whatever limitations persist to its practice, neo-liberalism as a set of principles rules undivided across the globe: the most successful ideology in world history.[46]

Elsewhere, Anderson has written of the contemporary 'saturation of every pore of the world in the serum of capital'.[47] What precisely Marxists – or, indeed, all those espousing progressive, broadly socialist politics – can do about this is a question on which, understandably, there is some paucity of analysis, not to say a shuffling of the ideological feet. And, to some extent, it would appear that the academy too has 'given up' on these questions.

Marxists express some considerable irritation, at the very least, with post-modernists' retreat into 'cultural style', but rarely have a clear alternative strategy for the Left, at least in the short term. Callinicos, for example, is driven to the rather ritualistic exhortation to revolutionary mobilization, at the close of his book critiquing postmodernism: 'unless we work towards the kind of revolutionary change which would allow the realization of this potential [that is, the potential of advanced technology and knowledge harnessed in the service of humanity] in a transformed world, there is little left for us to do, except, like Lyotard and Baudrillard, to fiddle while Rome burns'.[48] We return in the final chapter to a discussion of some of these questions of agency and political strategy.

For others in the Marxist tradition, though, it is not only politics, prescription and agency which present difficulties. Jameson, the prime theorist in this context, perceives the politics of postmodernism as a transformation not only economically but culturally. Although it takes place within a system that is unquestionably capitalist in nature and essence, this shift is, Jameson maintains, fundamental. As with Castells, Jameson identifies the new system economically with information technology based on modern electronics, and with global capital and the resultant outsourcing of manufacturing. However, he also emphasizes the 'rise of media conglomerates wielding unprecedented power across communications and borders alike',[49] and thus the centrality of culture. The result is that cultural industries, pre-eminently tourism (which now exceeds 'all other branches of global employment'[50]), and culture *per se* have 'become virtually coextensive with the economy itself'.[51]

The results of this, for Jameson, are profound. The class consciousness embodied, albeit in fractured, incomplete forms,[52] in industrial labour movements and social democratic and socialist political parties, has disintegrated. This, again, is not only an organizational disintegration but a cultural one too. With this has come 'the loss of any active sense of history, either as hope or memory'.[53] In terms of social class, Jameson thus argues that 'late capitalism remained a class society, but no class within it was quite the same as before'. There is brittleness and confusion in the new structures. However, both nationally and globally,

> no stable class structure, comparable to that of an earlier capitalism, has yet crystallized. Those above have the coherence of privilege; those below lack unity and solidarity. A new 'collective labourer' has yet to emerge. These are conditions, still, of a certain vertical indefinition.[54]

Jameson's less than convincing conclusion – from a socialist perspective, that is – is to emphasize the importance of analytical clarity preceding political action.

In terms of the analysis of social class and its place, if any, in the explanatory framework of late capitalist or postmodernist societies, much depends on definitions. Marxists are clearly correct, in our view, in maintaining that post-industrial societies have not dispensed with social class and its accompanying inequalities, exploitation and alienation. Still less has the capitalist system been transformed into some more flexible, complex, differentiated and pluralistic socio-economic entity. On the contrary, the undoubted hegemony of neo-liberalism – and the strengthening grip of economics, globally, in its capitalist forms[55] – have exacerbated capitalism's characteristics. Jameson, however, is equally clearly correct in asserting that the combined impact of the radical changes in occupational and employment patterns, the internationalization of capital and, not least, the huge expansion of the cultural industries of capitalism and their ideological force, has presented us politically with a new and complex situation.

What, then, of the wider political terrain of late capitalism and postmodernity? Some left-of-centre analysts – Anthony Giddens in particular – have argued that socio-political structures in late capitalism (late modernity, or postmodernity, depending upon ideological preference) are more complex than Marxists would have us believe. Two factors in particular stand out: the increase in the administrative power of the state and its bureaucratic apparatus and consequent social and cultural control; and the importance in most societies of military power, not only in terms of direct coercive force but as a major political actor. These political spheres, it is argued, although not separate from national and global capitalist interests and power, are significantly more autonomous than Marxists maintain.[56] From this perspective, Marxism is regarded as essentially reductionist, if not intellectually monolithic: all conflicts, inequalities and contradictions, it is argued, are essentially about class. And this contention is demonstrably untrue in relation to contemporary societies.

Such arguments are themselves reductionist of course. The relative autonomy of superstructural factors – in particular, cultural formations in all their variety – has long been a matter of detailed analysis and argument within the Marxist tradition.[57] Moreover, central to Marxism has been the notion of contradiction and the articulation, in the socio-political context, of the resultant conflict through a wide variety of processes and groups.

Postmodernism: a feminist critique

We now turn to the second aim of this chapter: to analyse, within the foregoing context, the evolution and nature of the feminist movement, and how it forms a powerful theoretical and practical challenge to both the ethical vacuum inherent in postmodernism and the cruder, more author-itarian manifestations of Marxism and other grand narratives.[58]

The feminist body of ideas, which interplayed powerfully with the women's movement throughout all western societies from the 1960s and 1970s on-wards, had a complex genesis. Its relationship to postmodernism, and to its definition of key issues, is similarly complex. Issues and topics often emerge from conflicts within academic fields that are produced and structured by much larger fields of cultural and political production. Carole Stabile, a North American socialist feminist theorist, has pointed out that postmodern-ist social theory was imported into the USA from European contexts (where it had emerged out of perceived hegemonic Marxist analysis), thereby gain-ing a different material context. Postmodernism and many feminists attracted to it thereby entered intellectual debates specific to European contexts.[59] Bizarrely, through obscuring the historical and material conditions that produced these debates, a backlash against economic analysis was appropri-ated by a society – the USA – in which a history of class struggle had been specifically and consistently repressed. The results of that appropriation were then bounced back to Europe and the United Kingdom (and the rest of the world) through the power of American publishing houses. The rest, as they say, is history.

The postmodernist social theory of Laclau and Mouffe had a particularly significant influence on feminism in the USA. This heightened already existing tendencies towards abstraction within American feminism, suggests Stabile. Social relations, according to Laclau and Mouffe, are 'discursively constructed'. Thus, in place of the so-called privileging of class – in the USA this is only so in very marginalized Marxist analyses in the academy or socialist organizations – we find the privileging, instead, of intellectuals and intellectual activity. Comforting for intellectuals, suggests Stabile; instead of having to participate in class struggle, they can participate in intellectual activity *in place of* class struggle. This conforms closely to the argument about the fate of Marxism in Western Europe, as analysed by Perry Anderson. In his account, Western European Marxist intellectuals retreated into the academy, because they could not resolve the complexities (and horrors) of real-world politics[60] (as we discuss in Chapter 9 and was noted in Chap-ter 1).

The idealist turn in postmodernist social theory is mirrored in anti-essentialist feminist theory. Jean Barr has recalled returning to academic life in the late 1980s and early 1990s after a gap of several years spent in the field of adult education:

> What I found there deeply disturbed me: a new feminist methodologism, a kind of feminist theoretical correctness, eschewing any generalisations about gender on *a priori* grounds, as 'essentialist' . . . Another aspect of this new theoretical turn . . . was that, whereas 'race' was foregrounded, 'class' seemed to have dropped out of much of the discussion.[61]

In all of these academic developments, there was not even a nod in the direction of the belief, central to critical social science, that in Marx's words, 'society does not consist of individuals but expresses the sum of interrelations, the relations within which these individuals stand'.[62]

This is unsurprising, given the anti-organizational bias that is an aspect of the postmodernist package. Offering only individualized solutions, it is incapable of addressing, far less resolving, structural problems, and the time-consuming work of building organized opposition is decried in favour of what Stabile refers to, witheringly, as 'discursive channel surfing'.[63]

In her 1999 book, *Why Feminism?*, Lynne Segal refers to the growing dominance of North American concerns within academic feminism that have elided some specifically British features of feminism.[64] Feminist scholarship began in the academy unashamedly in the name of feminism as a theory and practice of social transformation. As such, feminism did not separate women's concerns from wider struggles against inequality; and its distinct legacy and value lie in its insistence on the connections of the personal and cultural to the economic and political. Moreover, it has constituted a general cultural critique, not just a specific one concerning women – or even gender. How often, though, do we see feminist theorists listed alongside Foucault, Derrida, Rorty and so on as shapers of the disciplines, science, philosophy and culture? Rarely. More often we encounter a version of Edward Said's formulation:

> There are certainly new critical trends. We do know more about the way cultures operate thanks to Raymond Williams, Roland Barthes, Michel Foucault and Stuart Hall . . . and thanks to feminists like Elaine Showalter, Germaine Greer, Helene Cixous, Gayatri Spivak . . . it is impossible to avoid or ignore the gender issues in the production and interpretation of art.[65]

As Susan Bordo has commented, feminists are construed as engaging in specialist critique. 'One does gender or one engages in criticism of broad cultural significance; pick one.'[66]

In Segal's view, over the past thirty years of feminism there has been a shift in its focus from social structure to culture, politics to theory, collective to individual and material to symbolic, influenced by the growing dominance of North American concerns that have tended to lead to forgetting some of the most dynamic features of British feminism. A distorted version of feminism's past is becoming received wisdom, one which forgets that in

Britain many of the women involved were socialists, and which conflates the real world with the academic world. A crucial feature of the women's liberation movement in the 1970s was that it had a vision. And it is this vision – as a theory and practice of social transformation – that provides Segal with her reference point for the analysis of later developments.

In the late 1960s and early 1970s, the women's liberation movement developed in a critical dialogue with a broader left movement for a better, more equal, more socialist, world. Its distinct legacy, in Segal's view, lies in its potential to 'connect personal and cultural issues to economic and political affairs'.[67] Segal attempts to negotiate the increasingly tense relationship that has developed between feminist activisms and academic feminisms, a tension that is often wrongly reduced to clashes between the economic and the cultural. She believes that, at a time when welfare shrinks, the working day lengthens and inequality deepens, with working-class women and children at the cutting edge of all of this, the Left still needs feminism's potential 'to embrace complexity and conflict in the experiences of men and women'.[68]

Media repetition of dominant conceptions of late capitalism includes, crucially, a silence about capitalism, class, exploitation and inequality and divorces this ideological construction from material reality, especially in terms of both the mode of capitalist production and its social relations. This discourse has thus been transformed into a universal common sense – a hegemony that would have impressed, and horrified, Gramsci. This, of course, masks the fact that it expresses the 'complex and contested realities of a particular historical society', a society that is:

> characterised by the deliberate dismantling of the social state and the correlative hypertrophy of the penal state, the crushing of trade unions and the dictatorship of the 'shareholder-value' conception of the firm, and their sociological effects: the generalization of precarious wage labour and social insecurity, turned into the privileged engine of economic activity.[69]

Bourdieu and Wacquant point to the 'fuzzy and muddy' debate about multiculturalism in American universities as an example. It functions there as a 'screen discourse', they claim, masking what is really going on. Restricted to the academic/university level and expressed in an ethnic register, it masks the reality of the bankruptcy of public education at a time of intensifying competition for cultural capital and growing class inequality. What is really at stake is not the inclusion of marginalized cultures in the academic canon. The real issue is access to cultural capital, to the instruments – or means – of production of the middle and upper classes.[70]

North American multiculturalism is not really a theory or a social or political movement, claim Bourdieu and Wacquant, although it claims to be both of these. It is a specially North American discourse, which, although it sees itself as universal, actually emanates from the current historical predicaments of American academics. Cut off from the public sphere, they 'have nowhere to invest their political libido but in campus squabbles'. This is somewhat harsh. But it resonates with Lynne Segal's comment that multiculturalism is a problem not because it politicizes the academy, but because it constitutes politics as primarily *academic*,[71] as in Anderson's wider analysis of Western European Marxism, noted earlier.[72]

Contemporary feminism is increasingly distanced from the activities and goals of women's liberation as a social movement. This is simply because it is much easier to teach this as an academic topic. But, Segal points out, such amnesia about political movements is socially produced and perpetuated and it is dangerous. It is noteworthy, and not a little surprising, that such amnesia is a characteristic of many on the cultural left. Terry Eagleton, for example, in a critique of postmodernism, sees it as responsible for *installing* feminism on the political agenda; others see its influence as precisely the reverse!

In academic discussion, the perception of the women's movement, and its feminist ideology, as a social movement is downplayed; similar divorced views of theory and practice are applied to other social movements. The academy is played up and inflated: reference to the real world and its processes seems to drop out of view. Thus is produced the by now familiar story of feminism's history (simplistic, distorted and a caricature): first there was 'equality feminism' seeking liberal, egalitarian ends, followed by 'difference feminism' seeking exclusion from the 'masculine order', followed by 'post-feminist' deconstruction, critical of the binary of sexual difference itself. The problem many feminists tried to tackle all along was precisely how to avoid straightforward inclusion in, or exclusion from, the masculine (symbolic) order and a world organized primarily around men's interests. The difference was that, then, the conceptual tools used were borrowed from the likes of de Beauvoir, Marx, Gramsci and Freud rather than Kristeva, Derrida and Foucault.

Rowbotham argues, however, that the radical heritage of the women's liberation movement continues whenever feminists work to realize the dream 'that all human beings can be more than present circumstances allow'.[73] That vision, comments Segal, is not one of equal rights: '[i]t was called socialism and it was being reshaped to service feminism'.[74] It was a vision that recognized the need for developed imaginations as much as (or even more than) new theories – a socialist imaginary that combined with feminism to promote women's interests as a key part of fundamental progressive social, economic, political and cultural change.

All this withered away in Britain under the ferocity of Conservative rule in the 1980s. In this decade, a new romance with the feminine took precedence in the best known (and most popularly appealing) feminist thought, especially in North America – a sanctimonious form of cultural feminism that lauded women for being nurturing and non-violent and castigated men for being dominating and destructive. Later, developments in post-structuralism gave feminists useful conceptual tools for deconstructing such binary, dualistic thinking, for problematizing identity and social difference, and for engaging in battles over the discursive marginalization of women's lives and interests. But socialist feminists have continued all along to engage in social struggles over redistribution alongside issues of identity involving cultural recognition and respect.

If the Left is to become a popular and influential movement again, it has to acknowledge and embrace diverse cultural alignments and affiliations and also attend to what Segal terms 'the volatilities of "class" itself, as it is culturally produced and experienced'.[75] More than ever before these grass-roots movements for social justice, including women's movements, need scholarly servicing; they need, for example, theories of world markets and nation states, cultural understandings of identity formation and historical studies of social movements to combine with their own experiential know-ledge. Yet the disciplining of feminism within the academy and these fiscally contracting times make cross-disciplinarity less likely now. And when inter-disciplinary conferences on feminism do occur, they tend to be within the narrow boundaries of English and Cultural Studies.

In our view, there is no future in reductive positions that seek to divide the economic and political from the discursive and cultural. The least politically productive current intellectual efforts are those that defend the so-called 'real' left from the phoney cultural left.[76] There is no doubt that women's shifting fortunes worldwide are fundamentally enmeshed within cultural understandings of sexual difference that sustain misogyny, help promote male paranoia and contribute to violence against women as well as many men. The reason women worldwide do low-paid work cannot be reduced to capitalism *per se.* And the current sense that it is men/boys who are losing out is quintessentially cultural, claims Segal. Men, like women, are disparately affected by wider forces of economic restructuring, downsizing and job insecurity. The point is that although cultural and economic spheres are irreducible to one another, they are thoroughly intertwined.[77]

Conclusion

In the context of the women's movement – one specific social movement – and its accompanying ideological underpinnings, it is thus clear that the economic and cultural dominance of capitalism is pervasive. With all the complexities and qualifications noted, it remains the case that capitalism is dominant and accompanied necessarily by a hierarchical class structure. Indeed, there is a strong argument that capitalism has become *more* domin-ant. This is undoubtedly the case economically, as we have argued. Global capital and the penetration of the economic, defined in market, capitalist terms, have assumed unprecedented primacy. The common sense, eco-nomically, of capital is rarely challenged – and certainly not by either the theorists of postmodernism or the social democratic apologists of the Third Way. Similarly, in social and cultural terms, as we have argued, mass culture combined with the revolution in electronic technology have resulted in both a new prominence for mass culture and a cultural democratization controlled by large corporations. Not only is there a high level of political disillusionment and cynicism in most societies, there is a prevalent view that 'there is no alternative' to neo-liberal market capitalism.

As Segal has maintained, this interplays with issues of gender too:

> The most central global axes of economic and cultural oppression continue to construct and reconstruct themselves in the interrelated terms of 'gender' (tied in with sexual orientation), 'class' (tied in with nationality, ethnicity and religion), within what is currently *ever more* totalizing control of a transnational capitalist market. The invocation of specific differences can serve broadly based transfunctional ends, but only as a part of some *wider political project* seeking to dismantle these basic structures of domination.[78]

Blair's New Labour project in Britain is a prominent example of this ideological and political amalgam: liberal and welfare oriented but committed completely to working within the confines of capitalist structures and assumptions in terms of economic and political policy. The agencies of opposition to this and similar formations are hard to identify, not least of course because of the demise of communism not only in the former Soviet Union but throughout the more progressive parties of Western Europe and the severe weakening of socialist parties and movements internationally. (On the other hand, it is persuasively argued by Callinicos that the collapse of the USSR and the Communist regimes of Eastern Europe 'have simplified matters enormously. There can now be no doubt that we live in a single, unified world system. The illusion that there was "a socialist third of the world", that a separate, post-capitalist socio-economic system was in the process of construction, has been destroyed'.[79])

However cataclysmic the last decade or so of the twentieth century may have been in this political context, the fundamental socio-political structures of capitalism persist. Thus it remains the case, it is argued, that the structural injustices and economic instabilities inherent in capitalism are such that they are bound to produce large-scale movements of opposition. Even critical analysts acknowledge that contemporary capitalism has created systematic and global inequality.[80] There is also, demonstrably, a continuing volatility economically and inherent tendencies to unpredictable crises. As always, it is the interaction between objective circumstance and human agency that determines the outcomes of political conflicts. 'Men [*sic*] make their own history, but they do not make it just as they please; they do not make it under circumstances chosen by themselves, but under circumstances directly encountered, given and transmitted from the past'.[81] One of the biggest problems for developing a political consciousness in opposition to capital, and for mobilizing social movements and political organizations to overthrow capitalist hegemony, 'is the very belief that there is no alternative to capitalism'. This negativism 'is the main source of social despair in the contemporary world'.[82] The academy, currently, does little to provide an intellectual focus for opposition to this negativity. We should not, however, become carried away by such passionate, although rhetorical, socialist exhortation. While there is some point in Callinicos's political irritation, it is also clearly the case – as the postmoderns argue – that in the West large numbers of middle- and upper middle-class people enjoy and appreciate many of the conditions of social and cultural life in late capitalism. Never has there been such a cultural diversity in leisure, cultural and sporting activities. As well as the despair, and lack of perceived alternatives, there are elements of the ludic, the diverse – and the stimulating – in late capitalist culture. Although this, in turn, must be qualified by repeated survey findings that people generally, in all western societies, are unhappier and less fulfilled than ever before.

If the new social democrats and other apologists for market capitalism represent the political wing of this accommodation, intellectually it is the postmodernists who provide the ideological framework. Even those who are acknowledged advocates of Giddens's sociological analysis view postmodernism as 'a *trahison des clercs* – a safe consumer revolt, by the knowing, against a surfeit of indigestible knowledge'.[83]

Undoubtedly, postmodernists have provided valuable critical insights and contributed to the critiques of previously authoritarian socialist regimes with their often disastrous monolithic and constricting cultures and political practices. But the political negativity of postmodernism, with its cultural and philosophical relativism, and its eventual moral and political conformity with the *status quo*, has rendered it a politically conservative force. In the end, we agree with Terry Eagleton's verdict that 'postmodernism . . . is part of the problem rather than of the solution'.[84]

Notes

1. Kenneth Thompson (1992) Social pluralism and postmodernity, in Stuart Hall, David Held and Tony McGrew (eds) *Modernity and its Futures*. Buckingham: Polity Press and Open University Press, p. 229.
2. Ibid., p. 235.
3. Ibid., p. 237.
4. Perry Anderson (1998) *The Origins of Postmodernity*. London: Verso, pp. 23–4 (citing Charles Jencks (1986) *What is Postmodernism?* London: Academy Editions, pp. 44–7).
5. Zygmunt Bauman (1999) *In Search of Politics*. Cambridge: Polity Press, pp. 4–5.
6. Ibid., p. 49.
7. Anderson, op. cit., note 4, p. 46.
8. Gregor McLennan (1992) The Enlightenment Project revisited, in Stuart Hall, David Held and Tony McGrew (eds) *Modernity and its Futures*. Buckingham: Polity Press and Open University Press, p. 348.
9. Ibid., p. 330.
10. Ibid.

11. Alex Callinicos (1989) *Against Postmodernism: A Marxist Critique.* Cambridge: Polity Press, pp. 4–5.
12. See Frederic Jameson (1984) Postmodernism – the cultural logic of Late Capitalism, *New Left Review*, 146: 53–92; Jameson (1991) *Postmodernism or the Cultural Logic of Late Capitalism.* London: Verso; and Jameson (1998) *The Cultural Turn – Selected Writings on the Postmodern, 1993–1998.* London: Verso.
13. Frederic Jameson (1984) Postmodernism – the cultural logic of Late Capitalism, *New Left Review*, 146: 53–92.
14. Anderson, op. cit., note 4, pp. 64–5.
15. Arguably, modern Conservatism, at least in the United Kingdom, is also a creation of the Enlightenment environment, in the sense that the old aristocratic, Christian and hierarchical philosophy and political practice had to be radically reformed if it were to survive. For a sympathetic account of this process, see Robert Blake (1976) *The Conservative Party from Peel to Churchill.* London: Fontana (and subsequent editions); for a Marxist critique, see Nigel Harris (1972) *Competition and the Corporate Society.* London: Methuen. For more recent studies of Conservatism as an ideology, see Ted Honderich (1980) *Conservatism.* London: Hamish Hamilton; Noel O'Sullivan (1999) Conservatism, in Roger Eatwell and Anthony Wright (eds) *Contemporary Political Ideologies*, 2nd edn. London: Continuum.
16. Terry Eagleton (1996) *The Illusions of Postmodernism.* Oxford: Blackwell, pp. 56–7.
17. Ibid., p. 59.
18. Perhaps the most notable of twentieth-century Marxists who did not adhere to the centrality of social class in the transformatory process was Herbert Marcuse (see Marcuse: (1958) *Soviet Marxism.* London: Routledge and Kegan Paul; (1969) *An Essay on Liberation.* London: Allen Lane; (1974) *Eros and Civilization.* Boston, MA: Beacon Press; (1979) *The Aesthetic Dimension: Towards a critique of Marxist aesthetics.* London: Macmillan; etc.)
19. See, for example, Marx's own work: (1844) *Economic and Philosophical Manuscripts*, in Lucio Colletti (ed.) (1974) *Marx's Early Writings.* Harmondsworth: Pelican Marx Library; ([1846] 1968) *The German Ideology.* Moscow: CPSU; (with Engels) ([1848] 1969) *Manifesto of the Communist Party*, in A.J.P. Taylor (ed.) Harmondsworth: Penguin; ([1867] 1976) *Capital, Vol. 1*, translated by Ben Fowkes. Harmondsworth: Pelican Marx Library; cf. the voluminous amount of commentary and analysis. Particularly relevant in this context are: Tom Bottomore and Maximilien Rubel ([1956] 1963) *Karl Marx: Selected Writings in Sociology and Social Philosophy.* London: Pelican; Quentin Hoare and Nowell Smith (eds) (1971) *Gramsci, Selections from the Prison Notebooks.* London: Lawrence and Wishart; Georg Lukacs (1971) *History and Class Consciousness.* London: Merlin; David McLellan (1971) *The Thought of Karl Marx.* London: Macmillan; Ralph Miliband (1977) *Marxism and Politics.* Oxford: Oxford University Press.
20. Eagleton, op. cit., note 16, p. 22.
21. Ibid., p. 23.
22. Ralph Miliband (1994) *Socialism for a Sceptical Age.* Cambridge: Polity Press, p. 158.
23. Ibid.
24. Callinicos, op. cit., note 11, p. 128.
25. Ibid., p. 121.
26. Frederic Jameson (1991) *Postmodernism or the Cultural Logic of Late Capitalism.* London: Verso, p. 31 (cited in Thompson, op. cit., note 1, p. 237).

27. T. Allen (1992) Post-industrialism and post-Fordism, in Stuart Hall, David Held and Tony McGrew (eds), *Modernity and its Futures.* Buckingham: Polity Press and Open University Press, p. 172.
28. Ibid.
29. Alan Touraine (1971) *The Post-Industrial Society.* New York: Random House.
30. Allen, op. cit., note 27, p. 177. Among Daniel Bell's influential works on post-industrialism are: (1973) *The Coming of Post-Industrial Society.* New York: Basic Books; (1976) *The Cultural Contradictions of Capitalism.* New York: Basic Books; (1980) The social framework of the information society, in T. Forrester (ed.) *The Microelectronics Revolution.* Oxford: Blackwell.
31. Manuel Castells (1989) *The Informational City.* Oxford: Blackwell.
32. Ibid.; see also Allen, op. cit., note 27, pp. 176–84 for a discussion of this perspective.
33. See Allen op. cit., note 27, p. 179.
34. Callinicos, op. cit., note 11, p. 122.
35. Ernest Mandel (1975) International capitalism and 'supranationality', in Hugo Radice (ed.) *International Firms and Modern Imperialism.* Harmondsworth: Penguin, pp. 186–324; cited in Mark Murphy (2000), Adult education, lifelong learning and the end of political economy, *Studies in the Education of Adults,* 32(2): 166–80.
36. Murphy, op. cit., note 35, p. 173.
37. See Callinicos, op. cit., note 11, pp. 123–4.
38. Ibid., p. 124.
39. For an interesting discussion of left-wing intellectuals in the interwar period, and more generally, see Neil Wood (1959) *Communism and British Intellectuals,* London: Gollancz.
40. See, for example, Paul Kellogg (1987) Goodbye to the working class?, *International Socialism,* 2(36): 108–10; cited in Callinicos, op. cit., note 11, p. 125.
41. Callinicos, op. cit., note 11, p. 141.
42. Ibid.
43. On inequality in Britain, see Peter Townsend (1979) *Poverty in the UK.* Harmondsworth: Penguin; Ivan Reid (1998) *Class in Britain.* Cambridge: Polity Press; Vinod Kumar (1993) *Poverty and Inequality in the UK and the Effects on Children.* London: National Children's Bureau. On inequality within a more general and theoretical context, see Rosemary Crompton (1998) *Class and Stratification: An Introduction to Current Debates.* Cambridge: Polity Press; Erik Olin Wright (1997) *Class Counts: Comparative Studies in Class Analysis.* Cambridge: Cambridge University Press.
44. Perry Anderson (2000) Renewals, *New Left Review,* NS, 1(1): 13.
45. Ibid., p. 15.
46. Ibid., p. 17.
47. Anderson (1998) op. cit., note 4, p. 55.
48. Callinicos, op. cit., note 11, p. 174.
49. Anderson (1998) op. cit., note 4, p. 55.
50. Ibid.
51. Ibid.
52. For the original formulation of this 'deformation', see Perry Anderson (1961) The origins of the present crisis, and Tom Nairn (1961) The nature of labourism, in Perry Anderson and Tom Nairn, *Towards Socialism.* London: Fontana and New Left Books.

53. Anderson (1998) op. cit., note 4, p. 56.
54. Ibid., p. 62.
55. See Jean Dupuy (1980) Myths of the information society, in Kathleen Woodward (ed.) *The Myths of Information: Technology and Post-industrial Culture.* London: Routledge & Kegan Paul.
56. See, for example, Anthony Giddens (1990) *Consequences of Modernity.* Cambridge: Polity Press; (1991) *Modernity and Self-identity: Self and Society in the Late Modern Age.* Cambridge: Polity Press.
57. Raymond Williams (1980) Base and Superstructure, in *Problems in Materialism and Culture.* London: Verso. See also Frederic Jameson (1998) *The Cultural Turn.* London: Verso; Stuart Hall (1996) Cultural studies and its theoretical legacies, in David Morley and Kuan-Hsing Chen (eds) *Stuart Hall: Critical Dialogues in Cultural Studies.* London: Routledge.
58. Influential early works include: Sheila Rowbotham (1973) *Woman's Consciousness, Man's World.* Harmondsworth: Penguin; Helen Gavron (1968) *The Captive Wife: Conflicts of Housebound Mothers.* Harmondsworth: Penguin; Juliet Mitchell (1966) The longest revolution, *New Left Review,* 40, November/December; Betty Friedan (1965) *The Feminine Mystique.* Harmondsworth: Penguin; Annette Kuhn and Anne-Marie Wolpe (1978) *Feminism and Materialism: Women and Modes of Production.* London: Routledge & Kegan Paul; Barbara Ehrenreich and Deidre English (1979) *For Her Own Good: 150 Years of the Experts' Advice to Women.* New York: Anchor Press.
59. Carole Stabile (1997) Feminism and the ends of postmodernism, in Rosemary Hennessy and Christine Ingraham (eds) *Materialist Feminism: A Reader in Class, Difference and Women's Lives.* London: Routledge.
60. Perry Anderson (1976) *Considerations on Western Marxism.* London: New Left Books.
61. Jean Barr (1999) *Liberating Knowledge.* Leicester: NIACE, p. 120.
62. Karl Marx (1977) *Capital* (translated by B. Fowkes). New York: Vintage Books, p. 247.
63. Stabile, op. cit., note 59, p. 406.
64. Lynne Segal (1999) *Why Feminism?* Cambridge: Polity Press.
65. Edward Said (1991) *Musical Elaborations.* New York: Columbia University Press, pp. xiv–xv.
66. Susan Bordo (1998) The feminist as other, in Janet A. Kourany (ed.) *Philosophy in a Feminist Voice.* Princeton, NJ: Princeton University Press, p. 297.
67. Segal, op. cit., note 64, p. 5.
68. Ibid., p. 8.
69. Pierre Bourdieu and Loic Wacquant (2001) New Liberal speak: notes on the new planetary vulgate, *Radical Philosophy,* 105: 2–5.
70. Ibid., p. 4.
71. Ibid., p. 4.
72. Anderson (1998) op. cit., note 60.
73. Sheila Rowbotham (1983) *Dreams and Dilemmas: Collected Writings.* London: Virago, p. 354.
74. Segal, op. cit., note 64, p. 17.
75. Ibid., p. 218.
76. Ibid., p. 224.
77. Larry Ray and Andrew Sayer (eds) (1999) *Culture and Economy: After the Cultural Turn.* London: Sage.

78. Segal, op. cit., note 64, pp. 34–5.
79. Alex Callinicos (1991) *The Revenge of History: Marxism and the East European Revolutions.* Cambridge: Polity Press, p. 136.
80. Jeffrey C. Isaac (2000) Intellectuals, Marxism and politics, *New Left Review* 2, Second Series, March/April, pp. 111–15.
81. Karl Marx and Frederick Engels (1935) *Marx and Engels Selected Works*, Vol. 1, Moscow: CPSU, p. 147.
82. Alex Callinicos (2000) Impossible anti-capitalism?, *New Left Review* 2, Second Series, March/April, p. 120.
83. John Field (2000) *Lifelong Learning and the New Educational Order.* London: Trentham Books, p. 134.
84. Eagleton, op. cit., note 16, p. 135.

3

Revaluing the Enlightenment: The University and the Educated Public

Introduction: after humanity

In his seminal reconsideration of Kant's essay 'Was ist Aufklärung?' published in 1784, Michel Foucault wrote:

> You either accept the Enlightenment and remain within the tradition of its rationalism (this is considered a positive term by some and used by others on the contrary as a reproach); or else you criticise the Enlightenment and then try to escape from its principles of rationality.[1]

With some caution, Foucault decides that this is one burden of history we cannot escape. 'We must try to proceed with the analysis of ourselves as beings who are historically determined, to a certain extent, by the Enlightenment.'[2]

This chapter reviews some of the features of the Enlightenment that relate to higher education in the face of postmodern critique. We defend what we consider is still progressive in Enlightenment perspectives but take on board a necessary revisionism if it is still to be a persuasive force in education it the twenty-first century. As Tallis points out in his otherwise robust defence, the early promise of the Enlightenment has been proved deficient on at least three major counts: there have been no universal solutions to human ills guided by physical science; it failed to register that people might have fundamentally different ultimate aims rather than the common aims of 'mankind'; and that there has been a failure to establish a scheme of transcendental values. In short, the *philosophes* were themselves the product of a specific cultural conjuncture in a determinate time.[3]

It is perhaps not coincidental that the poststructuralist turn in philosophy and the opening up of mass higher education have coincided. Poststructuralist theory promoted widespread scepticism about the objectivity of knowledge and its universal application coupled with a prevalent belief in the cultural relativity of values and meanings. In poststructuralist accounts, the universalist values of the Enlightenment have given way to a general subjectivism and the notion of the human as the binding subject of knowledge, action and policy has fragmented before the onslaught of difference.

The question most asked by Enlightenment philosophers, 'What is it to be human?', has been replaced by 'What is it that makes us different?' Thus, the arts and the offspring of nineteenth-century positivism, human sciences, have yielded pole position to the study of culture or 'cultural studies'. Since there is no agreement on the 'essentially' human, essences themselves having been problematized, the emphasis has shifted in two ways: first, to the contextual study of signification and the social construction of individuals and, secondly, to the study of the unconscious determinants of behaviour, particularly the study of desire and sexuality. Above all, the 'linguistic turn', which has its roots in linguistic philosophy and formalist semiotics, has revealed that what was formerly regarded as the province of the human has now become the landscape of the text. We are, for the poststructuralist, creatures of discourse, spoken by the languages we attempt to speak and write, labelled and positioned by disciplinary discourses, authorless and robbed of agency. Once radical, even revolutionary, student activists have become quiescent, withdrawn and pessimistic. Habermas noted the air of resignation extant in so much post-sixties theorizing, with some understatement: '[t]he fact that poststructuralism, with its wholesale rejection of modern forms of life, finds an audience is surely connected with the fact that the efforts of praxis philosophy to reformulate the project of modernity along Marxist lines has suffered a loss of credibility'.[4]

Similarly, the stable male bourgeois ego (of myth) has been eschewed in favour of a stew of repressed desires that return morbidly in the nightmare of fantasy. While the stone carapace of the hu*man* has been turned over to reveal the woman underneath and the female inside, real women struggled to liberate themselves from patriarchy – only to be turned by deconstruction into a figure of speech. At first it looked as if the study of literature would succumb to the tidal wave of contextuality; instead, literariness is all and philosophy, the shining star of the Enlightenment, is regarded by many as just another branch of rhetoric.

The prominence given to the human by the Enlightenment emanated from a Protestant refusal of divine authority and priestly intermediaries as interpreted by the Roman church. As Brecht put it in his play *The Life of Galileo*,

> The pope, the cardinals, the princes, the scholars, captains, merchants fishwives and schoolboys believed themselves to be sitting motionless in the centre of this crystal globe. But now we are travelling headlong into space, Andrea. For the old age is past, and this is a new age.[5]

While the power of the priesthood by degrees gave way to a secular belief in the power of personal enquiry, reflective experience, rational justification and 'a great desire to fathom the causes of all things',[6] its

methods persisted in the new temples of learning. Even though this centrality of the 'human' has been problematized by postmodernist philosophers
(Foucault identified various forms of humanism that could not always be
reconciled with Enlightenment thought[7]), there is no corresponding urge
to return to divine authority as a guarantor of absolute *truth* (although
there might be for other reasons) or to abandon the methods of rational
debate.[8] Indeed the belief in personal enquiry into the truth has been
pushed by some to the extreme of asserting (paradoxically) that there is
only personal truth.

Post-colonialist critics argue that the Enlightenment theme of common
humanity and the common good has historically functioned only to sup-
press and conceal exploited minorities and those of a different culture,
race, gender, age or ability.[9] This vein of 'ideology critique' begins with
Marx's *German Ideology*, which was one of the first texts to explore the role
of ideology in constructing partial views of humanity, which masqueraded
as universals. Marx drew the conclusion that the celebratory narratives of
progress scripted by bourgeois historians occluded the perspectives and
struggles of the industrial working class. Feminist historians, adapting E.P.
Thompson's project of enabling those 'hidden from history' to speak, made
pathbreaking raids on the unarticulated to reveal counter narratives of
women's oppression and unacknowledged achievement. Post-colonial historians such as Edward Said, Gayatri Spivak and the Subaltern Studies group
in different ways challenge the grand narratives of imperialist historiography.
Kate Soper emphatically concludes that:

> without a deconstruction of the humanist subject we would not have
> had the feminist, anti-racist and gay movements; without a subversion
> of the modernist commitment to science and its productivist and tech-
> nocratic rhetoric (including that of Marxist Prometheanism) we would
> not have the green movement and ecological rethinking of the left.[10]

In one sense, it is remarkable how quickly the academy has responded
to these counter discourses, the implications of which are to fracture the
Enlightenment hope for the university as a repository of universal knowledge. Indeed, the vanguard of the attack on the validity of universities is
often to be found in the universities themselves.

The assumption of many Enlightenment philosophers was that humanity
(or Kant's 'mankind') was a singularity to which rights and duties could be
ascribed. The means to achieving this was education itself, through which
people could be trained to occupy appropriate functional positions within
an increasingly complex society and that also, through freedom of thought,
they could become morally responsible agents. The ideal of education was
to achieve a human civilization through rational argument, agreement over
values and ends and consent to the rule of law. The whole thrust of this
education was to release individuals from the thraldom associated with traditional custom and practice and unconditional submission to irrational
authority.

The educated public of the Scottish Enlightenment

An example of the new educational impetus can be taken from the Scottish Enlightenment of the eighteenth century, which took its lead from Bacon, Locke and Hume. The importance of the Scottish universities in creating a new kind of education based on Enlightenment precepts has been argued by Alasdair MacIntyre, who, in turn, is indebted to George Elder Davie's *The Democratic Intellect* (1964). MacIntyre argues that the primary achievement of the Scottish Enlightenment had been to create and develop an 'educated public' rather than a coterie of academic specialists.

The Scottish Enlightenment placed a heavy burden on collective rational activity. It fostered the belief in widespread social agreement upon standards and the subject matter for which *thinking* is required. Thinking, especially about first principles, should not be restricted to an elite of academics, but should be a fundamental activity of all those involved in public life. Debates between lawyers, doctors, ministers and other professional groups might then always return to a commonly agreed, rationally held substratum of belief.

However, it is clear that the peculiarity of the Scottish 'educated public' of the early eighteenth century was its small scale and local nature. MacIntyre suggests that there were three necessary conditions for this new public to exist. First, there had to be a tolerably large body of individuals, 'educated into both the habit and the opportunity of active rational debate', who understand the questions as being important for their shared social existence and recognize each other as constituting a public, not merely a group of specialists.[11] Secondly, there had to be agreement as to the standards of appeal by which arguments may be judged, which was quite distinct from appeal to the authority of custom and local precedent. A third condition was that, to a large degree, there should exist a shared background of beliefs and attitudes informed by reading a common body of texts 'which are accorded a canonical status' – not as a final court of appeal but such as are treated with a special seriousness in the context of 'an established tradition of interpretative understanding of how such texts should be read and construed'.[12]

Clearly there are dangers in this set of prescriptions, which, although they leap from a genuine concern for inclusiveness within the empire of the intellect, nevertheless steer dangerously close to an exclusive cultural orthodoxy. Nevertheless, what MacIntyre calls 'the philosophy of common sense' emerged from this milieu, which emphasized 'democratic intellect' rather than doctrinal authority. It meant that its alumni within the Kirk, the classroom and the law would almost immediately debate ideas cultivated in an academic context in court and house of business.

The particular educated public that emerged over these years was, of course, almost entirely male, middle class and centred in the Kirk, but included lawyers, small gentry, merchants and schoolmasters. In effect, the public that MacIntyre describes is centrally that of the male professional classes. Despite its small size and cultural and gendered exclusions, MacIntyre argues that it offered a model for the role of the modern democratic university. The existence of the public created by and sustaining of this model made it possible to fulfil both the educational obligations referred to earlier: social role modelling and individual enlightenment. Discussion in 'society' over the best way its members should live, both reflected and interchanged with academic debate in which a return to first principles made differences sharper but real agreement possible. It enabled thinking for oneself to be done in a public non-specialized context in which general social interest, concern for the general good, application of justice to effectiveness and the place of aesthetic goods in human life might be freely expressed and related.

Then, for MacIntyre, came The Fall: the link between social roles and appeal to first principles was broken and, within the century, the educated public was replaced by a heterogeneous set of specialized publics.

Could it have been otherwise? MacIntyre lists five historical moments that subverted the educated public of the Scottish Enlightenment. First, '[as] the philosophy of common sense became more complex in its response to a variety of questionings, it ceased to be able to articulate a common educated mind'.[13] Second, the change in the scale of political institutions fragmented local intellectual communities – the decline of small-scale communities and economic growth and poverty destroyed the *polis* aspect. Third, and related to this, was the conviction that the specialization of trades and professions in commercial society eroded those civic virtues by means of which individuals understood primary loyalties as being to society at large. Fourth, the exponential growth of economic classes that were not included in the original public, capitalist and proletariat gave rise to 'a class structure which made the educated class impotent and functionless in the face of the new class conflicts'.[14] Finally, knowledge itself became the problem: the effects of economic growth on knowledge and the curriculum meant that not only was there was too much to be known, but exclusive academic specialization increasingly isolated the 'disciplines' from each other. MacIntyre is drawn to conclude that: '[we] possess in our culture too many different and incompatible modes of justification. We do not even have enough agreement to be able to arrive at a common mind about what it is that we should be quarrelling about'.[15]

But can we assume that the project of the modern educational system was the creation of such an 'educated public', or was this merely the contingent effect of one particular conjuncture? Jameson, for example, while sympathetic to the Scottish Enlightenment, argues that the brilliance of the Edinburgh group was determined by the 'the space of coexistence of radically distinct zones of production and culture' – Highland clans, lowland agriculture and English industrialism.[16] While it has always been undeniably functional, the educational system has presupposed some social end beyond inculcating basic skills and professional specialization, through an education in liberal arts and sciences. However, in the absence of an educated public, MacIntyre doubts that these will be more than merely 'passively received consumer products'.[17]

The concept of an educated public, therefore, remains the ghost haunting our educational systems:

> Our inheritance from the culture of the Enlightenment is so pervasive that we cannot rid ourselves of attitudes to the arts and sciences which presuppose that the introduction into membership of an educated public of at least some of our pupils is one of the central aims of our educational systems. But, so we have claimed, there is no such public for them to be a member of.[18]

The rise and fall of the educated public of the Scottish Enlightenment, says MacIntyre, coincided with the rise and fall of the 'philosophy of common sense' taught in the universities, a coincidence which he takes as evidence for his belief that the existence of an educated public requires a widespread shared philosophical education.

MacIntyre acknowledges that this 'public' was very exclusive – of the working class, women, Catholics and anyone, it would seem, whose ability to reason in the required (disinterested) way could not be guaranteed. However,

> It is only through the discipline of having one's claims tested in on-going debate, in the light of standards on the rational justification of which, and on the rational justification afforded by which, the participants in debate are able to agree, that the reasoning of any particular individual is rescued from the vagaries of passion and interest.[19]

Such a small community, sharing a common culture and sense of purpose, could of course believe in its own universal character and 'disinterestedness' (the power of the best argument). But surely we cannot.

For feminists, MacIntyre's 'educated public' and, more generally, Habermas's related notion of the public sphere, are curiously devoid of the plurality of bodies that breathe and feel. According to Iris Young,

> the ideal of the civic public as expressing the general interest, the impartial point of view of reason, itself results in exclusion. By assuming that reason stands opposed to desire, affectivity and the body, the civic public must exclude bodily and affective aspects of human existence.[20]

The notion of the public sphere tends to elide actual inequalities of status. But as Nancy Fraser has suggested, proceeding as if inequalities do not exist does not actually foster participatory parity; on the contrary, such a 'level' playing field usually works to advantage dominant groups in society and to disadvantage subordinates. It assumes a public sphere can be a space of 'zero-sum culture', able to accommodate with perfect neutrality any cultural ethos. Against this, theorists like Jane Mansbridge have argued that,

Even the language people use to reason together favors one way of seeing things and discourages others. Subordinate groups sometimes cannot find the right voice or words to express their thoughts, and when they do, they discover they are not heard. [They] are silenced, encouraged to keep their wants inchoate, and heard to say 'yes' when what they have said is 'no'.[21]

And yet we cannot simply abandon the notion of the public sphere as a phantom: in radical struggles around education, health, economics, the media, architecture and many other sites, the 'public' has served as a progressive rallying cry, a code word for socialism. (Though we should note, too, the uncomfortable fact that the notion of the 'public' has been used to effect by Fascism and other ultra right-wing movements.)

A major thrust of the argument in this book is that the concept of the public sphere, in which the educated public can flourish as plural and critically engaged, has been erased in postmodern analysis. In our view, it is important for a reconceptualized higher education to reassert the centrality of these notions and of the need for universal principles of social justice, untrammelled intellectual enquiry and, we would add, an explicit *a priori* commitment to equality.

Re-imagining the human: education and the imaginary

Few contemporary discussions of the 'human' start from the assumption that there is some fundamental essence to which an appeal can be made. For many Enlightenment philosophers, reason or rationality was seen as a defining power or capacity of human beings, a critique of which was instantly made by Romantic writers such as Schiller and Lessing, and in Britain especially by Blake, whose figure Urizen was a caricature of 'your reason'. The legacy of this critique has been a suspicion of rationality as a disembodying process and a counter emphasis on other productive 'human' traits such as imagination.

The Greek/French philosopher Cornelius Castoriadis, for example, who as 'Paul Cardan' was a prominent member of the 1960s political group *Socialisme ou Barbarie*, maintains that the distinguishing mark of humanity is not so much the abstract rationality prized by MacIntyre and Habermas, but the creative power of the *radical imaginary*. Western thought, he argues, has systematically repressed the role of the imagination in favour of instrumental and calculating skills, which enable the books to be kept and facts to be recorded.[22] But the lived world is not just the unitary world of calculations. Like us it is fragments.

'Being' for Castoriadis is chaos; it lacks the inherent form which calculation believes pre-exists its technical instruments. From this chaos, societies forge institutions and what Castoriadis calls 'social imaginary significations' or common forms of recognition. New historic forms are imagined and brought into existence through purposeful activity. Only our capacity to imagine new forms for the chaos of life (which also includes decaying institutions and archaic significations) and live freely saves us from brute existence. Rationality is not absent but is only the servant of the imagination.

In common with much French post-war thought, Castoriadis believes that the project of 'autonomy' is central to becoming human, but this cannot remain individualized; personal autonomy is dependent on the autonomy of others. Castoriadis draws out the implicit connectedness of personal and social autonomy through the Aristotelian concept of *praxis*. However, as Habermas points out, 'Castoriadis goes beyond the Aristotelian concept by radicalising the specification that praxis is always directed toward others as toward autonomous beings, through adding the proviso that no one can seriously will autonomy without willing for *all*.'[23] His concept of individual autonomy is differentiated from the conservative idea of subjection to given rules by its insistence on constant questioning and critique of prevailing social norms in the light of reflection on and understanding of one's own unconscious life. For Castoriadis, the unconscious is not the feared 'other' to rational activity, but its partner in the process of creating a tolerable and sustaining communal life. Only through understanding our own deep fears and instinctual activity can we imagine what others might be feeling and why they might act in certain ways.

One of these fears is, of course, freedom itself. Castoriadis is strongly critical of the retreat into conformism of the French Nietzschean former left, which he feels has abandoned itself to the marketplace of consumption and has been fearful of asserting values in the face of obvious exploitation and discrimination. He appears to accept something like Foucault's 'technologies of the self' as forming the self-disciplining subject and some form of self-restraint. However, like Foucault, he has no clear programme for advancing along this particular road to freedom or why one should choose the frightening prospect of autonomy over passive obedience.

Education for Castoriadis is not about imparting knowledge but developing individual capabilities:

> At every age, pedagogy has to develop the self-activity of the subject by using, so to speak, this very same self-activity. The point of pedagogy is not to teach particular things, but to develop in the subject the capacity to learn: learn to learn, learn to discover, learn to invent.[24]

The problem that education has to contend with is that from the social-historical point of view, the adult, in order to become adult, has internalized virtually the whole of the existing institution of society and, more specifically, the 'imaginary significations that in each particular society serve to organise the human and non-human worlds and give them meaning'.[25]

While society is held together by individuals understanding and submitting themselves to the meaning of social institutions, these same institutions can become oppressive, as Althusser and others have argued. Castoriadis holds that although social solidarity is desirable in the abstract, actual social structures are frequently oppressive or 'heteronomous'. The 'impossibility' of pedagogy lies in the attempt to produce autonomous human beings within a heteronomous society and, beyond that, in the paradoxical situation of educating human beings to attain autonomy while – or in spite of – teaching them to absorb and internalize existing institutions.

Thus while Durkheim strove to dislocate education from politics and locate it in the realm of the sociological, Castoriadis holds that education is by its very nature political (which, of course, is a major strand in educational sociology). Education has to foster the capacity of the individual both to absorb social values but also to think critically and creatively about them; in other words, to work within the creative tension between the instituted and the instituting society, between the given laws on the one hand and the reflective and deliberating body politic on the other. A reflective society cannot be formed without reflective individuals acting democratically:

> The essential link between these two aims of politics is found in pedagogy, education, *paideia*, for how could there be a reflective collectivity without reflective individuals? Democracy in its full sense can be defined as the regime of collective reflectiveness: everything else can be shown to follow from this. And there can be no democracy without democratic individuals, and vice versa.[26]

Castoriadis sees all societies as in a constant flux of change in which new institutions emerge from the collective imaginary depths as alternative to and possibly oppositional to those in existence, which are seen as holding back the interests of certain groups. Whether the new institutions will be allowed to become effective is most frequently a political struggle and, when a complex of new such institutions is demanded, it can become a revolutionary struggle. A paradigmatic shift takes places in which a new universe of meaning leads to systemic historical change: 'the ultimate source of historical creativity is the radical imaginary of the anonymous collectivity'.[27]

Conservative hegemonic interests retain power in a number of ways: by forbidding certain kinds of thought, by blocking representational flux and by silencing radical imagination, for example. The educational system as a whole is required by such interests to reproduce society in ways that will preserve its values and significations. But since control over education is never total, room for critical contestation can and does exist. Education must enable the individual to come to terms with desire and the limits of the social. This has to be a complex negotiation of understanding where society might legitimately expect an individual to control her or his desires for the common good or, alternatively, where the law unjustly and even cruelly prevents the expression of personal desire for no good reason, simply because such a prohibition is institutionally encoded.

Drawing on Castoriadis, we can argue that the aim of education should be to enable adult individuals not to deny their desires in Puritan fashion but, through an understanding of their own unconscious life, learn to move within them. They should be capable of understanding the specificity of their own needs but also accepting the necessity of the social world, of obligations to fellow human beings and of the need for collectively imagined goals for the good of all. The question is how to educate the imagination to envision pathways to freedom that are both individually and collectively liberating from oppressive structures.

Imagining the other

While the Enlightenment tended to stress the identity and unity of humankind through rationality, Western contemporary thought emphasizes respect for and toleration of difference. Indeed, a trend towards pluralistic solutions to social and political problems is also a mark of current approaches. How far, then, can social justice and equality feature as goals for which there are educational implications? One of the more sustained pluralistic approaches, predating those of post-structuralism, has been that of Hannah Arendt. Arendt also lays great stress on cultivating and enabling the imagination, but rather than encouraging a purely philosophical critique which, she believes, can conceal a peculiar kind of 'male' language, she celebrates the power of narratives to release new meanings.

Arendt stresses plurality and conflict as conditions of public life – but, unlike Lyotard, who also stresses plurality and difference, Arendt's notion of plurality does not denote incommensurable differences, only their irreducibility to a common measure or standard. Nor does her stress on plurality 'flip over' into the validation and celebration of existing plurality (much of which is the result of oppressive relations), which we and other critics of postmodernism see as collusive with commodification and the neo-liberal ethos of contemporary capitalism.[28]

Arendt proposed storytelling as an alternative to impartial, detached reasoning as a way of constructing knowledge and as a way of engaging people in a different kind of critical thinking from an argument. What she calls 'thinking without a banister' requires explicitly judgemental storytelling situated in the 'living experience' of the theorist so as to teach a kind of critical understanding, which, in Martha Nussbaum's words, 'consists in the keen responsiveness of intellect, imagination and feeling to the particularity of a situation'.[29] Thus, in *The Human Condition*, Hannah Arendt writes about totalitarianism not to define it so much as to move her audience to engage with her in thinking 'what we are doing'.[30]

As with Nietzsche, philosophy takes second place to poetry in Arendt's view of critical thinking because, she insists, it is not abstraction but considered attention to particularity that accounts for 'enlarged thought'. For her, critical detachment does not require disinterest, detachment or withdrawal from political commitment but, instead, 'training the imagination to go visiting'. Through the device of storytelling she asks: 'how would you see the world if you saw it from my position?' The reader or 'visitor' is offered a bridge and invited not merely to assimilate the different perspectives but to converse with them and to consider how they differ from her or his own. Both the deliberate use of 'distancing' – the modernist technique of *entfremdung*, or making the familiar strange – and 'bridging' are necessary to critical thinking, believes Arendt. It is not a question of empathy or trying to feel like someone else, but of being and thinking 'in my own identity where actually I am not'.[31]

Disch suggests the term 'situated impartiality' to name the elusive critical position achieved by 'visiting'. It differs from the position of abstract impartiality, which (from this point of view) does away with human plurality, precludes reciprocity and slips too easily into what has been called by Spelman 'boomerang perception' – that is, accepting 'others' only on the assumption that they are *really* like 'us'.[32] Of course, for Arendt, travelling is in the mind. Nevertheless, what she says on this is suggestive for a reconstituted 'emancipatory' higher education. For Arendt, rationality is not simply within individuals; on the contrary, it is a possibility contingent on social arrangements. So her recommendation to 'train the imagination to go visiting' is offered as a model of rationality which does not violate plurality, which involves a commitment to disputation and does not fall into scepticism or relativism. In her view, civic mindedness can too often be a façade, which suppresses dissent.

Without doubt plurality is for her the political principle *par excellence*, since people bring their interests to the public view, to be shaped, tested and enlarged in encounters but not necessarily transformed into unanimous agreement. This political process depends on the creation of public spaces for collective discussion and deliberation where people's self-centred perspectives are open to challenge by the multiplicity of perspectives that make up public life. This, then, requires the creation of institutions and practices (like those familiar to adult education, or indeed to the original advocates of a liberal, critical orientation to the university) in which the perspectives of others, of diverse groups and communities, can be articulated in their own terms.

Like Arendt, Sheila Rowbotham uses a variety of styles and forms of writing to convey her view of history. In one such example – 'Dear Dr Marx' – she writes an imaginary letter as a fictional author, Annette Devereux, writing in 1851. In the letter she refers to Mrs Marx's view that working people might well suspect from the *Communist Manifesto* that an aristocracy of scholars is to replace an aristocracy of money. She writes (in character) 'we socialist women are similarly able to detect democratic dictators within our own ranks'[33] and she chides Marx for 'the exclusion of all reference to women's part in our own emancipation', saying (as did Hannah Arendt) 'I consider that the social emancipation of all will be based on the self-emancipation of all the pariahs of society.'[34]

The capabilities approach

While in many respects sympathetic to Arendt's approach, the American Aristotelian feminist Martha Nussbaum wants to show that the combination of gender inequality and poverty she depicts in *Sex and Social Justice* (1999) and in *Women and Human Development: The Capabilities Approach* (2000) makes clear the need for attending to what she and Amartya Sen call the 'central human capabilities'.[35] A truly human life requires the possibility of functioning in certain ways, according to the 'capabilities' approach to ethics favoured by Nussbaum and Sen. They ask us to consider what aspects of living comprise the good life for human beings. The capabilities approach seeks objective standards for assessing the extent to which persons realize the various capacities that enable living a good human life. Ten capabilities are laid out, including being able to have good health, reproductive health; 'being able to form a conception of the good and to engage in critical reflection about the planning of one's life'; 'being able to work as a human being, exercising practical reason and entering into meaningful relationships of mutual recognition with other workers'.[36] Such capabilities provide a template for norms of justice, which are universal standards, according to Nussbaum. However, a limitation of Nussbaum's Aristotelianism is that it is deeply rooted in Western philosophy and clearly it is the 'expert' who decides what is to count as a capability. Educationalists need to assess how far this expertise can become the common property of learners and how far the experts themselves can be assessed.

It will be objected that Nussbaum's reassertion of a 'common humanity' to be found winding through cultural difference is merely a continuation of Eurocentric arrogance. Against this, she argues that it is a necessary principle for confronting the injustice and inequality she believes are to be found in all cultures, that perspectives based in cultural relativism cannot confront. Andrew Sayer observes that it is unfashionable in cultural or political economic studies to pay much attention to norms and values and it is 'cool' to be suspicious of accounts of social life, which acknowledge these as anything but 'camouflaged power'.[37]

As we have consistently emphasized, this is associated with a relativist mood of postmodernism, which renders values beyond rational evaluation. Because non-relativists like Nussbaum see a connection between conceptions of the 'good' and human flourishing, they regard some needs as transcultural. As a consequence, they judge that at some level humans are of equal worth, which is grounded in an understanding of what humans are like and what their needs are.[38] Sayer makes the point that to accede to relativism is to render all resistance and struggle arbitrary.[39]

Zygmunt Bauman also notes, in a very rewarding short study of the idea of 'community', that cultural distinction can often take more malignant forms than language, dress or ritual expression and may include practices such as female humiliation that cannot be made palatable simply because they are 'traditional'. Bauman comments:

we [western intellectuals] may be readier to accept that, as much as we should respect the right of a community to protection against assimilatory or atomizing forces administered by the state or the dominant culture, we must respect the right of individuals to protection against choice-denying or choice-preventing communal pressures.[40]

Postmodern Enlightenment

It is unlikely that informed and reflective teachers will find much new in this argument for the renewal of commonality of values, because the social problems education now addresses – functionality, injustice, exclusion, inequality, doctrinal absolutism – are centuries old. However, we should have learned from critiques of Enlightenment rationalism and in particular feminist ones that value intuition, feeling, desire, positionality and difference, that there can be no return to reason alone. If some notion of an 'educated public' in which rational debate is a productive value, as described by MacIntyre, is still desirable, then it needs to be decided how this can be achieved in the context of large-scale economies, mass populations differentiated by class, culture, belief, gender, sexuality, age and ability. It could be argued that a necessary form of resistance to the negative aspects of globalization is a re-emphasized valuation of locality, especially the small-scale community that could furnish an educated public. However, such communities are inescapably located within a global network of influences and possibilities that cannot be ignored. The same inability to escape from the capitalist gaze that positions each 'new' place as little more than a retail outlet for corporate brands is, potentially at least, equally vulnerable to radically new ideas.

While all educational institutions must value and reflect their locations, with their diverse populations, cultural mix and economies, they have to be able to evaluate their own specific knowledge production. Universities in particular are highly sensitive globalized sites, participating in intensively networked research activity, frequently hosting international (no longer 'foreign') academics and conferences, and with highly developed Internet communications, second only to military usage. But the apparent internationalism that surrounds these activities can often obscure as we have noted their own customary epistemological parochialisms – the highly developed specialisms within science and increasingly the social sciences and arts, which leave the intelligent layperson bemused. Universities, too, have to examine what can be commonly shared from their learned discourses and what is merely the incommunicable rattling of myriad discrete specialisms. An educated public has to be able to deploy a common language, which is both subtle enough to decode specialist discourses, but at the same time intelligible to those who have the intellectual curiosity. Finally, as Luhmann has it, the very functionality of contemporary social systems both renders the 'objective' standpoint, beloved of the Enlightenment, illusionary, and overbalances the educational system towards the production of those who will fill functional roles in the economy.[41]

But is there, in the end, an alternative to the modes of thought and discourses of values promoted by the Enlightenment? Have the grand narratives of emancipation and reason really died or is news of their demise merely the profitable business of those who Tallis calls the new 'soul doctors'? This culture of 'Wasteland' pessimism, which took root in the nineteenth-century *fin de siècle* intellectual establishment, depressed both by the 'beating down of Art' (Yeats) and the rise of the untutored masses to democratic prominence, was the first to reject Whig progressivism. But the counter-Enlightenment strand of 'blood and soil' folkishness can have no appeal to liberal intellectuals, no more than any pre-lapsarian return to traditional pre-democratic societies, theistic despotism or small-scale agrarian utopias.

While pessimism, as Gramsci noted, is a necessary intellectual stance, it has to be balanced by 'optimism of the will'. Although the Enlightenment proposed a 'human' being that metaphysically transcended all its particular manifestations, we now have to work with a notion of the human stripped of the metaphysical but informed by what Nussbaum calls 'capabilities'. Agreement about what is 'human' need not simply level out all cultural differences irrespective of time and place. It can, moreover, have the effect of elevating the oppressed and unmasking the oppressor, who might hide behind 'culture' or 'faith'. It enables a discourse of human and civil rights, which can be applied anywhere. That such a discourse is, on occasion, scandalously used to justify manifestly imperialist adventures does not eradicate the reality that such a discourse has enabled substantial progress towards more just and equal societies over the last two centuries. Over this period, the effect of the serious adoption of 'Rights of Man' theses by progressive governments has incomparably raised the life expectations of whole populations. There is no evidence, Tallis believes, of moral degeneration within this movement or that it has been at the expense of other societies. Where persecution of ethnic or cultural minorities sadly occurs, it is normally *opposed* rather than supported by those with enlightened views, while such oppression is frequently the outcome of some *counter*-Enlightenment belief in religious, ideological, ethnic or national superiority.

Tallis convincingly argues that it is hard to propose an alternative discursive framework to Enlightenment thought for those who wish to promote the spread of egalitarian and socially just ideals and to critique, change or build afresh social institutions.[42] Those who do not share these ideals can, of course, choose other modes but are unlikely to be interested in education or believe that the welfare of their fellow beings can be attended to in this life.

While some aspects of the counter-Enlightenment critique are well grounded, many of the core practices of this tradition, we argue, remain entirely valid. These include, for example, the methodological testing of hypotheses and establishing of the limits of certainty. Although 'social engineering' has become a term of abuse on the Right, frequently aimed at any plan of reduction of poverty, redistribution of resources or labour protection laws, the antithetical term 'entrepreneurial freedom' is used by the Right to legitimate a variety of forms of labour exploitation. Tallis believes that there are common human values, such as individual accountability, the deployment of reason and hatred of cruelty that can be established regardless of culture. However, identifying the culturally invariant values has to be attempted while learning how to respect differences and that, despite being human, people do not all want the same thing. Such a reflexive revaluation of the Enlightenment does not, therefore, throw it out, unhistorically and improbably (since the very mode of arguing for abandoning it is saturated with Enlightenment rationality), but retains many of its key assumptions. Universities have, therefore, to become less rigid, bureaucratic and inward-looking and more generous and imaginative, less directive and more enabling. Their customary elitist stance as gatekeeper of the culture, moreover, has to be moderated in favour of more modest ambitions guided by democratic and ecological principles, as we elaborate further in subsequent chapters.

Notes

1. Michel Foucault (1986) What is Enlightenment?, in Paul Rabinow (ed.) *The Foucault Reader*. Harmondsworth: Peregrine Books, p. 43.
2. Ibid.
3. Raymond Tallis (1997) *Enemies of Hope: A Critique of Contemporary Pessimism*. New York: St. Martin's Press, pp. 397–8.
4. Jurgen Habermas (1987) *The Philosophical Discourse of Modernity*. Cambridge: Polity Press, p. 327.
5. Bertolt Brecht (1963) *The Life of Galileo* (translated by Desmond I. Vesey). London: Faber, p. 20.
6. Ibid., p. 21.
7. Foucault, op. cit., note 1, p. 44.
8. Eric Hobsbawm (1994) *The Age of Extremes, The Short Twentieth Century 1914–1991*. London: Michael Joseph, p. 566.
9. Ranajit Guha and Gita Spivak (1988) *Selected Subaltern Studies*. Oxford: Oxford University Press.
10. Kate Soper (1997) Realism, postmodernism and cultural values, in Ronald Barnett and Anne Griffin (eds), *The End of Knowledge in Higher Education*. London: Cassell, p. 42.
11. Alasdair MacIntyre (1987) The idea of an educated public, in Paul Hirst (ed.) *Education and Values: The Richard Peters Lectures*. London: Institute of Education, University of London, p. 18.
12. Ibid., p. 19.
13. Ibid., p. 46.
14. Ibid., p. 28.
15. Ibid.
16. Frederic Jameson (1998) *The Cultural Turn: Selected Writings on the Postmodern, 1983–1998*. London: Verso, p. 42.

17. MacIntyre, op. cit., note 11, p. 29.
18. Ibid., p. 34.
19. Ibid., p. 24.
20. Iris Marion Young (1987) Impartiality and the civic public: some implications of feminist critiques of moral and political theory, in Seyla Benhabib and Drusilla Cornell (eds), *Feminism as Critique*. Minneapolis, MN: University of Minnesota Press, pp. 59–60.
21. Jane Mansbridge (1990) Feminism and democracy, *The American Prospect*, 1: 127, quoted in Nancy Fraser (1993) Re-thinking the public sphere, in Bruce Robbins (ed.), *The Phantom Public Sphere*. Minneapolis, MN: University of Minnesota Press, p. 11.
22. Cornelius Castoriadis (1997) *World in Fragments: Writings on Politics, Society, Psychoanalysis, and the Imagination*. Stanford, CA: Stanford University Press.
23. Habermas, op. cit., note 4, p. 328.
24. Castoriadis, op. cit., note 22, pp. 129–39.
25. Ibid., p. 130.
26. Ibid., pp. 131–2.
27. Ibid., p. 134.
28. Andrew Sayer (2000) *Realism and Social Science*. London: Sage.
29. Martha Nussbaum (1986) *The Fragility of Goodness*. Cambridge: Cambridge University Press, p. 191.
30. Quoted in Lisa Jane Disch (1996) *Hannah Arendt and the Limits of Philosophy*. Ithaca, NY: Cornell University Press, p. 140.
31. Hannah Arendt (1997) *Between Past and Future*. New York: Penguin.
32. See Elizabeth V. Spelman (1988) *Inessential Woman: Problems of Exclusion in Feminist Thought*. Boston, MA: Beacon.
33. Sheila Rowbotham (1999) *Threads Through Time: Writings on History and Autobiography*. London: Penguin, p. 223.
34. Ibid., p. 228.
35. Martha Nussbaum (1999) *Sex and Social Justice*. Oxford: Oxford University Press; (2000) *Women and Human Development: The Capabilities Approach*. Cambridge: Cambridge University Press.
36. Ibid. (*Women and Human Development*), pp. 79–80.
37. Andrew Sayer (1999) Valuing culture and economy, in Larry Ray and Andrew Sayer (eds), *Culture and Economy: After the Cultural Turn*. London: Sage, p. 55.
38. Martha Nussbaum and Rorty Amelie Oksenberg (eds) (1992) *Essays on Aristotle's De anima*. Oxford: Oxford University Press; Len Doyal and Ian Gough (1991) *A Theory of Human Need*. London: Macmillan.
39. Sayer, op. cit., note 37, p. 60.
40. Zygmunt Bauman (2001) *Community, Seeking Safety in an Insecure World*. Cambridge: Polity Press, p. 138.
41. Niklas Luhmann (1998) *Observations on Modernity*. Stanford, CA: Stanford University Press; (1995) Why does society describe itself as Postmodern?, *Cultural Critique*, Spring, pp. 171–86.
42. Tallis, op. cit., note 3.

4

Universities as Epistemological Communities

In Roy Bhaskar's words, '[e]mancipation depends on the transformation of structures, rather than just the amelioration of states of affairs'.[1]

There are several critiques of the established, disciplinary and intellectual base of the university. This book addresses the most important of them, draws attention to their weaknesses, as we see them, and posits an alternative critique and prescription. These critiques are the postmodern (on which we focus most closely), the professional and the technicist (which we discuss in Chapter 8), and the feminist (which is the main, although not exclusive, focus of this chapter). We also critique throughout the established and establishment orthodoxy.

Critical sociology of education posits that education systems should be construed as 'sites of struggle' between reproducing and transforming processes, and that education's relative autonomy *vis-à-vis* state control means that alternative agendas can be introduced.[2] The identification of subversive space has been a theme, too, of radical writing in adult education.[3] If we see the field of higher education as a site of struggle, we cannot fail to see the significance of the shift in ideas that has been underway for some time, a shift that has been summed up as the ambition to dispense with 'things' and to value 'words' more.

> What we wish to do is dispense with 'things', to substitute for the enigmatic treasure of 'things' anterior to discourse, the regular formation of objects that emerge only in discourse.[4]

This shift is mirrored in a trend in Anglo-American educational writing towards treating education as 'discourse', in an engagement with postmodernist preoccupations and attitudes of doubt and irony as we have elaborated in earlier chapters. It is echoed in current fashions in academic feminism; and it is apparent in the shift in influential disciplines (in non-science areas), away from the social sciences and their concern for causal structural explanation, towards the arts, philosophy and humanities and their concern for the understanding and creation of cultural meanings. Such intellectual fashions themselves have material causes; they are not just the result of the evolution of ideas.

The world as text

In our view, there is now an urgent need to distinguish between ontology (theory of being) and epistemology (theory of knowledge). The text is *not* the whole story. Much confusion results from a failure to make this distinction. Mary Midgley believes that postmodernism encourages confusion between 'goofy relativism' and 'intelligent pluralism'; that is, the recognition that the truth is so complex, none of us has the whole of it.[5] We shall stress below the importance of 'epistemological communities' in the production of knowledge, and the dangers inherent in an overestimation of intellectual activity separated from the rest of life. The point we want to make here is that issues of materiality cannot simply be shelved. Yet this is implicit in postmodernism's predisposition to see language or discourse (or text) as the primary realm of human experience.[6] There are structural elements of power and oppression that go beyond what both Foucault and Marx had to say; and there are experiential realities that belie any easy over-investment in the 'word'. The limitations of such over-investment, and the importance of action, strategy (and organization), are nicely illustrated, we believe, in an extract from an evaluation report that one of us wrote some years ago, as an evaluator of a community-based educational programme in one of Glasgow's most depressed and disadvantaged areas. A woman, driven to distraction by her husband, tried the following tactic: 'I had his bags packed and he sits for two hours getting his shoes on. "My name's on the door", he says. So I says, "Well, take it with you and I'll get one wi' my name on it!" '[7] This sums up neatly what is missing from discursive renderings of the social (and what is central to 'critical' social science, for example); namely, that, as Marx argued, society consists not of individuals, but of the totality of the interrelationships within which these individuals stand.[8]

To be aware of the role played by language in shaping social realities is one thing, but to treat the world (social or natural) as just a construct of language is quite another. Language, comments Kate Soper,

> including its very considerable powers to order the universe of which it speaks . . . is only possible because of the existence of a realm of being which is both non-linguistic and always intrusively in play as a determinant upon what is or can be said. To . . . treat the world as the construct of language (or, in a more accurate description of the discourse perspective, to argue that there is nothing experienceable which is not linguistically constructed) is to create a Kantian divide between a 'phenomenal' realm of the discursive/textual, and a 'noumenal' realm of the unsayable and – *from the point of view of everything that matters in life* – ineffective materiality (emphasis added).[9]

It is a question, she maintains, of

> preserving a certain dialectic between the material and the linguistic,
> the verbal and the nonverbal: a complex dialectic which it is difficult to
> specify since it is true, as poststructuralist critique has rendered clearer
> to us, that the relationship here is not simply one of representation
> between word and thing.[10]

Despite insistence by many postmodernists that the phrase, 'there is nothing
outside the text', is not intended to be taken literally, the effect is the same.

On being ontologically bold and epistemologically cautious

We need to draw on much richer traditions to underpin a reconstituted
public higher education system. Traditions such as critical realism and critical
social science, for example, commit us to getting behind appearances, to
ferreting out the operations of power and deeply rooted relationships that
help explain more apparent phenomena.[11] We believe that C. Wright Mills'
'sociological imagination', the idea of a kind of imagination that is based
on understanding the forces that influence people's ordinary lives, provides
a compassionate and much needed counter to the abstractions and indi-
vidualizing impulses that are so powerfully present today. And we think that
the kind of 'critical realism' pioneered by Roy Bhaskar offers a promising
alternative to philosophical and methodological positions that we find
wanting. This is because it makes central the complex dialectic called for by
Kate Soper, endorsing a strong ontological commitment, while remaining
sensitive to meaning, language and complex subjectivity, the hallmark of
postmodernism and poststructuralism.[12]

The basic tenet of critical realism concerns the independence of the
world from our thoughts about it. It is different from empirical realism
(empiricism), which treats the world as if it were co-extensive with our
actual or possible experience of it, as if, that is, it has no unobservable qualities. Bhaskar rejects this kind of empiricist foundationalism. For critical
realism the real is whatever exists, whether natural or social, regardless of
whether it is experienced or understood by us. The world has 'ontological
depth'. It consists of objects and processes, their structures, possibilities and
powers. For Bhaskar, then, social relations and social structures (like the
economy, the state, the family and language) exist prior to, and in one
sense separately from, the individuals who enter them, and are thus relatively independent of individual and collective experience. Critical realism
accepts 'epistemic relativism', the view that the world (natural or social) can
only be known in terms of available discourses and descriptions. However,
it rejects 'judgemental relativism', the view that we cannot judge between
different discourses or believe with any justification that some judgements
and accounts are better than others. It maintains that 'notwithstanding the
daunting complexity of the world and the fallible and situated character of

knowledge, it is possible to develop reliable knowledge and for there to be progress in understanding'.[13]

It needs to be acknowledged, though, that the voice of certainty that sometimes booms out of such work and its central metaphors – 'digging beneath the surface', for example[14] – is inappropriate to its central stance, namely, that our knowledge of the complex underlying structure of advanced capitalism is always conjectural and indirect; reality is opaque; the existence of deeply rooted relationships that explain superficial phenomena is only evident in certain clues and signs that have to be 'read' and interpreted.[15] Thus, 'epistemological caution' seems the only stance to adopt in the face of critical social science's 'ontological boldness'.[16] Anti-realists seem not to appreciate that knowledge can be social and linguistic *and* capable of grasping something of the nature of the world.[17] They confuse knowledge with its objects and they ignore practice. What is needed after the linguistic turn, suggests Andrew Sayer, is a 'practical turn'.[18]

Pragmatism is a philosophical tradition well known for such a practical focus. In the philosophy of education, for example, John Dewey repeatedly criticized the distinction between liberal and vocational education for representing a separation of mind from body, head from hand and thought from action. Pragmatism, like critical realism, is at odds with the *epistemological* emphasis of modern philosophy and with the recent 'linguistic turn'. By putting experience centre stage, pragmatists like John Dewey, Herbert Mead and Jane Addams (a recently resurrected pioneer of the University Settlement movement in the USA[19]) respond to what all of us know at the level of lived experience: that experience is suffered, enjoyed, undergone, transformed, loved, as well as known. For Jane Addams, the situated knowledge of people located in different group positions is a resource for enlarging everyone's understanding. Different perspectives open up the possibilities of reality, she believes, and they must be reflectively validated after being acted upon. Thus, Addams drew on the experiences of factory and domestic workers in her own reflections early in the twentieth century, as well as on those of ethnic groups of immigrants and poor and working-class women. Like Hannah Arendt, she attributes many social ills to the 'lack of imagination which prevents a realisation of the experiences of other people' and her radical and far-reaching conclusion is that 'we are under a moral obligation in choosing our experiences since the result of those experiences must ultimately determine our understanding of life'.[20] For pragmatists, knowledge is always perspectival and includes values.

Feminist educators have argued the need for educational and pedagogical approaches that will enable the articulation of 'views from below'. So, too, have advocates of 'history from below'. They do so, not because by virtue of being from below they offer truer, more accurate accounts of the world (although this, on some accounts, is what standpoint epistemology maintains),[21] but because, in identifying and making available spaces where alternative ways of thinking and being can be worked up, such practices increase the *possibilities* of knowledge.[22]

Feminism has an uneasy relationship with postmodernism, as we discussed in Chapter 2. Both are interested in how power pervades intellectual discourse. Postmodernism rejects standard notions of rationality and objectivity; feminists, too, have been involved in a sustained critique of these. But, as Kate Soper maintains, to criticize is not necessarily to reject; we must not confuse the 'critique of various forms of rationality, objectivity and power with the triumph of irrationalism, relativism and impotence'.[23] Some, indeed, see in feminism a further unfolding of the Enlightenment project conceived as an unfinished cultural journey and programme for critique and social change.[24] Often it is an *expanded* notion of knowledge and reason that is demanded to replace the narrow notions that dominate. Mary Midgley, for example, has commented on how extraordinary it is that, traditionally, epistemology has almost wholly neglected a very important aspect of knowledge – knowing people.[25]

The critique of reason carried out by feminists since the 1980s does not aspire to a 'female thought' style, as some have argued. Rather, it is the articulation of the different strands – intellectual, imaginative and affective – that are involved in *human* thinking and a resistance to their polarization. Feminist epistemology has stressed the situated and embodied nature of knowledge, criticizing mainstream science and social science for presuming that knowledge is disembodied, unmarked by the social position and character of those who practise it. This has been called 'the God trick' and it rests on the notion that embodiment and situatedness have to be transcended to achieve objectivity. On the contrary, claims Sandra Harding, denial of the situatedness of knowledge leads to 'weak objectivity'. In other words, unexamined dominant ideas, values and assumptions of the scientific (and wider) community are likely to intrude and a view from above to prevail; in contrast, acknowledging and taking into account different standpoints and the perspectival nature of knowledge makes possible the achievement of 'strong objectivity'.[26] Feminist work in epistemology has developed notions of objectivity that allow for detachment from one's own standpoint without commitment to the possibility of ways of knowing that transcend *all* standpoints.[27] Jean Grimshaw stresses that although knowledge is always selective (it always is from some point of view), we are not locked into closed worlds of meaning.[28] And Donna Haraway, an historian of science, speaks of 'responsible knowledge', learning to take responsibility for the social position from which we speak: 'struggles over what will count as rational accounts of the world are struggles over *how* to see'.[29]

A kind of social disengagement accompanies the relativist and highly individualistic spirit of the times. In our view, the more extreme forms of unmediated relativism encourage closed rather than open minds, because they protect one's favoured theories from outside criticism. We should not easily surrender the ideas of rationality and truth (or the belief that criteria of validity and legitimacy can be formulated), even though there may be real differences in what people think about, in how they organize their thoughts and in the concepts they use – depending on background and class, for instance.[30]

The need to insist on both the public nature of truth and the kind of social engagement alluded to above has never been more pressing. We live in a thoroughly internationalized economy where the activities of the most powerful global actors are *not* public. Currently, the most powerful transnational regulatory bodies – the International Monetary Fund, the World Bank and the World Trade Organization – are controlled by the world's richest nations, which, in turn, are increasingly dominated by the world's most powerful private, global corporations. In the face of this there is a growing civil society that is fostering new public spaces through which people and groups are exposing the doings of powerful state and economic actors and holding them to account. Since the 1980s, millions of people have been engaged in transnational organizing, in aid work and in arts exchanges to put pressure on transnational corporations like Gap. At Seattle, in 1999, hundreds of thousands of people protested at the World Trade Organization's proposal to allow corporations to circumvent existing regulations of nation states – to enhance their own freedoms, not for the sake of coordinated global regulation. Some of the most creative social movements today involve people whose aim is to focus *transnational* attention on issues of democracy and justice. In such a world, where there are vast injustices and where public spaces give way daily to private places, democratic politics *have* to be a process of struggle and conflict, as many have maintained; and these struggles are often with powerful agencies of systemic exploitation.[31]

Epistemological communities

It is an argument of our book that if universities are to develop more democratic and inclusive practices of knowledge development, they need to abandon the prevalent individualistic notion and myth of knowledge development that is enshrined in our education system. What needs to be acknowledged is the part played by social processes, epistemological communities and collective change in the development of knowledge.[32] Susan Bordo has spoken of the 'messy, slippery, practical struggle' to create institutions and communities that will not permit some groups of people to make determinations about reality for all.[33] Knowledge is in the end based on *acknowledgement* (whatever else it also depends on, including empirical evidence). We know as social beings, as members of interpretive communities and we do not all have access to the 'rhetorical spaces' where authoritative interpretations are made.[34] Thus, with relativists, we are in agreement that 'knowledge is constructed in positions of varying power and privilege; yet against extreme relativists, that knowers are accountable *to* a reality that is often quite precisely specifiable, and *for* the products and consequences of their constructive activities'.[35]

Lyn Nelson believes that to enlarge 'what it is possible to know' means recognizing that groups and communities, rather than individuals, are the primary knowers. Hers is a philosophical argument for the recognition of epistemological communities as the primary generators and repositories of knowledge.[36] It could be argued that the real agents of this insight were not primarily academics and philosophers, but the liberation movements of history including those varied groups of the 1960s and 1970s that staked a claim for the legitimacy of 'subjugated knowledge' and which, at the same time, exposed the partiality of 'official' knowledge. 'Whose knowledge?' was the historical and social question that dispelled the fantasy of disembodied knowledge and marked a crucial moment in, for example, feminism's history.[37] In relation to science, Evelyn Fox Keller comments that it too should be seen for what it is: 'the name we give to a set of practices and a body of knowledge delineated by a community, not simply defined by the exigencies of logical proof and experimental verification'.[38] To say that the practice of science would be enhanced if it had a more diverse constituency and if it were more open to public understanding and scrutiny is a rational claim.

Recent efforts to seek out enlightening ideas in popular action and community-based projects show what can be learned from attending to what E.P. Thompson called 'disregarded forms of knowing'. Feminist scholars like Cynthia Cockburn are a minority group who have conducted systematic critiques of the main academic disciplines since the early 1970s *and* who have consciously located themselves in a position both inside and outside the academy. A theme to which Cockburn returns again and again in her recent book is the knowing use of silence – that is, knowing when to keep your mouth shut – and the virtue of tact.[39] Cockburn's interest in popular and practical projects as a source of insight and knowledge is refreshing. It runs counter to the usual norms of the university, which tend to decry the practices and problems of everyday life.

Doreen Massey's research on the high-technology industry is suggestive here. Her focus is on highly qualified research scientists employed in the private sector designing and researching new products in high-technology companies. These are some of the core workers of the so-called new knowledge economy. They are overwhelmingly male and they work extremely long hours, first, because of the competitive nature of the industry and, second, because they quite simply love their work.[40] Massey notes that some of the reasons for such long hours – the nature of the labour market and the love of the work – are shared by other sectors of the economy, 'perhaps most particularly academe'.[41] Within the economy, jobs such as these represent the domination of reason and science and this is what lends them much of their status: what is demanded is the ability to think logically. Indeed, Massey maintains that such sectors of the economy are structured around two of the oldest dualisms in Western thought: Reason and non-Reason, and Transcendence and Immanence. Reason has been culturally constructed and inscribed as masculine.[42] So, too, has Transcendence – that is, making breakthroughs, being involved in change, in opposition to the static realm of Immanence, or, living-in-the-present, simple reproduction: he who gets out and makes history as against she who merely lives and reproduces.

Massey claims that the continuing power of these connotational or symbolic structures became apparent through analysis of the research interviews. It is there in what people say, in the way they organize their lives, in the unvoiced assumptions that keep emerging. Glorifying tales of their scientific work, of 'struggle', 'quest', 'always reaching higher', contrast with self-perceptions in the face of domestic labour and caring for themselves and anyone else. The idea of being good at both is not on the cards. The pressure, then, is for someone else to carry the 'other' side of life. If there is a form of masculinity bound up with all of this, suggests Massey, then it seems to be the case that companies in high-technology parts of the economy give it its head and benefit from it. Men and partners speak of minds being elsewhere when playing with their children; while domestic time is permeable, work time is not, and in its current constitution cannot be. This is because, in the nature of such work, it demands total concentration; and in Western society, the production of knowledge has for long been associated with detachment from the real world.

There are parallel pressures in academic life, where, in its increasingly intensified and competitive form, 'workaholism' is becoming commonplace, even required, says Massey. Referring to her dilemma after years of criticizing de-skilling, and finding herself now criticizing jobs for being too absorbing, Massey ventures that what is at stake, indeed the root of the problem, is the social division between conception and execution, between intellectuals and the rest.

More mundanely, but equally importantly, we would maintain, it is the subjugation of the whole public sector in terms of resourcing and the importing of elements of the 'macho' culture of private capital into the public sector. Rather than being critical of de-skilling *or* super-skilling, it is precisely their polarization which should be the focus of critical attention, Massey believes. The problem that she intuits in the kind of compartmentalized lives represented by the scientists, lies in the 'postulated separation-off of the isolated intellect from the rest of one's being and calling the product of the working of that (supposedly) isolated intellect: knowledge'.[43]

Massey's research brings to light the 'strangeness' of this state of affairs and invites us to see what we do as academics in a fresh light. Such separation-off of 'spaces of the mind' has a long history of course. David Noble has written of the long struggle to create a priesthood (more recently, an academy) through which knowledge was seen to be produced and legitimated.[44] Noble's history of a 'world without women' (the title of his book) tells of the capturing by enclosed masculine societies of the kind of knowledge production that was to be accorded the highest social esteem. Noble's story is one of continuity between some early Christian forms, male monasteries, early European universities and today's academy. He shows how the sphere of the production and legitimation of knowledge was a world without women.

But it was not a world created without a struggle. The conventional story about the origins of the university is one of the forces of good (democracy, reason) against the forces of evil (hierarchy, irrationality, faith). Noble tells a more complicated tale of the process of the separation-off of spaces of the mind (which is arguably also a history of the production of the form of scientific rationality depicted by Massey). His history depicts periodic challenges to how knowledge should be organized, who could have access to it and who could be thought to be a maker and producer of legitimate knowledge. It also documents challenges from those who had other ideas about gender.

From early androgynous Christian sects, through the Cathars of France, the radical dissenters of the sixteenth and seventeenth centuries, to feminist arguments today, this challenge has been directed not only at the exclusive possession of knowledge and spaces of knowledge by men. It has also questioned the nature of the knowledge itself and its attendant form of elite and class-based masculinity. At one level, the spaces of high-technology research and development are just part of a long line of spaces that are, in Massey's view, 'integral to the hegemony of particular sorts of knowledge and particular sorts of masculinity'.[45]

It is precisely this idea of knowledge as a set of institutional arrangements founded on the separation of mind and body that feminists among others have criticized in theory and in practice. The logical conclusion is to challenge the construction of the spaces themselves and the social arrangements that support them. Such a challenge lies behind, for example, the early developments in women's education as it arose out of the women's liberation movement within adult education throughout the 1970s and early 1980s.

The mind has no sex?

In fact, some feminist philosophers have argued that culturally and symbolically, the limits of reason have been fixed to exclude certain qualities that are then assigned to women.[46] Their claim is that femininity is constituted partly by this exclusion: 'Rational knowledge has been construed as a transcending, transformation or control of natural forces and "the feminine" has been associated with what rational knowledge transcends, dominates or leaves behind'.[47] This notion of reason as a method of thinking that sheds the non-intellectual and contextual and which requires rigorous training is culturally specific. Yet it functions in our education system as if it were entirely obvious and the only way of being rational.[48] Although there is an active academic debate about whether, and if so in what ways, men and women differ cognitively, the widespread assumption that they do has had far-reaching consequences; it shapes in subtle and profound ways people's educational and other experience.

A telling example of how this works out in practice is provided in Valerie Walkerdine's empirical research on secondary school maths teaching.

Walkerdine recounts striking incidents of how girls who are actually doing well at maths are still seen by their teachers as not really having what it takes. Boys, on the other hand, who are actually doing poorly, are still credited as having potential, just being lazy. According to Walkerdine, girls end up in a double-bind: no matter what methods they adopt in their pursuit of mathematical knowledge, none appears correct.

> If they are successful, their teachers consider that they produce this success in the wrong way: by being conscientious . . . and hard-working. Successful boys were credited with natural talent and flexibility, the ability to work hard and take risks. Further, teachers tend to think that boys fit the role of 'proper learner' – active, challenging, rule-breaking.[49]

Ann Ferguson believes that we need a theory that acknowledges both that the association of reason with men and emotion with women *is* an ideology, not necessarily a reality, and that patriarchal relations have made this ideology generally true. She criticizes grounding women's and men's different personalities (to the extent that these exist) in the private sphere of the family and in early childhood relations to the mother. Instead, she locates gender differences in a type of labour that cuts across the public–private sphere. She calls this sex/affective labour. This is work done in the home, community and wage labour, which meets sexual, affective and nurturance needs, as well as physical maintenance needs (cooking, cleaning, nursing, wiping bottoms). In the sexual division of labour, it is women who generally meet these needs, by serving men, children and other women in ways not generally reciprocated by men. This is as true in education as elsewhere, both institutionally and in the classroom. Thus women develop communication, nurturing and ego-flattering skills to meet men's needs, reinforced by peer bonding, in the same way as men's gender identity is formed. It is only now, when the public–private split is breaking down as a result of contemporary social, economic and cultural developments, that the reason–emotion split may have the possibility of being de-gendered, suggests Ferguson. This can occur only if feminists (both male and female) pursue a re-organization of the sexual division of labour, in which concern for concrete others, nurturing skills and physical maintenance are revalued for both men and women, and if social policies and economic and status rewards and recognition support this.[50]

Universities as they are presently constituted enshrine the dualisms criticized here. There has been little place in them for education of the body, hence for the education of action. Nor has there been room for education of the emotions or 'other-regarding' feelings.[51] In *Cultivating Humanity*, Martha Nussbaum defends a reformed, critical, liberal education, whose goal, the cultivation of humanity, is derived from Socrates's concept of the examined life, Aristotle's notion of reflective citizenship and the Greek and Roman ideal of world citizenship.[52] The book is based on empirical research on a number of higher education institutions and departments in the USA and it defends inclusion in the liberal education curriculum of the study of non-Western cultures, women's studies, African-American studies and the study of sexuality. Nussbaum does not ask if the development of all of the capacities which constitute 'cultivating humanity' is consonant with the academy's mission as it is or has been culturally defined. Liberal education as we know it has been a cultivation only of that part of the human being captured by the term 'mind'. This has been the subject of feminist critiques, as we have indicated above.

Foucault's model of power may be useful here, as some feminist educators (and many others) believe. An important reason for this is that it offers insights into how education works on bodies and emotions as well as minds. For Foucault, modern power is productive: it produces and normalizes bodies to serve prevailing relations of dominance and subordination. To understand how such power works requires two conceptual changes, Foucault believes.[53] First, we have to stop thinking of power as a possession of individuals and groups and see it instead as a network or dynamic of non-centralized forces. Secondly, we have to recognize that such forces are not random but assume certain historical forms in which specific groups and ideologies do have dominance. Techniques of power are captured by institutions and colonized by privileged groups. However, such dominance is not maintained from above but through multiple processes, from below, which regulate the most intimate aspects of personal and social life. Where power works from below, prevailing forms of subjectivity, including gender, are maintained, not mainly through coercion (although that may also be present) but chiefly through self-discipline. 'Just a gaze. An inspecting gaze' is all that is required.[54] External discipline is replaced by self-discipline, and various forms of confessional practices proliferate.

In education, guidance and counselling, learning contracts, records of achievement and self-directed learning have all been subjected to Foucauldian analyses. According to Foucault, through certain practices and techniques, people's inner lives are brought into the realm of power, through educating them to govern themselves. Education and learning, then, involve the disciplining of bodies and passions as much as minds. Foucault believes that the Marxist location of power in class obscures how power is also 'capillary' – how, that is, it invests the body and soul. In proposing his relational and productive model of power, power as process, Foucault does not deny the existence of centralized state power, for example in the state. But he maintains that this model of power as a possession, as centralized and flowing from top to bottom and as potentially repressive, is not adequate to capture those forms of power that make centralized, repressive power possible: the myriad of power relations at the micro-level of society. As emergent, this power is produced in concrete sets of relations; importantly, it is produced in 'certain coordinates of knowledge'. These are the practices of disciplinary power that he sees as emergent from the rise of the human sciences in the nineteenth century. There are, he says, 'no power relations without the constitution of a field of knowledge, nor any knowledge that does not presuppose at the same time power relations'.[55]

Some analyses of current trends in higher and lifelong learning draw on a Foucauldian perspective. John Field has commented that what lies at the heart of the rise of the concept of lifelong learning is *individual attitudes and behaviour*, at a time when 'values of autonomy and independence are deeply embedded in our culture'.[56] In a learning society where lifelong learning is the norm, people are individually responsible for obtaining the information and training they require for their own well-being. This becomes at the same time a justification for reducing public services and an encouragement to search for individual solutions to public issues. The trend to lifelong learning thus shifts the burden of responsibility onto the individual, at the same time as the welfare state in other areas of public life switches from passive support to 'active strategies of insertion', including strategies to form individuals who 'need', desire and take responsibility for acquiring the training and education necessary for their own well-being. (For a discussion of lifelong learning, see Chapters 6 and 7.)

Resources for the future

The massification of higher education was welcomed by many on the Left, in the belief that such expansion would be a significant and supportive factor in the development of a more egalitarian society. Some years ago, Basil Bernstein spoke of the 'secret' of higher education, a secret to which the vast majority were denied access: *only* at the level of higher education (unlike school education), the level of the elite, was knowledge presented as an activity and ongoing process in which undergraduates were encouraged to participate.[57] That was the privilege and secret of higher education which was held to be inappropriate for the majority of the labour force in a capitalist society. Bernstein's arguments belong to a time when critiques of capitalism were far more common in the public domain than they are in the early years of the twenty-first century. Yet their spirit is pertinent today where pressures to prepare students for employment often conflict with the desire to develop their critical faculties and to encourage them not only to participate in the production of knowledge, but to believe, too, that if they want to, they can change things.

According to Michele le Doeuff, history shows us philosophical moods that differ markedly from one another. She identifies two classic ones, the architectonic, concerned with building theoretical systems, and the corrosive, aiming to criticize and demolish. Sometimes these come together, but sometimes one dominates and suffocates the other. Since the 1980s, she observes,[58] interest seems to have lain in the possibility of destroying all language and undermining all speech, and although affirmatory works 'about something' have been produced, such production has tended to go unnoticed because of the 'mood of the times'.[59] According to le Doeuff, 'the major contradiction of our times' is the loss of language among the learned (through postmodernist underminings) and the need to articulate urgent problems with people other than academics.[60] In stressing that what is needed is a system of education that is not an apprenticeship into a hierarchy of power, feminist educators, among others, have emphasized a model of education based on dialogue and a recognition that there are diverse groups and communities that the university should serve. The complexity of those links with real groups struggling in the real world has yet to be explored; and the demands for equality, recognition and material entitlement represented by the current exclusion of these groups have still to be met. Meeting both conditions offers significant challenges for the future.

Many have made much of Lyotard's description of the demise of the 'emancipatory narrative'.[61] Alison Assiter has proposed that another way of viewing this very same phenomenon might be to suggest that the scope for knowledge creation has been increased. Many more people now have the possibility of gaining access to high-level knowledge; the hope must be that, as more and more people from dispossessed and underprivileged groups gain access to such high-level knowledge (and to Bernstein's 'secret'), they will begin to challenge the link between knowledge and power which Lyotard and Foucault have described. We might then see the inauguration of a post-postmodern reconstituted university founded on radical principle.[62] University educators who are interested in such a repositioning have to engage in two principal tasks: to develop an improved *critical* understanding of the relationship between our work (and the ongoing restructuring of higher education) and the *wider* processes of capitalist restructuring already underway; and, secondly, to devise tactics and strategies that can transform that improved understanding *into action*.

We have suggested that if we are to engage in such a positive and practical project, we need to draw on ideas and practices that break with the post-modernist mindset and delineation of 'interesting' issues that still holds so many academics in thrall. To this end, we have drawn on ideas from polit-ical economy, from philosophy (especially critical realism and pragmatism), from critical social science and from feminism as a theory and practice of social transformation; we have also made reference to the role of social movements and social groups as a source of new knowledge and ways of working. One major intention of the book is to urge that we *move on* from the linguistic turn towards a new practical turn. The practical turn we are calling for signals, too, a return to politics.

Notes

1. Roy Bhaskar (1989) *Reclaiming Reality*. London: Verso.
2. Roger Dale (1989) *The State and Education Policy*. Buckingham: Open University Press.
3. Richard Johnson (1988) Really useful knowledge, in Tom Lovett (ed.) *Radical Approaches to Adult Education*. London: Routledge.
4. Michele Barrett (1992) citing Foucault, Words and things: materialism and method in contemporary feminist analysis, in Michele Barrett and Ann Phillips

(eds) *Destablilizing Theory: Contemporary Feminist Debates.* Cambridge: Polity Press, p. 201.

5. Mary Midgley (1997) Visions of embattled science, in Ronald Barnett and Anne Griffin (eds) *The End of Knowledge in Higher Education.* London: Cassell, p. 78.
6. Kate Soper (1990) *Troubled Pleasures.* London: Cassell, p. 78.
7. Jean Barr (1999) *Liberating Knowledge.* Leicester: NIACE, p. 56.
8. Karl Marx (1977) *Capital* (translated by Ben Fowkes). New York: Vintage, p. 247; see also Bhaskar, op. cit., note 1.
9. Soper, op. cit., note 6, p. 10 (emphasis added).
10. Ibid., p. 11.
11. See Roy Bhaskar (1979) *Philosophy and the Human Sciences.* Brighton: Harvester Press; see also Bhaskar, op. cit., note 1.
12. See Roy Bhaskar (1991) *Philosophy and the Idea of Freedom.* Oxford: Blackwell; see also Bhaskar, op. cit., notes 1 and 11 and Alison Assiter (1996) Citizenship re-visited, in Nira Yuval-Davis and Pnina Werbner (eds) *Women, Citizenship and Difference.* London: Zed Books.
13. Andrew Sayer (2000) *Realism and Social Science.* London: Sage, p. 30.
14. Lee Harvey (1990) *Critical Social Science Research.* London: Unwin Hyman.
15. Carlo Ginzburg (1980) Morelli, Freud and Sherlock Holmes: clues and scientific method, *History Workshop Journal,* 9: 5–36.
16. Bhaskar, op. cit., note 1, p. 186.
17. Roy Bhaskar (1991) *Philosophy and the Idea of Freedom.* Oxford: Blackwell.
18. Sayer, op. cit., note 13, p. 71.
19. See Robert Hamilton (1995) The educational vision of Jane Addams: the formative years. Unpublished Master's thesis, University of Glasgow.
20. Jane Addams (1964) *Democracy and Social Ethics.* Cambridge, MA: Berknap Press of Harvard University Press, pp. 9–10.
21. Sandra Harding (1986) *The Science Question in Feminism.* Milton Keynes: Open University Press; (1991) *Whose Science? Whose Knowledge?* Milton Keynes: Open University Press.
22. Lyn Hankenson Nelson (1993) Epistemological communities, in Linda Alcoff and Elizabeth Potter (eds) *Feminist Epistemologies.* London: Routledge; Jean Barr (2000) Engaging educational research, *Discourse,* 21(3): 311–21.
23. Soper, op. cit., note 6, p. 13.
24. Pauline Johnson (1993) Feminism and the Enlightenment, *Radical Philosophy,* 63: 3–12.
25. Mary Midgley (1994) *The Ethical Primate: Humans, Freedom and Morality.* London: Routledge.
26. See Sandra Harding (1991) *Whose Science? Whose Knowledge?* Milton Keynes: Open University Press; Donna Haraway (1991) Situated knowledges, in Donna Haraway (ed.) *Simians, Cyborgs and Women: The Reinvention of Nature.* London: Routledge; Jean Grimshaw (1996) Philosophy, feminism and universalism, *Radical Philosophy,* 76: 19–28; Nelson, op. cit., note 22.
27. See Genevieve Lloyd (1998) Rationality, in Alison Jaggar and Iris Young (eds) *The Companion to Feminist Philosophy.* Oxford: Blackwell.
28. Grimshaw, op. cit., note 26, pp. 19–28.
29. Haraway, op. cit., note 26, p. 194.
30. See Seyla Benhabib (ed.) (1986) *Critique, Norm and Utopia.* New York: Columbia University Press.

31. See Midgley, op. cit., note 25; Stuart Hampshire (1999) *Justice is Conflict.* London: Duckworth; Iris Marion Young (2000) *Inclusion and Democracy.* New York: Oxford University Press; John Pilger (1998) *Hidden Agendas.* London: Vintage; George Monbiot (2000) *Captive State: The Corporate Takeover of Britain.* Oxford: Macmillan; and Naomi Klein (2000) *No Logo.* London: Flamingo.

32. Barr, op. cit., note 7.

33. Susan Bordo (1990) Feminism, postmodernism and gender scepticism, in Linda Nicholson (ed.) *Feminism and Postmodernism.* London: Routledge, p. 142.

34. See Lorraine Code (1995) *Rhetorical Spaces.* London: Routledge, p. 231; Barr, op. cit., note 7; Nelson, op. cit., note 22.

35. Code, op. cit., note 34, p. 196.

36. See Lyn Hankenson Nelson (1990) *Who Knows: From Quine to Feminist Empiricism.* Philadelphia, PA: Temple University Press; Nelson, op. cit., note 22.

37. See Bordo, op. cit., note 33.

38. Evelyn Fox Keller (1985) *Reflections on Gender and Science.* New Haven, CT: Yale University Press.

39. See Cynthia Cockburn (1999) *The Space Between Us.* London: Zed Books.

40. See Doreen Massey (2001) Blurring the boundaries: high-tech in Cambridge, in Carrie Praechter, Margaret Preedy, David Scott and Janet Soler (eds) *Knowledge, Power and Learning.* London and Milton Keynes: Paul Chapman in association with the Open University.

41. Ibid., p. 21.

42. See also Genevieve Lloyd (1984) *The Man of Reason.* London: Methuen; Londa Schiebinger (1989) *The Mind Has No Sex?* Cambridge, MA: Harvard University Press.

43. Massey, op. cit., note 40, p. 33.

44. David Noble (1992) *A World Without Women.* Oxford: Oxford University Press.

45. Massey, op. cit., note 40, p. 34.

46. See, for example, Lloyd, op. cit., note 42.

47. Ibid., p. 2.

48. See Elizabeth Minnich (1989) *Transforming Knowledge.* Philadelphia, PA: Temple University Press.

49. Valerie Walkerdine and Girls and Mathematics Unit (1989) *Counting Girls Out.* London: Virago, p. 155.

50. See Ann Ferguson (1993) Does reason have a gender?, in Roger Gottlieb (ed.) *Radical Philosophy: Tradition, Counter-Tradition, Politics.* Philadelphia, PA: Temple University Press, pp. 21–47.

51. See Jane Martin (2000) *Coming of Age in Academe.* London: Routledge, p. 132.

52. See Martha Nussbaum (1997) *Cultivating Humanity.* Cambridge, MA: Harvard University Press.

53. See Michel Foucault (1979) *Discipline and Punish.* New York: Vintage Books; (1980) *Power/Knowledge: Selected Interviews and Other Writings, 1972–77* (edited by Colin Gordon). New York: Pantheon Press.

54. Susan Bordo (1993) *Unbearable Weight: Feminism, Western Culture and the Body.* Berkeley, CA: University of California Press, p. 27.

55. Michel Foucault (1979) *Discipline and Punish.* New York: Vintage Books, p. 27.

56. John Field (2001) Lifelong education, *International Journal of Lifelong Education,* 20(1/2): 11.

57. Basil Bernstein (1972) *Class Codes and Control,* Vol. 1. London: Routledge & Kegan Paul.

58. Michele Le Doeuff (1991) *Hipparchia's Choice: An Essay Concerning Women, Philosophy etc.* Oxford: Blackwell.
59. Ibid.
60. Ibid., p. 179.
61. J.F. Lyotard (1984) *The Postmodern Condition.* Manchester: Manchester University Press.
62. Assiter (1999) op. cit., note 12.

Part 3

Policy Development
in Higher Education

5

The Policy Context

The primary focus of this book is the postmodern perspective – or series of perspectives – on higher education, in terms of policy development and cultural attitude, and the reasons, in our view, why these perspectives are both inadequate analytically and produce a cultural and political climate that is not conducive to progressive change. The intention in this chapter is to present an overview of the policy context in higher education in Britain since the 1960s.[1] In Chapter 6, we address these issues in some detail focusing on lifelong learning.

Although universities are among the oldest continuous social institutions in Britain, indeed in the Western world generally, the contemporary system is predominantly a modern, arguably modernist, creation. In Britain, the cultural influence, as well as the sheer material wealth, international prestige and intellectual pre-eminence, of Oxford and Cambridge, is clearly very great. (And, it can be argued, there is a handful of other institutions of similar prestige in more specialist worlds – Imperial, LSE and so on.) Nevertheless, as Peter Scott has noted, the fact that even as late as 1963, the year the Robbins Report was published, there were still only twenty-four universities, 'demonstrates that the ancient pedigree of the universities is largely a myth. The universities themselves are recent creations'.[2] The interweaving of the culture and traditions of the prestigious, ancient universities and the modernity of the overwhelming majority, typifies the way in which British culture and social structure have evolved since the industrial revolution. As Perry Anderson noted many years ago, the legacy of the aristocratic, landed society and the ideology it produced remains centrally important, despite the socio-economic system's demise long since.[3]

Obviously, therefore, at a level of generality, the higher education system as it has developed since the 1960s is highly heterogeneous. There is no single, simple model, or even collection of exclusive generic characteristics, of 'the university'. Indeed, Peter Scott identifies twelve sub-sectors in the system at the beginning of the twenty-first century.[4] Again at a level of generality, the development and culture of the university system at any given period reflects the socio-economic needs, as they are perceived. Thus, in pre-industrial times, universities 'were largely concerned with the training of clergymen and teachers, entwined professions. Their mission, in today's terminology, was to sustain intellectual hegemony, the established Anglican (or Presbyterian) order'.[5] As industrialism took hold in the nineteenth century, so there was both a need for far more technologically and professionally trained people for the economy, and for access to universities for the new middle classes: hence the creation of the big civics in the then new industrial centres of the Midlands and the North. During the twentieth century, developments in higher education have broadly mirrored the corresponding needs, as they were perceived, of the wider society.

There are two further preliminary points to be noted by way of introduction. The first is that universities have always been and remain, as is argued below, an important means of social reproduction. This applies in particular, of course, at what are perceived to be the higher levels, so that the elite universities have acted as key agents for the reproduction of the governing classes; but, in the twentieth century, this has been extended to the more complex process of reproducing a number of intermediate strata through generally relatively less prestigious institutions. It should thus come as no surprise that, in an era of performativity criteria, higher education is increasingly geared towards the skills training agenda and the generation of transferable skills. In the past, when the governing class was composed of 'Renaissance men' whose attributes were, not a vocational training, but 'rather ... an ability to handle men and affairs that [depended] more on character than on knowledge',[6] the elite liberal culture imbued by the universities was highly congruent.

The final introductory factor to note is the growing importance of the state in higher education.[7] Again, this obviously connects to the growth of corporate and state structures from the late nineteenth century onwards, which, in turn, has its origins in the radical development economically and organizationally in the national and international economy.

All these factors are general determinants of the change that took place in the system from the time of the Robbins Report[8] onwards. The specific and fundamental developments since the 1960s are framed by an inherited culture characterized by very diverse organizational forms and objectives, by the continuing role of universities as agencies of social reproduction and by the increasing role of the state. Above all, though, universities and their activities, missions and cultures are determined by the changing wider socio-economic environment. As with that environment, the higher education system is thus characterized by a series of contradictory pressures and ideological forces.

The Robbins period

From the time of Robbins onwards, the most notable feature of higher education in Britain – to an even greater extent than in comparable societies

Table 5.1 Growth in participation in higher education, 1979 to 1992

	1979	*1992*
Age Participation Index (API)	12.4%	27.8%
Percentage of first-year home full-time students on undergraduate courses aged 21 or more	24.0%	33.0%
Women as percentage of all first-year full-time students	40.8%	47.3%
Social class: clerical and working	37.0% (1978)	42.0% (1993)

Sources: DES, 1991; DfE, 1994; A. Smithers and P. Robinson (1995) *Post-18 Education: Growth, Change, Prospect*, Executive Briefing. London: Council for Industry and Higher Education.

– has been the rapid growth in student numbers and, to a lesser extent, in the overall size of the system. However, this growth has been uneven: the post-Robbins and post-Baker phases 'were characterised by distinct spurts of growth, followed by governmental second thoughts'.[9] The overall impact of the expansion has been dramatic. A snapshot illustration of this can be shown graphically by comparing 1979, by which time the full effects of the post-Robbins reforms had come into force, and 1992, when Kenneth Baker's expansionary policies had created the next major 'spurt' of expansion.[10]

The Robbins Report was, of course, very positive about universities and their social, as well as educational, potential. The Report recommended that 'the university sector should be enlarged by promoting, first, the Colleges of Advanced Technology and, subsequently, selected regional Colleges of Technology (which became the core institutions of the future polytechnics)'.[11] Although it is true that the incoming Labour Government of 1964 rejected Robbins's view of 'expansion built round autonomous universities in favour of expansion based on accountable polytechnics', the influence of Robbins was, according to Peter Scott, 'immense'.[12] Scott argues, correctly in our view, that the legacy of Robbins was fundamental. The large-scale expansion entailed a step change: from the later 1960s onwards, the state was the key player (and funder) of higher education. As a result of Robbins, higher education was 'enlarged . . . to embrace the leading technical colleges and teacher training colleges as well as the universities'.[13]

However, the Labour Government did not follow Robbins's policy of the enlargement of the university sector; instead, the colleges of advanced technology became a subset of the system, administered through the University Grants Committee (UGC); and the polytechnics were created, as announced by Anthony Crosland in his famous Woolwich speech in 1965, as a new public sector higher education 'formally in local government control but with a strong national dimension'.[14]

This deliberate creation of a binary system was the clearest possible indication that, first, the state regarded high-level vocational skills training for much larger numbers of people than hitherto as a high priority and, secondly, that the universities, construed within the broadly liberal, humanistic culture articulated by Robbins, were not the appropriate vehicles for this task. Crosland, himself a product of Oxford, was thus the instigator of a dichotomy, which, although it had long existed as part of the contradictory processes referred to earlier, had not previously had a formal articulation.

The subsequent, complex relationship between the UGC representing the universities and the National Advisory Body (NAB) absorbed much energy, wasted much time on political in-fighting and exacerbated the tensions within the system. Through the 1970s the universities – and the UGC – pressed for a continuation of the traditional high-cost university system, operating alongside a separate, cheaper and local authority controlled polytechnic system. In effect, universities were asking for an explicit re-endorsement of a separate university economy, which was expensive primarily because of the practice of residence for undergraduates and the costs (in terms of both staff and capital plant) of research.

Almost by default, governments in the 1970s tolerated this system, though with periodic assaults on the unit of resource and a continuing tug of war over university costs in general, because their attention in the post-compulsory sector was elsewhere. They were 'too absorbed by the difficulty of redefining, or unravelling, the complex relationship between polytechnics and local education authorities to insist on the illogicality of the UGC's position'.[15] With hindsight, this was always a temporary respite from a virtually inevitable and fundamental change in the whole system. Although the 1981 UGC cuts gave a brief new lease of life to the UGC, and inflicted sharp and genuine misery on the old universities, by the later 1980s it had become clear that 'the UGC, and the "old" universities, were only a part of [the system of higher education] . . . and a dwindling part. The system's centre of gravity subtly shifted from universities to polytechnics'.[16] This is certainly true in terms of government focus, reflecting perceived national needs in terms of vocationalism, skills strategies and cost-effectiveness.

However, as always, there were and are contradictory pressures. The high status and power of the more prestigious universities was, and is, in effect unassailable. The research reputations and the accompanying funding became increasingly – and increasingly explicitly – concentrated upon the 'old' universities, especially Oxford and Cambridge. Equally important, the power networks in the wider society and the central function of elite social reproduction continued to be centred firmly within the higher echelons of the university system. In these ways, the higher education system reflects the hierarchical society of which it is a part; and, a recurring theme of this book, this finds its primary, though not exclusive, articulation in the continuing, pervasive power of the social class structure.

The beginnings of mass higher education

In the twenty years since the Robbins Report, the higher education system had thus undergone its most profound transformation in history. The resultant, uncomfortable, structures clearly needed rationalization. As Peter Scott notes, 'the fact that the creation of NAB did not resolve the tensions between the DES and local education authorities over the management of the polytechnics and colleges of higher education set off a chain reaction which led to the creation of a unified system and – sad necessity – the abolition of the UGC'.[17]

The removal of the polytechnics from local authority control became almost a formality: this rendered the NAB an anachronism. The creation of the Polytechnics and Colleges Funding Council (PCFC), the government's priority so that it could plan, regularize and develop the public sector higher education bodies and thus orient the system to the primary goal of higher level skills training on a cost-effective basis, necessitated the creation of a parallel body for the 'old' universities. Thus the Universities Funding Council (UFC) was created, as noted, almost by default.

In retrospect, it is clear that this was, yet again, always going to be a short-term transitional, not to say messy, structure. The UFC had both a brief and an unhappy life. The PCFC was from the outset dynamic, representing the new freedom of the polytechnics and seizing the initiative; it was clearly and inherently more attuned to the instrumental and vocational aspirations of the Conservative Governments of the 1980s. In practical and important terms, it was the polytechnics that delivered increased student numbers in the 1980s, while the universities expanded – on the whole and with notable exceptions – only slowly. Their 'instinct [was] to defend the unit of resource' and resist any rapid expansion.[18]

In 1992, the whole post-compulsory system was rationalized with the creation of unified Funding Councils for Higher Education, though significantly as a result of the climate of devolution, with separate bodies for England (HEFCE), Scotland (SHEFC) and Wales (the Welsh Funding Council). Equally important, further education was taken out of local authority control and with the establishment of the FEFC put on a primarily national basis. Thus, in a sense, a new binary system, between higher education and further education, was created. However, with the Learning and Skills legislation in 2000, the FEFC was abolished and dissolved into the Learning and Skills Council, with a broader and more comprehensive post-compulsory brief. Whether this final binary system will be abolished in its turn is an interesting and contentious issue, and it is clear that the boundaries were *de facto* blurring though not dissolving in the early years of the twenty-first century.

The nature of the emergent system

This almost frenetic pattern of organizational change was a consequence primarily of the transition, or partial transition, from an elite to a mass system of higher education. From an APR (age participation rate) of fewer than 8 per cent of the standard age group in the early 1960s, the system expanded so that, by the late 1990s, there was an APR of over 30 per cent. Moreover, there has been a huge growth in the numbers of part-time, mainly mature, students within higher education, concentrated heavily on the post-1992 universities. However, with the introduction in England and Wales of tuition fees and the extension of the loans system to replace maintenance grants for all but those students in hardship, the numbers of mature entrants have declined noticeably. This was, perhaps, one of many examples of the much-vaunted 'joined up government' not working. Significantly, with partial autonomy brought about by the devolution process, Scotland opted for a radically different system, thanks to pressure from the Liberal Democrat partners in the ruling coalition with Labour. A committee under the chairmanship of Andrew Cubie formulated a system dependent upon a graduate tax, triggered by subsequent income, and abolished the tuition fee element for Scottish higher education students. The new system also introduced a relatively generous bursary scheme for students from disadvantaged backgrounds.

Another notable area of expansion has been in taught postgraduate programmes, very largely geared towards specific professional training, again an indication of the strongly vocational, high-level skills orientation of much of the development in higher education. (This is the subject of analysis in Chapter 8.)

Overall, student numbers in higher education in the United Kingdom grew from 200,000 in 1960–61 to almost 1.8 million in the late 1990s. There has been a marked increase in participation in higher education by women – particularly young middle-class women – and by all social classes except the traditionally defined working class: the C2, D and E categories of employment. This testifies, again, to the persistence of social class inequalities in the wider society and the way in which higher education reflects this. Generally, higher education has expanded 'not so much by reaching out to new student constituencies, as by exploiting existing constituencies more fully'.[19]

There are thus contradictory processes at work: on the one hand a massive expansion in the system, on the other an intensification of the diversity of the sector. This diversity is often proclaimed as a pluralistic benefit of the new, broader and at least quasi-mass system. This chimes nicely with postmodernism's celebration of difference; and, indeed, there *is* much to celebrate in having a more flexible, differentiated sector that can respond to a variety of learners and their necessarily diverse needs – in terms of mode of study as well as disciplinary, or increasingly interdisciplinary, fields of interest.

However, overarching all these positive factors is the pervasive hierarchy and elitism of the system. The 'Russell Group' universities – not only Oxford and Cambridge – have changed relatively little. Their student intakes are very largely middle class, standard age, full-time, residential and well-qualified. And their subject mix is predominantly traditional. There *are*, of course, many differences in the 'old' universities between the 1960s and 1970s and the 1990s and beyond: student numbers have expanded, there are far greater numbers of female students, modular systems have been introduced in many institutions, the subject mix has been significantly extended (the growth of Business Studies, for example). The predominant pattern, though, is for these universities to continue culturally in the same vein as before: hence the oft repeated claim that, rather than a radically changed and mass system, we have in practice a crowded traditional system.

The pressures for accessibility for non-traditional learners, for curriculum innovation and the rest, have been heavily, though by no means exclusively, focused on the post-1992 institutions. Even this, arguably, has not been a wholly progressive impetus. It is precisely in this part of the sector that the change to more vocationally driven (and frequently business driven) provision has been most pronounced; similarly, it has been in the *pre*-1992 parts of the sector that adherence to the liberal, disinterested, models of higher education has been strongest. It may be argued that this is unsurprising, as the elite universities, after all, historically have provided the all-round education for the higher strata of society and their subsequent employment. And the appropriate education has been seen as liberal and arts based; to that extent the elite universities have been historically vocational too, ensuring the social reproduction of governing elites. But it is also from within this framework that the critical, sceptical spirit of enquiry has grown, flourished and been protected. There is thus a paradox in the jealous protection, by the most establishment institutions, of often the most socially and politically deviant and least 'relevant', most esoteric forms of learning, scholarship and research; and, on the other hand, the incorporation within the established market culture of many of the most seemingly progressive, access-oriented, newer universities and other higher education institutions.

The explanation for this lies perhaps in two related factors. The pre-1992 universities, including those created in the 1960s, generally had a strong representation of arts and social sciences and had a culture of decentralized, independent academic activity. The defining and to an extent controlling unit of the university was the 'department' rather than the 'management' of the institution. To an extent, this has changed in the last decade of the twentieth century and the early years of the twenty-first century; but it remains largely the case. In contrast, the post-1992 institutions have a strongly managerialist culture, allied to a much more vocational and applied science mix of provision. And, of course, they have historically been subject to bureaucratic control through local authority structures and then bodies such as the Council for National Academic Awards (CNAA) and the NAB. The second factor is the influence of the 'external world' on both sorts of institution. For the pre-1992 universities, both the development of perspectives and knowledge paradigms such as cultural studies and the impact of social movements directly relevant to the arts and the social sciences – feminism, minority ethnic identity movements and so on – were influential. In contrast, the increasingly dominant Thatcherite tenor of the 1980s and 1990s impacted strongly on the post-1992 universities.

These factors should not be overestimated, however. There is a clear trend in the system as a whole towards a business culture, a dominance of finance criteria for policy, and a diminution of the longstanding critical thinking, independent core of the university's identity.

On a more mundane and specific level, there are also sector-wide cultural practices that have been inherited from different parts of this diverse, though now formally unified, higher education system. One of the two most prominent is the so-called 'audit culture', stemming from the old polytechnic system of the CNAA *et al.*, and now dominant within the teaching and learning structure of the whole sector. This is articulated through such bodies as the Quality Assurance Agency (QAA) and potentially the Institute for Learning and Teaching inaugurated in 1999, and through the new emphases (new for the pre-1992 universities, that is) on outcomes-based curriculum, regular monitoring and review of teaching and learning against explicit criteria, criterion-referenced procedures for staff promotion and so on.

The second prominent example is the peer review process for assessing and grading research quality and the subsequent allocation of research funding accordingly. This has been implemented through a periodic Research Assessment Exercise (RAE), based upon traditional subject-based disciplinary units of assessment, conducted through elite peer assessment, and articulated within an almost unchanged UGC cultural framework. (This, too, in one sense can be seen as part of the trend towards an audit culture that measures and grades *all* aspects of the academy's work.) Needless to say, both systems sit extremely uneasily as sector-wide practices and have caused mounting resentment and anger within the sector and beyond, from the 1980s onwards.

Undoubtedly, the pace of change in higher education in the last twenty or so years of the twentieth century has been unprecedented. Moreover, it is not only the speed of the change and its wearying persistence that is remarkable: it has also been the fundamental challenge, or series of challenges, it has presented to the very bases of the system. In some ways, the emergent system of the twenty-first century is unrecognizable from its precursor at the time of Robbins. The parallel with broader political institutions across the same period is instructive: how different, qualitatively, ideologically and in many other ways, is the New Labour Party of Tony Blair compared with that of Harold Wilson, who had just assumed leadership of the Party in 1963, the time of the Robbins Report, and was to become Prime Minister the following year. British society overall, then, has changed fundamentally over these years. Although this is hardly a revelatory statement, it does lead back clearly to the issue of the socio-economic and political context within which the changes in the particular world of higher education have taken place.

Changes in society, the economy and politics

Throughout the turbulent changes of the post-war period, consistently and increasingly governments' priority for the whole post-compulsory sector of education has been the enhancement of vocational skills. Indeed, it is arguable that the very beginnings of university expansion in the industrial era were stimulated primarily by the perceived need 'to enlist [higher education] in the war against national, regional and local economic decline'.[20] This policy objective has taken different forms at different times: it has sometimes been directed primarily at one part of the sector rather than another; it has at times, naturally, been a higher priority than at others; but it has generally become more dominant as the so-called knowledge society has become a reality, and the demands for a much more highly skilled workforce have increased.

Although rarely in economic crisis since the 1930s, the British economy has been predominantly towards the bottom of the league of developed capitalist economies, by all the usual measures. The underlying causes of this relatively poor performance – judged by economic indicators of overall gross national product, growth rates, investment levels and the like – are contentious.[21] However, most analysts have laid stress among other factors upon a range of deficiencies in the British educational system. In part, these have focused on the steeply hierarchical nature of the British system, whereby a small number of people (almost exclusively, in the past, white, male, late adolescents of middle- or upper-class backgrounds) have received a very good university education, whereas most of the population have been inadequately trained (or indeed educated) for entry into the labour market.

In the 1990s and beyond, the context is frequently characterized as fundamentally changed, as a result of the post-Fordist analysis discussed earlier (see Chapter 1) and the New Labour, postmodern take on the 'new classless Britain' within an international, post-industrial context (see Chapter 2). It is thus worth noting that, as Ralph Miliband has argued, the fundamentals of the socio-economic system remain unchanged:

> Capitalism is more firmly embedded in the social order than it ever was, notwithstanding all the transformations which it has undergone over the years. Market relations are insistently pronounced as the most desirable form of individual and social interaction; and there never has been a time when commercialization has more thoroughly come to pervade all spheres of life.[22]

The labour market employment framework has, of course, changed radically; but the marketization of culture and the gross inequalities of both material wealth and social and political power have increased. This was largely the result of deliberate policy, driven by a lethal mix of monetarist, neo-liberal economics and an ultra-right wing political project of the Conservative Governments from 1979 to 1997. By 1993, '10 per cent of the population . . . [o]wned 50 per cent of all wealth, and . . . 25 per cent owned 71 per cent. In other words, 75 per cent of the population had to make do with 29 per cent of the remaining wealth.'[23] Whether or not this pattern of increasing inequality will be ameliorated to any extent by the Labour Government elected in 1997 and its successor Labour Government of 2001 remains to be seen. The evidence so far would seem to suggest some very modest alleviation of the poorer sections of the community as a result of the equally modest redistributive policies of the Chancellor.

What is beyond doubt is that, at the very least as a sub-theme of New Labour's higher education agenda, the Labour Governments post-1997 have had the objective of widening participation and offering far more people the opportunities for personal enhancement and education and training that an involvement with higher education can bring. (For a discussion of the problems with the widening participation agenda, see Chapter 9.)

Whatever the future development of the policy of the Labour Government, it is clear there has been a long-term and serious undermining of the industrial labour movement, which has reduced the collective power of working people to resist these trends of inequality: trade unions were attacked quite explicitly during the years of Conservative Governments, most dramatically of course during the prolonged miners' strike of the 1980s. As unemployment rose and trade unions were defeated, and the Labour Party was partly powerless and partly unwilling to defend them, so trade union membership declined from the 1970s highpoint of around 12 million to below 7 million. Perhaps even more fundamental was the decline in the traditional heartland constituencies of Labour: most of the old heavy industry and manufacturing unions virtually disappeared, and within a short period of time. The systematic and ideologically motivated destruction of Britain's manufacturing base by Conservative Governments exacerbated long-term economic and social trends. The resultant political and industrial weakening of Labour was, of course, one of the Conservatives' primary aims.

This was closely related to broader trends in the international economy that affected Britain as they did other capitalist economies. In some ways, these are encapsulated in the post-Fordist analysis discussed in Chapter 1. Principally, these changes have been: the expansion of multinational capital and its related globalizing strategy; the diminution in power of national economies as a consequence; the growth of finance capital and high-technology industries, and the associated decline of heavy industry and manufacturing in all developed economies; the ruthless exploitation by multinational capital of a range of developing countries, with the most appalling human, social and ecological consequences;[24] and the increasing sophistication of technology through the rapid development of information technology (IT), the Internet and telecommunications generally.

These changes have produced a very different environment for graduate employment. The increasing importance of the sectors referred to, and of the service sector too, which has also expanded rapidly, has been complemented by the growth of specific new skills and occupations – for example, in design, marketing and IT. The organizational pattern of economic activity has also changed to an extent, with more people employed in small and medium-sized companies. All these trends can be seen as in part cause and in part effect of a growing trend of atomized, individualistic structures and attitudes in the workplace. There has also developed a whole rhetoric of flatter management structures, quality assurance (TQM *et al.*) and the perceived need for a multi-skilled and flexible workforce.[25] How far this rhetoric corresponds to reality is a lot more dubious. Nevertheless, the organizational changes and the radical restructuring of employment are combined with far less job security to produce a very different economic configuration. (For a brief discussion of the relationship in this context between higher education and work, see Chapter 9.)

An aspect of the 'turn to culture' discussed in this book is that capitalism itself seems to be undergoing its own cultural turn, as knowledge – it is argued – becomes its main asset.[26] This has important political implications and consequences for those working at the heart of the knowledge industry and it presents those in higher education who are troubled by the current state of affairs with new threats and opportunities.

Certainly, the academic study of business – a growth industry itself – increasingly emphasizes the importance of information and knowledge to cope with change and uncertainty. This includes an emphasis on harnessing the full potential of the knowledge incorporated in workers, including the potential to innovate. Educationalists are by now used to seeing their more progressive ideas and practices, which have origins in emancipatory movements, being re-packaged, as here, in the service of very different ends. Experiential knowledge has for long been a mantra of liberal and radical adult education, and 'embodied knowledge' is something made much of in feminist scholarship and education especially.[27] And the increasing commodification of knowledge has 'only pointed to the value of knowledge which cannot be commodified, and especially to the value of practical knowledge, knowledge that can't be written down and packaged'.[28]

There is a growing emphasis on *learning* in business, especially learning by doing. And there is increased interaction between business and the academy. Business has become more academic as the academy has become more business-oriented; in consequence, comments Thrift, it is no longer possible to write off business as the haunt of the 'epistemologically challenged'.[29] It is becoming a commonplace idea that the old hierarchy of knowledge, with the universities at the top and able to offer the most validated knowledge, is being replaced by a flatter, more diverse set of interconnected knowledge communities which challenge the pre-eminence of universities by concentrating on learning by doing – often at a distance. In addition, theoretical developments routinely leak across old boundaries between the academy and business, producing, it is claimed, a new form of 'soft' capitalism: a new managerialist discourse of work reform is heralding new ways for people 'to be' at work.

In considering the real meaning of capitalism's own turn to culture, it helps to understand that this managerial discourse describes a world that literally does not exist, a world of 'learning organizations'. This rhetoric (although not yet preponderant in small and medium-sized enterprises (SMEs) where most paid work takes place) is, as Thrift maintains, part of the 'background hum' of business around the world (including universities, and not just in their management studies departments). It is a form of rhetoric spoken by management professions and professors and it is being used more and more as a rationale for decision making. Its concern is with 'looser and more agile' organizational forms, able to 'go with the flow' to be open to a complex and ambiguous world, and to produce 'subjects' who can fit these forms. Such a business organization is meant to use experiential learning, draw on tacit knowledge in the workforce and rely on trust. Above all, it must be made up of willing and willed subjects whose work is vital to their self-fulfilment. MBAs transmit this new knowledge and a whole set of powerful new management gurus and consultants propagate it. The shelves heave with books about it and management seminars proliferate. To take just one example, *The Seven Habits of Highly Effective People* has sold 5 million copies since 1989 and is available in 28 languages. Yet, cautions Thrift, despite this emphasis on knowledge, culture and creativity inviting the label of 'soft' capitalism, it has its hard edge in the downsizing of work-forces (of multinational companies) and the exploitation of managers and key workers.

Managers, like many other contemporary individuals (including lifelong learners), are enjoined to live as if running a project of themselves, aided by various expert languages or discourses and by various techniques that promise self-transformation.[30] Thus IBM offers 'I Ching' courses; others offer 'Release the Power Within' courses and yet others, 'Charisma Training'. British Gas sends its executives to do 'Whirling Dervish Dances' and the Scottish Office has sent thousands of employees on 'New Age Thinking' courses.

The company, increasingly multinational and multicultural, becomes itself a learner: a networked, virtual, looser form of business that can 'ride the swell' and still go forward. This may be an exaggeration, admits Thrift, commenting on his own flowery metaphors (which, however, echo those of 'management talk'). Nevertheless, this new managerialism is becoming the hegemonic account of what the business world is like and should become across the world. The material effects of this conceptualization, says Thrift, are 'measured out in shattered lives'. Organizations that take the discourse – or ideology, to call a spade a spade – most to heart tend to downsize, and the supposed commitment to an open-ended view of people (or 'subject-hood') is often super-exploitative. It exploits managers, who are now expected to commit themselves body and soul to the firm; and it exploits workers, who are now expected to commit their embodied knowledge to the organization's epistemological resources as well.[31] The new managerialism of universities, in their rush to become businesses, even 'business-like', fails to take stock of the possible consequences if they continue on course. The situation is, as usual, rife with contradictory currents. Universities are themselves subject to countervailing forces. Global processes of economic, cultural and workplace restructuring are having an increasing impact on our work as educators – at the same time, of course, postmodernists want us to focus on the local and particular. Many workers, including teachers and many university employees, are in fact being turned more and more into narrow technicians with competences; their work (and, arguably, their training) is being restructured precisely to exclude wider, social, political and cultural understandings and engagements. The increased activities to accredit teachers in higher education is relevant here. Janice Malcolm and Miriam Zukas point to the current oddity, in teaching and learning staff development programmes, of separating teaching from other forms of disciplinary activity: knowledge and research. They claim that this separation of pedagogy from the disciplines and research 'has serious implications for the status of teaching in higher education, the prospects for "connective specialization", and the process of knowledge production itself'.[32]

Social changes have similarly been fundamental and these too are linked closely to higher education developments.

> The traditional nuclear family, characterised by permanent and early marriage, the bearing of children at an early age, and women remaining in the home rather than in paid employment, has become far less prevalent since the 1960s. People marry at an older age, more women remain childless, and those who do have children have fewer and start their families later in life. There is an increasing number of single parent families.[33]

The position of women in society, as the trends noted indicate, has changed significantly. Although social and economic inequality based on gender remains endemic, there has been a marked increase in awareness of gender issues, particularly among the middle class. Second-wave feminism generated a consciousness that produced what might be termed at least a partial 'desubordination' of women. This cultural shift, combined with specific social developments, such as changes in sexual attitudes, has created a new environment in terms of gender.

The growth of global culture has also been a key factor in the last quarter of the twentieth century. The growth of IT, the dominance of the media monopolies – Murdoch *et al.* – have led to what one analyst has described as a process of 'global cultural convergence, the production of universal cultural products and global market consumers'.[34] It is also, however, an increasingly important influence in socializing the population into an ever more homogeneous international culture whose function is to legitimate the existing social and economic order; however, in a good example of contradiction, it has also enabled the development of a new and accessible *alternative* culture.[35]

For postmodernists, this loosening up and globalization of social organization and cultural forms leads to a consumer society that is permeated by difference and that is dynamic, free and flexible: the barriers between elite, old high culture and mass, modern popular culture are being broken down.

It is within this complex and contested context that the future development of higher education will take place. Definitions of policy objectives such as lifelong learning, accessibility, skills development, socially and economically relevant research, are neither discrete nor value-free. In the following analysis, these key issues will be discussed in this context and the relevant postmodern perspectives examined.

In our view, the defining characteristics of the contemporary policy debate are volatility within a contradictory and contested agenda. There are real possibilities for progressive change: at present, there is something of a strategic policy hiatus. As Peter Scott has argued, 'the absence of strategic direction is not new in British higher education';[36] but perhaps the need for a coherent, strategic perspective is greater than in the past, because of the volatility in the system, and in the wider society, and also because the potential and importance of higher education are greater than ever before.

The following chapter examines these issues, concentrating in particular on postmodernist perspectives and alternatives to them.

Notes

1. This chapter draws heavily on: David Watson and Richard Taylor (1998) *Lifelong Learning and the University: A Post-Dearing Agenda*. Brighton: Falmer Press; Peter Scott (1995) *The Meanings of Mass Higher Education*. Buckingham: SRHE and Open University Press.
2. Scott, op. cit., note 1, p. 11.
3. Perry Anderson (1961) The Origins of the Present Crisis, in Perry Anderson and Tom Nairn (eds) *Towards Socialism*. London: Fontana and New Left Books.
4. Scott, op. cit., note 1, pp. 44–7.
5. Ibid., p. 12.
6. Sir Geoffrey Butler (1957) *The Tory Tradition*. London: Conservative Political Centre, cited in Samuel H. Beer (1969) *Modern British Politics*, 2nd edn. London: Faber & Faber, p. 93.
7. There is a large literature on the nature of the state. For a particularly illuminating and continuingly relevant debate of some of the issues, see Ralph Miliband (1969) *The State in Capitalist Society*. London: Weidenfeld & Nicolson; see also his subsequent polemical interchange with Nicos Poulantzas, reprinted in John Urry and John Wakeford (eds) (1973) *Power in Britain*. London: Heinemann. For a discussion of the role of the state in the specific context of higher education, see Scott, op. cit., note 1, p. 13ff; W.A.C. Stewart (1989) *Higher Education in Postwar Britain*. London: Macmillan; Robert Berdahl (1959) *British Universities and the State*. Berkeley, CA: University of California Press.

8. Robbins Report (1963) *Report of the Committee on Higher Education.* London: HMSO.
9. Watson and Taylor, op. cit., note 1, p. 3.
10. Sources for statistical information: DES, 1991; DfEE, 1994; A. Smithers and P. Robinson (1995) *Post-18 Education: Growth, Change, Prospect,* Executive Briefing. London: Council for Industry and Higher Education.
11. Scott, op. cit., note 1, p. 17.
12. Ibid.
13. Ibid.
14. Watson and Taylor, op. cit., note 1, p. 9.
15. Scott, op. cit., note 1, p. 18.
16. Ibid., p. 19.
17. Ibid.
18. Ibid., p. 21.
19. Ibid., p. 23.
20. Watson and Taylor, op. cit., note 1, p. 14.
21. For two interesting analyses, see Martin Wiener (1983) *The Decline of the Industrial Spirit.* Cambridge: Cambridge University Press; Gordon Roderick and Michael Stephens (eds) (1982) *Performance, Education and Training in Britain Today.* Brighton: Falmer Press. For an overview, see David Coates and John Hillard (eds) (1986) *The Economic Decline of Modern Britain.* Brighton: Wheatsheaf.
22. Ralph Miliband (1994) *Socialism for a Sceptical Age.* Cambridge: Polity Press, p. 10.
23. Ibid., p. 17.
24. See, for example, John Pilger (1994) *Hidden Agendas.* London: Vintage.
25. See Robin Usher, Ian Bryant and Rennie Johnston (1997) *Adult Education and the Postmodern Challenge: Learning Beyond the Limits.* London: Routledge; Scott, op. cit., note 1, pp. 90–117; Peter Scott (ed.) (1998) *The Globalization of Higher Education.* Buckingham: SRHE and Open University Press.
26. Nigel Thrift (1999) Capitalism's cultural turn, in Larry Ray and Andrew Sayer (eds) *Culture and Economy: After the Cultural Turn.* London: Sage; for an account of how capitalism is turning from 'things' to 'ephemera', and the very real devastation that this is wreaking in people's lives worldwide, see Naomi Klein (2000) *No Logo.* London: Flamingo.
27. Lorraine Code (1989) Experience, knowledge and responsibility, in Ann Garry and Margaret Pearsall (eds) *Women, Knowledge and Reality.* London: Unwin Hyman.
28. Thrift, op. cit., note 26, p. 138.
29. Ibid., p. 137.
30. Ibid., p. 151.
31. Ibid., p. 157.
32. Janice Malcolm and Miriam Zukas (2000) Becoming an educator: communities of practice in higher education, in Ian McNay (ed.) *Higher Education and its Communities.* Buckingham: SRHE and Open University Press, p. 55.
33. Watson and Taylor, op. cit., note 1, p. 17, based on statistical evidence from HMSO (1996) *Social Trends 1996.* London: HMSO.
34. J. Kenway *et al.* (1997) Marketing education in the post modern age, *Journal of Education Policy,* 8(2): 105–22.
35. For the classic statement of this argument, see Ralph Miliband (1969) *The State in Capitalist Society.* London: Weidenfeld & Nicolson.
36. Scott, op. cit., note 1, p. 31.

6

Contested Concepts of Lifelong Learning

It is impossible to reach consensus on the nature of the contemporary university and the higher education system. Several analysts, somewhat paradoxically, have claimed this impossibility as a central, defining characteristic of the university in the postmodern knowledge society.[1] In the past, universities were based solidly on certain broad principles, in conceptual terms, albeit with major differences in the various national, cultural contexts; and organizational, curricular and role variation has, of course, been very great indeed in different institutions. Nevertheless, as noted in Chapter 1, there were generic commitments to Humboldtian notions of university research culture; to Kantian concepts of reason and to scientific, rationalist methodology; and to broadly liberal educational objectives in the tradition of Cardinal Newman. Overall, though, universities have had a clear function as institutions of elite vocational training and thus of social reproduction. (See Chapter 5 and, on professional training and vocationalism in the contemporary context, Chapter 8.)

This latter function remains central, although its nature and articulation have been transformed radically. Commitments to any broad ideological and cultural identity, as in the Humboldtian or Newman frameworks, are no longer universal. The system is heterodox and diverse and nobody can seriously maintain that there is uniformity across all universities, let alone all higher education institutions, in all their various cultural and institutional contexts and in all their highly differentiated faculty areas. There is much talk in contemporary analysis of the collapse of the 'idea of the university'[2] as both a consequence and a constituent part of the postmodern condition. In the British context some, such as Usher and Edwards,[3] celebrate this development; others, such as Scott and Barnett,[4] envisage new complex formations eventuating; while more critical voices, such as Webster, Coffield and, in North America, Readings,[5] are both more negative and more radical.

In this chapter, rather than entering directly into that debate, we concentrate on *concepts* of lifelong learning and, in the next chapter, in more detail upon some of the central formulations within this framework. There are several reasons for the high profile accorded to lifelong learning in the policy context in the early years of the twenty-first century. First, the massification and increasing diversity of the higher education system have led most policy-making bodies to point to lifelong learning as the new unifying concept for higher education (and for the whole post-compulsory sector). This is not confined to Britain but is dominant, too, in most of the European Union.[6] Second, lifelong learning is also conceptually dominant. Across the spectrum of analysis, and politically from right to left, lifelong learning is usually the agreed starting point for discussion.

Third, lifelong learning, although often held to be a cluster of complementary and dynamic approaches, is in reality highly contested ideologically.[7] By examining some of the detail of this contention, a choice of policy frameworks becomes clearer. Finally, lifelong learning provides in all its contexts a dynamic, organizing concept for higher education development. However contested its definition and policy implications may be, it is clearly not a conceptual framework that endorses the orthodox, established approach to higher education.

Concepts of lifelong learning

Although lifelong learning, and preceding concepts such as *education permanente*, have been debated in policy circles for some years – for example, the Faure Report of UNESCO[8] in 1972 – not until the late 1990s did the concept and its underlying implications become so pervasive and powerful. Governments and policy makers have seen the term as a suitably broad and progressive rhetorical vehicle encompassing a variety of policy orientations within a framework, which, it is implied, has both coherence and complementarity. Thus, in the British context for example, the Labour Government elected in 1997 was intent on portraying lifelong learning as having the complementary objectives of skills development, social inclusion and personal growth and fulfilment.[9]

However, as argued above, such formulations in reality mask very different ideological stances. Nor should this be a matter of remark: virtually all interesting and dynamic concepts and developmental frameworks are ideologically contested. Any attempt to delineate positions, inevitably, runs the risk of becoming overly schematic. Almost always, the reality is of overlap, blurring of boundaries, shifting coalitions and so on. However, with this caveat, we believe that there are at least five distinct and to an extent conflicting conceptions of lifelong learning. These may be characterized as having the following definitional focal points for lifelong learning policy and development. Lifelong learning is seen, variously, as concerned essentially with:

• vocationalism and performativity;
• social control and incorporation;

- pluralistic complexity within a postmodern framework;
- personal development and growth;
- radical social purpose and community development.

Lifelong learning as vocationalism and performativity

Governments have long seen skills development, education for employ-ability and a generally vocational approach as keynotes of higher education, indeed of post-compulsory education as a whole. Numerous government reports and commissions in virtually all developed countries, and higher education institutions themselves, have emphasized this orientation. Predictably, this has been echoed through the European Union, with the development in the 1990s of a range of training programmes and initiatives through the European Commission, for example the Leonardo scheme.[10] Certainly, recent studies have shown clearly that this policy orientation is the main thrust underlying the development of lifelong learning. In western European societies generally, 'the emphases have been upon Continuing Professional Development and high income earning provision. This type of high level work, with the already well-educated and professionally experienced, is also well-attuned to the cultural perceptions and missions of most higher education institutions'.[11]

It is also true that universities have always had a vocational element. As we have already noted, in one sense their origins in Europe were bound up with vocationalism, initially in the education and training of the clergy and, subsequently, in fulfilling a similar role for the elite professions of medicine and law (see Chapter 8).

What is quantitatively so different in the twenty-first century, as we move to what is generally acknowledged as being a knowledge society, is that education and training are held to have become key commodities, necessary attributes at a relatively high level for most of the labour force. The general phenomenon of the development of professional and vocational education perspectives in higher education is discussed in some detail in Chapter 8. Here, in the context of the conceptualization of lifelong learning, it is our argument that this commodification, and in a sense reification, of education has had a powerful cultural impact. As with all such hegemonic ideological constructs, the phenomenon is now generally accepted as inevitable and uncontentious. It is, in fact, a product of an increasingly marketized perspective on western culture and society in general. The massification of higher education is fuelled largely, but not exclusively, by this realization. It was this new conception of education that led, for example, the British Government in 1995 to merge the previously separate Ministries of Education and Employment to form a single, and supposedly unified, Department for Education and Employment (short-lived, as it turned out, with the successor Labour Government of 2001 reforming the ministry to become the Department for Education and Skills (DfES)). This has led some analysts to claim that the fundamentals of post-compulsory education in general and perhaps higher education in particular have been changed: the practices, the language and terminology, and the dominant curricula in higher education – in short, the culture of higher education – have now become incorporated into free market, capitalist ideology. One of the leading figures of postmodernism, J.F. Lyotard, identified this trend with some prescience as early as 1979:

> The question . . . now asked by the professionalist student, the State or institutions of higher education is no longer 'Is it true?' but 'What use is it?' In the context of the mercantilisation of knowledge, more often than not this question is equivalent to 'Is it saleable?' And in the context of power-growth: 'Is it efficient?'[12]

The National Committee of Inquiry into Higher Education in the United Kingdom (the Dearing Committee) recommended in 1998 that higher education institutions should not only expand their programmes in direct technical training, but should also develop 'professional skills, such as communication, self-management and planning'.[13]

The Report similarly recommended that higher education institutions should 'consider the scope for encouraging entrepreneurship'.[14] In an earlier study analysing the Dearing Report in the context of lifelong learning development, David Watson and Richard Taylor noted that in Britain 'during a period in which undergraduate numbers went up by 70 per cent the above average increases were all in professional and vocational areas, notably the professions allied to medicine . . . , business and financial studies and information sciences'.[15] There has also been widespread development in the newer institutions across the European Union – the post-1992 universities in Britain, for example, and the polytechnics in the still binary systems of higher education in countries such as Finland and the Netherlands[16] – of a whole raft of applied, training programmes in subject areas such as tourism and leisure studies, media and communications, and marketing.[17]

Running alongside this development of the vocational orientation in higher education has been a series of attempts to introduce vocational qualifications at higher education level to parallel or supplement (or even replace) traditional academic degree awards. Thus, since the 1970s in Britain, the following schemes among others have been introduced, most of them with an explicitly vocational purpose (this has also often been linked to bridging and access functions): BTEC, DipHE, HNCs and HNDs, NVQs and GNVQs, and two-year Foundation Degrees.[18] Of course, many of these – in particular NVQs and GNVQs – address primarily levels below higher education, but the principle of the vocational orientation remains the same.

In the higher education context, all such qualifications, and proposed frameworks for credit transfer,[19] have foundered as the honours degree continues to be regarded by students, employers and indeed government and higher education itself as the 'gold standard'. (There is a strong parallel here, in the British context, to the 'A' level system in secondary education and the deep-seated difficulty of introducing flexibility while this remains the perceived benchmark of quality.)

Higher education, therefore, has a new relation to the market: in common with much else in the institutional and cultural environment of the late capitalist world, higher education has adopted, in Perry Anderson's words, 'a culture of accompaniment, rather than antagonism, to the economic order'.[20] This uncritical acceptance of the market system and its values represents, in Anderson's view, the hegemony of postmodernism, which 'may be said to be the first specifically North American global style'.[21]

This is the broad context in which to place our focus on the specific phenomenon of vocationalism in the emerging new higher education systems, and the ways in which this undoubted shift in orientation in higher education has been analysed and received. By no means everyone has welcomed such developments. Although there are, in the early years of the twenty-first century, relatively few critics of the Kingsley Amis, 'more means worse' school of thought, there are nevertheless genuine and widespread anxieties about the maintenance of quality and standards, given the rapid expansion of the higher education system and its persistent under-funding in almost all developed societies,[22] the undoubted phenomenon of grade inflation,[23] and the wide diversity of curricula and programme areas that qualify now for higher education study, but fall outside any previously recognizable framework of academic disciplinary areas.

More fundamentally, however, critics have pointed to the narrowing of the criteria both for provision and for performance in higher education. Richard Bagnall, for example, has characterized

> the valorization of Lifelong Learning . . . to be overwhelmingly the product of economic determinism . . . ultimately driven, framed or determined by considerations of cost and benefit as measured through the economy . . . The value of education and learning are reduced to . . . assessments of their contribution and cost to individual, local, national, regional or global economic well-being . . . It is expressed in the general vocationalization of education, wherein the value of education is assessed in terms of its contribution to occupational skills development.[24]

Higher education is thus seen primarily if not exclusively as a financial investment, and its value assessed on the basis of the financial returns on that investment. Students and learners are seen as customers[25] and higher education institutions as at least in part supermarkets, selling higher education in the marketplace.[26]

For Bagnall, the lifelong learning agenda is becoming essentially concerned with the development of skills 'required by business and industry. This is arguably more a deskilling and a disempowerment, than it is an empowering education'.[27] Transformative learning, on this argument, translates straightforwardly into the socialization and incorporation of learners and ultimately their institutions into global capital and its cultures.

Bill Williamson, similarly, sees this strong emphasis on skills acquisition and instrumental education as in opposition to his concept of the essentially humanistic purposes of the academy. The main emphasis of lifelong learning development, Williamson argues, has been on an instrumental conception of employability. 'The thrust has been to make modern capitalism work more effectively to steal a lead on competitors and keep shareholders – still the major "stakeholders" of the modern economy – happy.'[28] Whereas in his view learning for employability and skills have their place, 'the fundamental challenge . . . is to enable more people to be able to join in critically in the discussion and decisions which shape their lives'.[29] In other words, lifelong learning is essentially concerned with learning for democracy and empowerment.

As higher education across the developed world becomes more dependent upon private sector, capitalist funding streams, and more responsive to the stakeholder interests of employers, so these trends – towards learning being valued for its role in vocational development within a capitalist free market context – are likely to increase. This perspective on lifelong learning, therefore, is highly contested. Its advocates see this model as bringing the academy into a much more constructive, relevant and 'real world' structure and culture, serving the interests economically of the whole community. Its opponents, however, characterize these developments as, in Bill Readings's words, constituting the transformation of the university into a 'ruined institution'.[30] Rather than a liberating, progressive force, therefore, lifelong learning viewed from this perspective leads ultimately to the death of the university. There could hardly be a more extreme difference of view of the import of lifelong learning, defined within the vocational and performativity perspective.

Lifelong learning as social control and incorporation

For many on the Left, especially those who have adopted a broadly Marxist framework of analysis, all educational institutions and processes have been seen as primarily, although not exclusively, agencies for socializing the population into the culture and assumptions of capitalism. Brian Simon, in his classic work *Education and the Labour Movement*, argued this case in historical detail for the late nineteenth and early twentieth centuries.[31] Ralph Miliband, too, in his analysis of the state laid great stress upon the role of 'legitimation' in the maintenance of capitalist hegemony, and highlighted education's class-confirming functions; the classic sociological study of these issues, in the broader context, by Bowles and Gintis, reached similar conclusions.[32]

In the more specific field of adult and continuing education, Roger Fieldhouse has analysed the diverse roots of modern developments and argued that, in the nineteenth century, 'the bourgeoisie needed to control and direct the thoughts and actions of the increasingly powerful working class'.[33] This has been a continuing theme throughout the twentieth century too, or arguably so. Always, however, this has been part of a *contradictory* process. With the development of trade union education, for example, the primary motivations were skills development and industrial relations training; but sub-themes, so to speak, included at one end of the spectrum both worker empowerment and revolutionary cadre education and, at the other, the concern of employers, government and often trade union establishments to ensure that potential militancy was as far as possible deflected into more legitimate, social democratic frameworks.

> It was felt [in relation to the Workers' Educational Association, but the point has more general application] that it was likely to educate the leaders of the Labour Movement to exercise their influence moderately and in the interests of social harmony, thus helping to keep class conflict and full-blooded socialism at bay . . . a sound political investment against extremism.[34]

This general line of analysis is followed through, albeit in a developed and amended form, by some analysts of the concept of lifelong learning. Far from being liberatory and empowering, lifelong learning, it is argued, is a mechanism both for social control and for pathologizing the educationally unsuccessful.[35] Frank Coffield and Bill Williamson, for example, argue that initially lifelong learning was inspired by a genuinely democratic and socially progressive spirit, as exemplified in the 1972 UNESCO Report by Edgar Faure.[36] However, since the concept of lifelong learning has come to real prominence in the 1990s and beyond, it has been hijacked for quite other purposes. Education in general, and lifelong learning in particular, is construed increasingly within a cultural framework that has adopted, explicitly, both the language of capital and the criteria for academic legitimacy and success that are those of business.

Thus, 'students have become "customers" or "consumers" . . . heads of departments . . . "line managers" . . . and many vice-chancellors "chief executives" . . . scenarios for the future of this country are called "visions for UK plc"'.[37] This is not an isolated phenomenon. Private sector business representatives are now routinely expected to form at least a substantial minority of the membership of the more important national higher education bodies (HEFCE, for example). Other parts of the post-compulsory sector are similarly structured. Thus, for example, the Learning and Skills Council structure in England and Wales, responsible in effect for all post-compulsory education and training (except for higher education), draws all the chairs of its major committees from the private sector, and at each level of the structure 40 per cent of committee members are required to come from the business community. The term 'community' itself, as discussed in more detail in the next chapter, is increasingly defined largely as the *business* community.[38]

Related to this, Frank Coffield has argued that the dominant conception, ideologically, of lifelong learning has been defined by government (and the business community) in terms of human capital. According to Coffield, the 'central tenets' of the 'prevailing orthodoxy' include the following elements:

- the new economic forces unleashed by globalization and technology are as uncontrollable as natural disasters and so governments have no choice but to introduce policies to 'upskill' the workforce.
- . . . in some formulations, education becomes the mere instrument of the economy, e.g. 'Education is the best economic policy we have', as the Prime Minister [Tony Blair] expressed it.
- the responsibility is passed to individuals to renew their skills regularly to ensure their employability.[39]

Moreover, higher education is explicitly encouraged, if not compelled, to model itself upon business, in terms of curriculum, processes and overall approach. As Coffield points out, given the acknowledged poor performance of the British economy – judged by its own capitalist criteria – over the last one hundred years and more, and the equally demonstrable success of British higher education, this seems an especially perverse perspective.[40] The value and purpose of lifelong learning is construed primarily in terms of skills development to increase the competitiveness of individuals, through education, and thus of the economy as a whole. Thus, for example, the Department for Education and Employment stated in 1997 that: 'Investment in learning in the twenty-first century is the equivalent of investment in the machinery and technical innovation that was essential to the first great industrial revolution. Then it was physical capital; now it is human capital.'[41] This applies, too, to developments in lifelong learning elsewhere in Europe, as recent research has shown.[42]

However, even while stressing this dominant interpretation, we should note again that social inclusion perspectives are also present, and arguably prominent, in the lifelong learning programmes and policy stances of most European governments. This is exemplified by the British Government's *Learning Age* policy statement.[43]

Coffield's view, however, is that lifelong learning is quite clearly and preponderantly the latest in a long line of governmental attempts to exercise social control:

behind the benevolent intentions and the high flown rhetoric, lifelong learning, the learning society and the learning organisation are all being propounded to induce individuals to become more – or – less willing participants in learning for life and to bear an increasing proportion of the costs of such learning without end. In the sense that society always employs a variety of social processes to ensure that its members conform to its changing expectations, lifelong learning is viewed [by some] . . . as the latest form of social control.[44]

John Field asserts that the rise of the concept of lifelong learning should be seen as a tool for the reform and modernization of education and training systems.[45] As such, it is just one aspect of a much wider transformation in the relationship between civil society and state in the western nations. Lifelong learning, he argues, is becoming one among many other factors that are transforming the governance of late modern societies, part of wider moves towards a new settlement between state and civil society, 'as the state sheds directive powers both downwards (to individuals and associations) and upwards (to transnational corporations and intergovernmental bodies)'.[46] While many previously politically radical academics turn inwards to ever increasing 'reflexivity', educational policy (including lifelong learning) continues to be shaped by the forces of modern capitalism in fundamental and often subtle ways. We need to develop a better understanding of these processes if lifelong learning is to become a valuable and progressive force for social change.

Other analysts, such as Jackie Brine, have also argued that there are structural rather than purely altruistic motivations at play here. Brine suggests that as the nation state's control of economics dwindles, because of the growing power of transnational corporations, so the need for its hold on social policy increases.[47] This is especially the case in the fields of welfare and education in order that any potential for social unrest resulting from the effects of globalization can be countered.

Walter Heinz, contrasting some aspects of the lifelong learning policy context in Germany with that prevailing in Britain, elaborates this perspective. 'At least for the UK and North America the slogan "let them eat skills" is changing to "let them buy skills" with their own money . . . [The trend is] to turn lifelong learning into a moral obligation and in many cases an external constraint.'[48] There is thus a 'normative expectation' that people will participate in, and pay for, lifelong learning wherever the increasingly volatile capitalist market system demands retraining or redeployment. 'Furthermore, it socialises people to become more flexible or more employable without promising them job security.'[49]

Overall, then, the *reality* of lifelong learning policy on these analyses is quite at variance with its rhetorical proclamations. Far from marking a break with previous policy orientations, it is argued that lifelong learning is, in its present formulations, a rhetorical smokescreen for the continuation – even intensification – of the longstanding ideology of social control and incorporation. These analyses are by no means wholly negative and gloomy, however. Rather, they are couched within Marxist notions of contradiction and struggle. Lifelong learning has the *potential* to help to bring about democratic, participatory practice, where learning can be not only democratized but can also play its part in progressive social and political transformation. This perspective, therefore, sees lifelong learning, again, as contested territory, where the debate over policy definition and emphasis is integrally connected to humanistic notions of education and learning, and to wider ideological conflicts over social and political change.

Lifelong learning as a postmodern framework of pluralistic complexity

Postmodernists, and those sympathetic to the broad and amorphous ethos of postmodern thinking, have a characteristically ambivalent attitude to lifelong learning. On the one hand, postmoderns are suspicious of, if not downright hostile to, the increasing domination of higher education by global, corporate capital and the criteria of the market. After all, as Kenneth Wain has reminded us, 'all the thinkers usually labelled postmodern (Lyotard, Derrida, Foucault, Rorty, Deleuze, and so on) regard themselves as, in some sense, and with plenty of ambiguity, on the Left'.[50]

The dystopian characteristics of the contemporary university as sketched by Lyotard, for example, who decries the performativity criteria discussed earlier,[51] the negative effects of the growth of ICT and the 'e-society', as described by Baudrillard,[52] and the impersonal authoritarianism of Foucault's disciplined society[53] – all point to an almost nightmarish future for higher education and, indeed, for the wider postmodern society.

At a somewhat more meso level, there are two factors in particular in the transformation of higher education that concern those analysts who are postmodern in orientation. First, there is a realization of the dangers of the increasing marketization of the higher education system and consequent commodification of knowledge. Secondly, such analysts have acknowledged the cultural threat to the university posed by the increasing dominance of ICT within a context where neither the physical identity of the university nor its legitimate intellectual parameters are clear. As Anthony Smith remarked in a perceptive review of Ronald Barnett's book *Realizing the University*,

> there are cognitive as well as operational challenges in an environment increasingly subjected to managerial disciplines and expectations of performance ... In a production-dominated knowledge economy, academic texts are increasingly reduced to the status of data ... Postmodernism means that the epistemological slate is being scraped clean, while, in performativity, a new unifying narrative is emerging.[54]

Anthony Smith goes on to assert, in classic liberal terms, that this narrative 'strikes at the core' of the western university, which is disinterested reason. This is all too rosy a view, in our opinion, as will have been abundantly clear. Nevertheless, his main point is well made and significant.

These are among the concerns of those who have a broadly postmodern perspective on lifelong learning. Those concerns, however, are heavily out-weighed for such analysts by the perceived benefits, potentially, of a life-long learning model within the new higher education context. For Robin Usher, for example, the contemporary world is viewed as 'irreducibly and irrevocably pluralistic, split into a multitude of sovereign limits and sites of authority'.[55] Higher education should reflect this pluralism, fragmentation and intellectual flexibility.

Intellectually, there are arguably two main focuses of postmodernism's deconstruction of the traditional university's cultural self-identity, which were alluded to in Chapter 1. There is, first, postmodernism's vehement rejection of all grand narratives, as discussed in Chapter 1. In part, this results from the failures of all such meta-ideologies, which invariably posit unrealizable utopian objectives: Marxism and socialism generally, liberal individualism and, of course, Christianity. None of these ideological and political constructs has produced social and human results that remotely approximated to their stated objectives.[56] Indeed, in many instances, the results of trying to develop and implement these perspectives have been morally grotesque and barbaric: obvious examples include the Holocaust and Stalin's regime of terror and liquidation in the USSR.

These fallacies and inadequacies, however, result also, it is argued, from the second major flaw with the intellectual structures of western societies in general and higher education in particular: the assumption that scientific, rational enquiry, formulated within discrete disciplinary areas, produces disinterested, objective and 'scientifically reliable' bodies of knowledge. This assumption, or series of assumptions, has now been thoroughly discredited, it is argued, not only through 'real world' experiences but also through intellectual and theoretical deconstruction of established ways of constructing and practising academic methodologies and disciplines.

Reference points, landmarks, benchmarks and maybe criteria of *any* sort for *any* type of higher education activity are thus arguably removed. As Zygmunt Bauman has observed: 'Everything the universities have been doing for the last nine hundred years made sense inside either the time of eternity or the time of progress; if modernity disposed of the first, post-modernity put paid to the second.'[57]

Postmoderns regard this realization as essentially beneficial and liberatory. By jettisoning all the baggage of illusory moral, political and generally teleological objectives for higher education, we can appreciate the rich differentiation, the endless variety of experience and perspective that the world has to offer. It is, in effect, a process of growing up, intellectually: of throwing aside childish dreams of a simple, monolithic and progressive pathway to human happiness and fulfilment. Higher education, for the postmoderns, is a 'knowledge product' to be bought and consumed for its own intrinsic interest and use – not for some moral or social betterment. The aim of higher education is, at least in part, to enable as many as possible to acquire the direct material, utilitarian benefits it bestows subsequently on its graduates.

There is clear evidence that higher education does indeed provide such benefits. A research report from the Smith Institute in 2000 found that, by tracking surveys of 16,000 people born in Britain in single weeks in 1958 and 1970,

> men born in 1970 with no qualifications were 12 times more likely to be out of work by the age of 26 than those with degrees. Of those who

were in work, their pay was also considerably lower than the children of professional parents. Women's chances of being in full-time employment – rather than in part-time work or staying home with children – were eight times higher for graduates than for those with no qualifications . . . In both generations, those with no qualifications were about three times more likely to be classed as depressed at ages 33 and 26 than graduates.[58]

The Dearing Report concluded similarly that 'higher education has proved to be an excellent personal investment with a return averaging between 11 and 14 per cent and we expect it to continue to be a good investment, even after further expansion'.[59]

Dramatic though this empirical evidence would seem, we would add that the picture presented is almost certainly misleading because of an assumed monocausality. That is, it is assumed that the expansion of degree level qualifications *per se* has created these significant social changes. What are omitted implicitly from such survey data are both cultural and, crucially, social class factors.

Nevertheless, there can be no doubt that significant social changes *have* taken place, and that educational credentialling through higher education has been an important element in this process. Nor is it only these material benefits that the perceived, new, pluralistic and open system can offer. Freed of all modernist illusions, the higher education system, centred on lifelong learning it is argued, enables individuals to 'try on a new identity. Experience itself is the end, leading to further experience. It is the very openness and unteleological quality of experience which is desirable'.[60]

Higher education in the past has been straitjacketed not only through now anachronistic disciplinary boundaries and methodologies, but also through a pedagogy that saw the teacher and the traditions of knowledge as the fount of received wisdom and the learner as recipient, albeit on occasion through 'Socratic dialogue'. In postmodernity, the learner becomes a more active player and is empowered as knowledge is decentred. For postmodernists, teachers can thus become facilitators (though not transformative intellectuals) and learners not only consumers but free agents intellectually, ranging across the huge diversity of knowledge and experience opened up by higher education.

The plurality and diversity of higher education in its greatly expanded form is held to reflect appropriately the differentiation and fragmentation of the wider society. For Zygmunt Bauman,

> it is precisely the plurality and multi-vocality of the present-day collection of the gatherings . . . that offer the universities, old and new and altogether, the chance of emerging successfully from the present challenge. It is the good luck of the universities that there are so many of them, that there are no two exactly alike, and that inside every university there is a mind-boggling variety of departments, schools, styles of thoughts, styles of conversation, and even styles of stylistic concerns . . . In

the world in which no one can anticipate the kind of expertise that may be needed tomorrow, the dialogues that may need interpretation ... the recognition of many and varied ways to, and many and varied canons of, higher learning is the condition *sine qua non* of the University system capable of rising to the postmodern challenge.[61]

In this new, flexible world, 'traditional class, gender and other distinctions fall away, individuals are freer to write their biographies', so it is argued.[62] Higher education also reflects the increasing orientation to leisure, media and ludic culture in postmodernity: 'playfulness now produces profit; images [and ideas] are commodities. In short, superstructure is now structural'.[63] As Tessa Perkins has put it, 'the individual, no longer a class member, no longer a woman, is now the site of conflicting and competing discourses; the fluidity and instability of identity are celebrated'.[64]

Lifelong learning as the underlying educational concept, not only for higher education but for education and learning in conditions of postmodernity generally, can provide the means for individuals to cope successfully with uncertainty. 'In postmodernity uncertainty, the lack of a centre and the floating of meaning are understood as phenomena to be celebrated rather than regretted. In postmodernity, it is complexity, a myriad of meanings, rather than profundity, the one deep meaning, which is the norm.'[65] Moreover, as social class and identity defined through work decline in importance, 'individuals will seek alternative indicators of their worth and status ... postmodernism in higher education may come increasingly to provide these alternative indicators'.[66]

There are two points to be made in conclusion to this part of the discussion. First, it is clear that within this perspective on lifelong learning there is a deep division of view – often reflected in ambivalence within individual protagonists themselves – over whether or not postmodernity is conducive to the positive development of a progressive framework of higher education. Secondly, and quite clearly given the overall argument of this book, we disagree, often fundamentally, with the arguments made here. These arguments, already broached in Chapters 1, 2 and 3, are taken up again in Chapter 9.

Lifelong learning as personal development and growth

Lifelong learning as a central means of achieving personal development and fulfilment is a cornerstone, at least rhetorically, of most governmental education policies in the developed world.[67] This emphasis upon self-actualization through education has obvious resonances with the postmodern perspectives discussed above. Centre stage in this model is the autonomous individual, freed from the intellectual tramlines of modernity and the confines of a stratified society hidebound by socio-economic and cultural distinctions of class, now able to 'surf the network' of learning experience. The individual, too, has a central place in the lifelong learning ambitions of progressive politicians and policy makers. David Blunkett, for example, the Secretary of State for Education and Employment in Britain from 1997 to 2001, expressed this in his introduction to the British Government's policy paper on lifelong learning, *The Learning Age:*

> *For individuals:*
> learning offers excitement and the opportunity for discovery. It stimu-
> lates enquiring minds and nourishes our souls. It takes us in directions
> we never expected, sometimes changing our lives. Learning helps
> create and sustain our culture ... There are many people for whom
> learning has opened up, for the first time in their lives, the chance to
> explore art, music, literature, film, and the theatre, or to become cre-
> ative themselves.[68]

On the other hand, individualist concepts have been at the centre of a much older tradition too, in liberal constructions of the purposes of educa-tion. The 'liberal tradition', developed in particular in nineteenth- and twentieth-century English *adult* education in university extramural depart-ments and organizations such as the Workers' Educational Association (WEA),[69] has itself been both a complex and a contested ideological frame-work, as Richard Taylor, for example, has argued in detail elsewhere.[70] At its heart, and certainly central in terms of its intellectual evolution, however, are general liberal precepts about the moral, political, social and economic nature of society. As Alan Ryan has noted, the development of education in the late capitalist societies of the western world (and perhaps of adult education in particular, at least as far as Britain is concerned), has been 'part of a long process of democratization, industrialization, and secularization'.[71]

It is no accident that the early missionaries for adult education, from the 1870s onwards, were for the most part committed Liberals, or, later, consti-tuted a significant element in the Labour Party, which had firm ideological roots in Liberalism.[72] The individual and his or her freedom to pursue social and personal life as untrammelled as possible by state, bureaucratic or any other collective interference, are at the heart of this perspective. The 'good society', so it was argued by liberal educators rather optimistically in those far-off days, would result from as large a number as possible of free individuals gaining access to education and enlightenment. Social progress would then be possible, not only though greater technical and practical competence, but also through an understanding of and identity with the values, practices and mores of civilized society.

In the lifelong learning age, where mass higher education has become a reality and where objectives of democratization are a high priority, these individualist perceptions are rather differently contextualized. It is arguably a modest and attainable goal to aspire to create a general educational system that ensures that everyone, or virtually everyone, acquires not only the vocational skills to earn a living but also a level of cultural literacy whereby they 'leave school able to live a tolerably happy and useful life'.[73] It is rather a different objective, and 'maybe an impossible [one], to wish everyone both to have the skills they require to earn a living, and *to possess the sense of cultural ownership that was once the prerogative of the few* (emphasis added).[74]

It is here, perhaps, that the new lifelong learning perspective parts company with the longstanding liberal tradition. The latter was characterized strongly by the aim of bringing high culture to the mass of ordinary people. Depending on the particular protagonist involved, and depending too upon the analytical perspective in historical and political terms that is adopted to explain this objective, this can be construed in either positive or negative terms, measured by democratic criteria. Thus Albert Mansbridge, founder of the WEA, believed passionately in the *a priori* good of enabling working people to appreciate great art, literature and music. The cultural enrichment of the individual was all important. Others in the established order, wary of political emancipation generally and universal male suffrage in particular, saw that 'the preservation of "high" culture in the face of the erosion of social privilege and the erosion of the religious framework that once gave that culture its particular meaning'[75] was a difficult task. The incorporation into the established order of potentially discordant, if not revolutionary, elements was a high priority. Socialization through education, both to legitimate the existing culture (political as well as artistic) and to incorporate working people and their representative organizations, was seen as a means to this end and, therefore, a primary objective.[76]

At the time of the first major post-war enquiry into higher education and its future in Britain, in 1963, the Robbins Report gave continuing prominence to the cultural dimensions of higher education. Robbins's fourth principle for the roles of higher education institutions was the 'transmitting [of] a common culture and common standards of citizenship'.[77] Robbins took little if any cognizance of the increasingly complex and multicultural nature of British society. The 'common culture' was clearly *high* culture, and the 'common standards of citizenship' shorthand for British parliamentary democracy and the deep-rooted cultural assumptions which this embodied. The point here is not to criticize such an approach but rather to note that the priority given to high culture in the context of higher education was still very much in evidence in the 1960s. By the time of the Dearing Report in 1997, this commitment had been reformulated as an 'admonition to higher education to be part of the conscience of a democratic society, founded on respect for the rights of the individual and the reciprocal responsibilities of the individual to society as a whole'.[78]

There is, finally, a crucial corollary to this description of the liberal, individualist perspective on lifelong learning:

> the University experience should challenge received wisdom, and especially analyse critically the often implicit ideological assumptions upon

which contemporary society operates. *Alternative* ways of seeing and analysing the world should be studied, and often unpalatable ideological perspectives explored ... education should be about developing students' powers of independent judgement, and the process of teaching and learning should not be 'confused with the process of winning souls for God, liberalism or the revolution'.[79]

The individual, therefore, should be learning in a sceptical intellectual environment. In Alan Ryan's words, the role of the academic in the context of teaching and learning interaction with students is to be 'unkind to ideas' – although, as he goes on to say, this should be complemented by being 'extremely fastidious about being courteous to those who hold them'.[80]

Historically, all these elements have been seen as essential for the social reproduction of the governing class, as Marxist analysts would describe the process; or in Cardinal Newman's terms, the 'creation of gentlemen'. In the somewhat monastic culture of the old elite universities of the past – in Britain as elsewhere – 'Renaissance men' were prepared as wise, knowledgeable and culturally aware members of the governing class. In the twentieth century, this has been recast from its pure pre-industrial expression in more modernist terms. In our earlier chapters, we, as other critics of such precepts, have pointed to its strongly elitist, patriarchal[81] and anglocentric ideology. It inculcated, to a very restricted and homogeneous upper and upper middle class elite of young men, liberal culture by producing, or attempting to produce, 'the "liberal" citizen, individualistic, rationalistic, with a faith in benevolent progress through science and "truth"'.[82]

In our view, while such criticisms have real force, a revitalized liberal social purpose approach, couched within a radical and egalitarian framework, can provide an appropriate starting point for lifelong learning. Here, we leave this as assertion and return to these issues in Chapter 9.

Lifelong learning as radical social purpose and community development

The final perspective in this catalogue of interpretations of lifelong learning can be described much more briefly and follows on from the last point in the preceding section. The ideas inherent in the framing of lifelong learning as essentially concerned with social purpose and community development form a central element in our concluding argument in Chapter 9.

In one sense, the radical social purpose orientation can be seen as a part of, or a development from, the liberal educational model.[83] The differences, both in substance and emphases, are marked, however. Most fundamentally, this perspective is collective rather than individualistic. Individuals are certainly important, of course; but their disadvantaged position, alienation and disempowerment have to be seen, it is argued, within the structures of inequality that characterize all developed societies.[84] Without entering into the detail, factually there is no doubt that chronic, pervasive inequality characterizes late capitalist societies – to say nothing of the huge disparities of wealth and power between the developed world and the poor societies of Asia and Africa.[85] In many late capitalist societies, including pre-eminently Britain and the USA, relative inequalities of wealth increased significantly in the last decade of the twentieth century and continue to do so in the early years of the twenty-first century.

The historical commitment of radical social purpose educators to view education as a central part of the movement for egalitarian social change, thus seems eminently justified in contemporary circumstances. In the past, this perspective has been linked to socialist, normally labour movement, politics.[86] From the time of the 'moral force' Chartists in the mid-nineteenth century, workers' education has been seen as a key means of emancipation. 'Knowledge is Power' has been a powerful motivating force for socialists of all hues. Higher education has been heavily skewed in its social class composition, as is generally acknowledged.[87] Despite all the democratizing changes in the wake of the massification of higher education,[88] the under-representation of the lower socio-economic groups remains an endemic characteristic of all, or virtually all, late capitalist societies.[89]

What were effectively compensatory, albeit large-scale, programmes of workers' education were an important part of the provision of post-compulsory education and training from the 1920s onwards in many late capitalist societies.[90] From the 1970s this has been complemented by community education,[91] women's educational initiatives[92] and more general Access provision.[93] Such developments reflect the broadening of both radical social analysis and European political movements (Eurocommunism *et al.*) in the 1970s and 1980s, to encompass a much broader and more inclusive conception of disadvantage. This represented the realization in the educational context of the importance of groups other than the traditional, male, manual working class: disadvantaged women, ethnic minority communities, disabled people, tenants and the unwaged among them.[94]

However, these perspectives within higher education have been, historically, relatively marginal. In the older universities, including Oxford and Cambridge, there has been a strong outreach tradition, but it has been confined generally to specialist departments or units that have been organizationally and culturally separate. Social purpose and equity issues have been seen, within universities by both academic staff and managers, as the concerns of other parts of the education and training structure. Universities, it has been argued, are concerned by definition with excellence and the highest academic standards – they are, by extension, inherently elitist.

Arguably, the concept of lifelong learning, within a context of mass higher education, has changed all this. Lifelong learning provides potentially a flexible framework, both conceptually and structurally, to enable the development of a broad-based, community-oriented and egalitarian system. This assertion, the arguments supporting it and its implications for future development form one of the bases of the discussion in the final chapter.

We should note that there are connections here both to postmodernist and liberal approaches to lifelong learning policy (see above); and there is, of course, a range of criticisms that can be levelled at this generally optimistic assertion. Apart from the argument as described earlier, that lifelong learning discourses are dominated by the agenda of global capital and its perceived needs for both social control and the development of an instrumental skills agenda, postmodernist critics have cogent criticisms of such a perspective. Essentially, these centre on two related points. First, it is argued that the external social-political world has changed out of all recognition with the demise of the 'socialist project' and what is perceived as the fragmentation and cultural dislocation of the post-Fordist, post-industrial and post-work society.[95] Secondly, the deconstruction of the academy and its traditional disciplinary universe and methodological assumptions of scientific rationality, signifies, it is argued, the need for wholesale changes in curriculum and pedagogy. Both of these factors are held to undermine fatally any educational framework that centres on what is, effectively, the grand narrative of socialism.

Many critics,[96] and we ourselves, dissent from such conclusions, as already noted. Here, however, the point is to note yet again the contested nature of this, as of all the other lifelong learning perspectives discussed here.

The next chapter continues this theme of exploring the contestation underlying the lifelong learning debate, by examining in some detail three of the key concepts central to the lifelong learning framework, and indeed other policy analysis.

Notes

1. See, for example, Ronald Barnett (2000) *Realizing the University in an age of supercomplexity.* Buckingham: SRHE and Open University Press; Peter Scott (1995) *The Meanings of Mass Higher Education.* Buckingham: SRHE and Open University Press.
2. See, for example, Barnett, op. cit., note 1; Scott, op. cit., note 1; Bill Readings (1996) *The University in Ruins.* Cambridge, MA: Harvard University Press.
3. Robin Usher and Richard Edwards (1994) *Postmodernism and Education.* London: Routledge; Richard Edwards (1997) *Changing Places? Flexibility, Lifelong Learning and a Learning Society.* London: Routledge.
4. See Barnett, op. cit., note 1; Scott, op. cit., note 1.
5. Frank Webster (1998) The post modern university? The loss of purpose of British universities, paper presented to the SRHE Conference, Lancaster University, December; Anthony Smith and Frank Webster (eds) (1997) *The Postmodern University? Contested Visions of Higher Education in Society.* Buckingham: SRHE and Open University Press; Frank Coffield (1997) Can the UK become a Learning Society? Fourth Annual Education Lecture, King's College, London; Frank Coffield (ed.) (1999) *Why is the Beer Always Stronger up North?*, Studies of Lifelong Learning in Europe. London: Policy Press; Readings, op. cit., note 2.
6. See Richard Taylor (2001) Lifelong learning in higher education in Western Europe: myth or reality?, *Adult Education and Development Journal* (DVV, Germany),

56: 127–46. This is based on detailed research on lifelong learning in higher education in Britain, Germany, Holland and Finland, undertaken through a SOCRATES (European Commission) project in 1998 and 1999.

7. See, for example, the *International Journal of Lifelong Education*, 19(1), special issue on lifelong learning, January–February 2000.

8. UNESCO Report (the Faure Report) (1972) *Learning to Be: The World of Education Today and Tomorrow*. Paris: UNESCO.

9. See Department for Education and Employment (1999) *The Learning Age: A Renaissance for a New Britain*. London: HMSO.

10. There have been successive Leonardo programmes. At the time of writing (Summer 2001), the latest programme is concerned with 'community vocational training' and aims to link lifelong learning training policies with 'the aptitudes and skills necessary for successful integration into working life and the full exercise of citizenship'. Quotations are from the Leonardo 'further details' document for the second phase of the programme, from 1 January 2000 to 31 December 2006.

11. Taylor, op. cit., note 6.

12. J.F. Lyotard (1984) *The Postmodern Condition: A Report on Knowledge*. Manchester: Manchester University Press, p. 51; cited in Usher and Edwards, op. cit., note 3, p. 175.

13. National Committee of Inquiry into Higher Education (the Dearing Report) (1997) Recommendation 31.

14 Ibid., Recommendation 40.

15. David Watson and Richard Taylor (1998) *Lifelong Learning and the University: A Post-Dearing Agenda*. Brighton: Falmer Press, p. 68.

16. Making it Work: European Universities and Lifelong Learning, Socrates Project, September 1997 to September 1999.

17. See Nick Frost and Richard Taylor (2001) Patterns of change in the University: the impact of 'Lifelong Learning' and the 'world of work', *Studies in the Education of Adults*, 33(1): 49–59.

18. See Gilbert Jessop (1991) *Outcomes: NVQs and the Emerging Model of Education and Training*. Brighton: Falmer Press; George Hargraves (1998) The origins of the National Vocational Qualification, with special reference to the Manpower Services Commission, 1974–1986, and to the review of Vocational Qualifications, 1985–1986, unpublished doctoral dissertation, University of Leeds.

19. The Dearing (NCIHE) recommendations are discussed in Watson and Taylor, op. cit., note 15, pp. 47–54.

20. Perry Anderson (1998) *The Origins of Postmodernity*. London: Verso, p. 63.

21. Ibid., p. 64.

22. See NCIHE (1997) for a comparative analysis of ten OECD countries and their lifelong learning policies, see Hans Schuetze and Maria Slowey (eds) (2000) *Higher Education and Lifelong Learners: International Perspectives on Change*. London: Routledge Falmer.

23. For a graphic example of grade inflation in the USA, see Alvin Kernan (1999) *In Plato's Cave*. New Haven, CT: Yale University Press, pp. 278–9, 298–9.

24. Richard Bagnall (2000) Lifelong learning and the limitations of economic determinism, *International Journal of Lifelong Education*, 19(1): 21.

25. Richard Taylor (2000) Concepts of self-directed learning in higher education: re-establishing the democratic tradition, in Jane Thompson (ed.) *Stretching the Academy: The Politics and Practice of Widening Participation in Higher Education*. Leicester: NIACE, pp. 68–79.

26. Barnett, op. cit., note 1; David Watson (2000) The two worlds of Ron Barnett: a pragmatic critique, paper presented to the SRHE and Open University Press Symposium on the Work of Ron Barnett, January.
27. Bagnall, op. cit., note 24, p. 28.
28. Bill Williamson (1998) *Lifeworlds and Learning.* Leicester: NIACE, p. 20.
29. Ibid., p. 8.
30. Readings, op. cit., note 2, p. 169.
31. Brian Simon (1965) *Education and the Labour Movement 1870–1920.* London: Lawrence & Wishart.
32. Ralph Miliband (1969) *The State in Capitalist Society.* London: Weidenfeld & Nicolson; Samuel Bowles and Herbert Gintis (1976) *Schooling in Capitalist America.* London: Routledge & Kegan Paul.
33. Roger Fieldhouse and Associates (1996) *A History of Modern British Adult Education.* Leicester: NIACE, p. 12.
34. Ibid., p. 169.
35. See, for example, Bagnall, op. cit., note 24.
36. UNESCO Report, op. cit., note 8.
37. Frank Coffield and Bill Williamson (eds) (1997) *Repositioning Higher Education.* Buckingham: SRHE and Open University Press, p. 1.
38. John Goddard *et al.* (1994) *Universities and their Communities.* London: CVCP.
39. Frank Coffield (1999) Breaking the consensus: lifelong learning as social control, Inaugural Lecture, University of Newcastle, February. The quotation from Tony Blair was included in the policy paper from the Department for Education and Employment, op. cit., note 9, p. 9.
40. There is, of course, a whole literature of economic and historical analysis that details this weak economic performance and its effects and causation. In the 1990s, this relative weakness, and the accompanying low levels of investment in British industry, showed no signs of abating. For example, the British Treasury calculated in 1998 that the UK's productivity gap with the USA was around 40 per cent, and with France and Germany 20 per cent. HM Treasury (1998) *Pre-Budget Report.* London: HMSO; cited in Coffield, op. cit., note 39, pp. 2–3.
41. Department for Education and Employment (1997) *Excellence in Schools,* Cm 3681. London: HMSO, p. 15; cited in Coffield, op. cit., note 39, p. 4.
42. For example, detailed analysis undertaken in 1998 and 1999, through the SOCRATES (European Commission) project *Making it Work: European Universities and Lifelong Learning.* For a summary of the main findings, see Taylor, op. cit., note 6.
43. Department for Education and Employment, op. cit., note 9.
44. Frank Coffield (ed.) (1999), op. cit., note 5, p. 11.
45. John Field (2001) Lifelong education, *International Journal of Lifelong Education,* 20(1/2): 3–15.
46. Ibid., p. 3.
47. Jackie Brine (1999) *underEducating Women: Globalizing Inequality.* Buckingham: Open University Press.
48. Walter Heinz (1999) Lifelong learning for life? Some cross-national observations, in Coffield, op. cit., note 44.
49. Heinz (1999) in Coffield, op. cit., note 44, p. 15.
50. Kenneth Wain (2000) The learning society: postmodern politics, *International Journal of Lifelong Education,* 19(1): 45.

51. Lyotard, op. cit., note 12.
52. Jean Baudrillard (1983) *In the Shadow of the Silent Majorities*. New York: Semiotex.
53. Michel Foucault (1979) *Discipline and Punish*. London: Penguin.
54. Anthony Smith (2000) Review of Ron Barnett, 'Realizing the university in an age of supercomplexity', in *Times Higher Education Supplement*, 21 April, p. 33.
55. Robin Usher, Ian Bryant and Rennie Johnston (1997) *Adult Education and the Postmodern Challenge*. London: Routledge, p. 10.
56. See Chapters 1, 2 and 9 for further discussion of these, and counter-, arguments.
57. Zygmunt Bauman (1997) Universities: old, new and different, in Anthony Smith and Frank Webster (eds) *The Postmodern University? Contested Visions of Higher Education in Society*. Buckingham: SRHE and Open University Press, p. 21.
58. Research Report by the Smith Institute, commissioned by the Department of Health of the UK Government, 2000. Reported in the *Guardian*, 12 May 2000, p. 1.
59. National Committee of Inquiry into Higher Education (Dearing Report), Summary Report, 1997, p. 25.
60. Usher *et al.*, op. cit., note 55, p. 10.
61. Bauman, op. cit., note 57, p. 25.
62. Peter Scott (1997) The postmodern university?, in Smith and Webster (eds), op. cit., note 5, p. 44.
63. Ibid., p. 44.
64. Tessa Perkins (2000) Who (and what) is it for?, in Christine Gledhill and Linda Williams (eds) *Reinventing Film Studies*. London: Arnold, p. 86.
65. Usher and Edwards, op. cit., note 3, p. 10.
66. Scott, op. cit., note 62, p. 46.
67. See Schuetze and Slowey, op. cit., note 22.
68. Department for Education and Employment, op. cit., note 9.
69. See Norman Jepson (1973) *The Beginnings of English University Adult Education*. London: Michael Joseph; Roger Fieldhouse (1977) *The Workers' Educational Association: Aims and Achievements, 1903–1977*. New York: Syracuse University Press; Fieldhouse and Associates, op. cit., note 33.
70. Richard Taylor (1996) Preserving the Liberal tradition in 'New Times', in John Wallis (ed.) *Liberal Adult Education: The End of an Era?* Nottingham: University of Nottingham Continuing Education Press, pp. 61–75; Richard Taylor, Kathleen Rockhill and Roger Fieldhouse (1985) *University Adult Education in England and the USA: A Reappraisal of the Liberal Tradition*. Beckenham: Croom Helm; Richard Taylor (1998) Lifelong learning in the 'Liberal tradition', *Journal of Moral Education*, 27(3): 301–12.
71. Alan Ryan (1999) *Liberal Anxieties and Liberal Education*. London: Profile Books, p. 32.
72. See Jepson, op. cit., note 69. For an examination *inter alia* of the profound Liberal influence in the early Labour Party, see Ralph Miliband (1973) *Parliamentary Socialism*, 2nd edn. London: Merlin Press.
73. Ryan, op. cit., note 71, p. 30.
74. Ibid., p. 31 (emphasis added).
75. Ibid., p. 32.
76. For the classic Marxist argument, within the British context, about the importance of the legitimation process, including the role of education, see Miliband, op. cit., note 32.

77. Lionel Robbins (1963) *The Report of the Committee on Higher Education*. London: HMSO.
78. Lord Dearing (1997) Dearing's summary, *Times Higher Education Supplement*, 25 July, p. i; National Committee of Inquiry into Higher Education (the Dearing Report), p. 8, cited in Watson and Taylor, op. cit., note 15.
79. Richard Taylor (1993–94) Continuing education and the accessible university, Inaugural Lecture delivered on 26 April 1993, *University of Leeds Review*, 36: 314–15. (Citation is from Thomas Hodgkin (1950–51) Objectivity, ideologies and the present political situation, *The Highway*, XLII: 80; cited by Roger Fieldhouse, in Taylor *et al.*, op. cit., note 70.)
80. Ryan, op. cit., note 71, p. 48.
81. See Jane Thompson (1983) *Learning Liberation: Women's Responses to Men's Education*. Beckenham: Croom Helm.
82 Usher *et al.*, op. cit., note 55, p. 11.
83. See Taylor, op. cit., note 70.
84. For the specifically educational dimensions of this inequality, see Ryan, op. cit., note 71; Griff Foley (1999) Workplace learning: back to basics, *Studies in the Education of Adults*, 31(2): 181–96; Griff Foley (2001) *Strategic Learning: Understanding and Facilitating Organisational Change*. Sydney: Centre for Popular Education, University of Technology Sydney.
85. On the international patterns of pervasive inequality and capitalist exploitation, see John Pilger (1998) *Hidden Agendas*. London: Vantage Books.
86. See, for example, Simon, op. cit., note 31; Taylor *et al.*, op. cit., note 70; Kevin Ward and Richard Taylor (eds) (1986) *Adult Education and the Working Class: Education for the Missing Millions*. Beckenham: Croom Helm.
87. See Scott, op. cit., note 1; NCIHE, 1997.
88. See Watson and Taylor, op. cit., note 15.
89. Schuetze and Slowey, op. cit., note 22.
90. For a history of elements of this provision in Britain, see John Holford (1993) *Union Education in Britain*. Nottingham: University of Nottingham.
91. See, for example, Tom Lovett (ed.) (1988) *Radical Approaches to Adult Education: A Reader*. London: Routledge; Ian Martin, 1996, Community education, the dialectics of development, in Fieldhouse and Associates, op. cit., note 33.
92. Thompson, op. cit., note 81.
93. On England and Wales, see Gareth Parry (1995) England, Wales and Northern Ireland, in Pat Davies (ed.) *Adults in Higher Education: International Perspectives in Access and Participation*. London: Jessica Kingsley. (Davies's book also includes chapters on Australia, Austria, Belgium, Denmark, France, Germany, Italy, The Netherlands, Scotland and Spain.)
94. See, for a mainly regional case study, Ward and Taylor, op. cit., note 86.
95. See Scott, op. cit., note 1; Tom Steele (2000) Common goods: beyond the world of work to the universe of the imagination, in Thompson (ed.), op. cit., note 25; Usher and Edwards, op. cit., note 3.
96. See, for example, J.C. Alexander (1995) Modern, anti, post, neo, *New Left Review*, March/April, 290: 63–101.

7

Community, Globalization and Learner Autonomy

This chapter pursues the themes discussed in Chapter 6 by analysing in turn some of the key concepts within the lifelong learning policy debate. As with the central concept of lifelong learning, these are all, it is argued here, contested ideologically. These are not merely matters of abstract argument of course: differing ideological definitions entail different policy implementation, curriculum content, funding structures and so on. Far from there being a consensual plurality, providing a constructive dynamic for future learning as most postmodernists writing on education have argued,[1] the policy landscape resembles more a series of manoeuvres, battles and compromises between the ideological interpretations of social reality and purpose in this particular area of the public and political arena.

The concepts to be discussed are representative, but constitute some of the main areas of contestation in the debate. It is our contention that the seeming solidity of the conceptual framework of lifelong learning and the prevailing – although by no means unanimous – consensus that lifelong learning is a progressive policy framework is, in fact, riven with contradictions and contestation as we argued in Chapter 6. A number of the central facets of lifelong learning could be analysed to argue this point. Here, we have selected three, which we maintain are both particularly important and particularly contentious. They are all held, in their different ways, to define the new, classless, flexible environment in which higher education, as everything else, now operates. They are: community, globalization and, at a rather different level, the individualistic approach to learner autonomy.

Community

Managers of the more prestigious higher education institutions tend to define community in elitist terms.[2] That is, for most pre-1992 higher education institutions in Britain, it is the international community that has priority in terms of research and other links with peer institutions and, of increasing importance for largely financial reasons, the recruitment of international students. However, more regional as well as national perspectives on community have developed in recent years, as analysed by John Goddard and his colleagues in a 1994 report for the British Committee of Vice-Chancellors and Principals (CVCP – since 2001, retitled Universities UK), and in the development of a whole complex of regional and higher education consortia. In Yorkshire and Humberside, for example, in the North of England, the Yorkshire and Humberside Universities Association (YHUA) – renamed in 2002 Yorkshire Universities – is an active body with a full-time secretariat and a number of committees with representation at senior level of all the universities in the region.

The concepts of community in this new context are certainly multifaceted and pluralistic, but they are dominated by an emphasis upon the economic role of higher education working in conjunction with local, regional and national capital as articulated through individual employers and their representative organizations. In the 1994 CVCP Report referred to, for example, the main headings of cooperation are listed as: Technology Transfer (considered to be the most important by far); Tourism and Conferencing; the Built Environment; and Social and Community Development.[3] In other words, 'community' is largely equated with 'business'.

In the proclaimed 'New Times'[4] of postmodernity, however, the term 'community' has taken on a wider, almost ubiquitous, meaning. Tony Blair, Prime Minister of the British New Labour Government elected in 1997 and re-elected in 2001, homes in on community as a symbol of a society characterized by a new absence of social class tensions and divisive 'old Labour' attitudes. Peter Wilby, for example, noted in the *Observer* in June 2000 that the Prime Minister repeatedly mentions the word community. In a high-profile speech in June 2000, 'we have "active community", "renewal of community", "core values of community", "fragile web of community", "idea of community", and much else on the same lines'.[5] This 'Third Way' view of community stresses the perceived diffusion, fragmentation and complexity of contemporary society and celebrates its pluralism and multiculturalism. This is combined, of course, quite harmoniously with New Labour's market orientation and embrace of business. As Ian Martin has observed, 'the conflation of democracy with the marketplace combined with a widespread disillusionment with representative politics to generate an equally widespread sense of a democratic deficit'.[6] This use of community thus follows on directly from the American functionalists, such as Robert Dahl, who argued in the 1950s and 1960s in the political science context that American democracy was alive and well and vibrant despite obvious disillusion with formal politics, as indicated by very low participation in voting, in political party membership and a clear consensus between the Democratic and Republican parties on all essentials. Ingeniously, if not perhaps convincingly, Dahl argued that the plethora of *community* involvement in his case study of New Haven, Connecticut, proved that democracy worked and that through such community involvement ordinary people were both involved and empowered in a more fundamental sense than could be provided through formal politics.[7]

In the New Labour, postmodernist framework, however, community has stronger overtones of caring, compassion and emotional warmth. Nor is this confined to New Labour: the 'compassionate conservatism' of the American Republican Party in the lead-up to the presidential election in 2000 was, for example, enthusiastically endorsed by the moderate Right in Europe, in particular by the leadership of the British Conservative Party (not that it did them much good: they suffered a severe electoral defeat).

Community, as a concept for facilitating control and incorporation by the ruling order, also has a relatively long history politically. As early as the nineteenth century, British imperial civil servants, for example, were invoking 'community' to instil British attitudes, cultural mores and, not least, British-style institutions.[8]

For most people in education, though, very different perceptions of community have dominated. Henry Morris, for example, developed the now much-celebrated Community School and College movement in the 1920s and 1930s.[9] The village college, he proposed, 'should become the focal point for communal regeneration: an holistic institution, integrating educational, social, cultural and recreational activity in a "new institution, single but many-sided for the countryside"'.[10] Morris was a strong advocate of community education as a catalyst for the regeneration of the *whole* community. His ambition was to create an 'organic provision of education for the whole adult community . . . our places of education [must] become centres of corporate life and not congeries of classrooms for discourse and instruction'.[11] As Martin points out, although Morris's view of community was 'radical and imaginative', [he] 'was also a paternalist'.[12] Morris romanticized the pre-industrial rural society and wanted to recreate what he believed to have been an organic, consensual society, with 'the village colleges . . . replacing the churches as centres of community cohesion'.[13]

This model of community education, although initially centred in Cambridgeshire and then developed in broadly similar ways in other rural counties of England (Cumberland, Devon, Leicestershire, etc.), was eventually generalized into more urban contexts. Often this degenerated, as Martin has noted, into a rhetoric of integration;[14] but it led to the foundations of the idea of recurrent education and lifelong learning. However, this concept of community, although radical in some ways in Morris's original context, became bureaucratized and essentially 'an imposed rather than a popular politics of education'.[15]

Through the 1970s and 1980s, as social and economic problems and ideological tensions in the wider society predominated, so community became increasingly associated with notions of disadvantage, and with the need to incorporate or co-opt disadvantaged communities into the mainstream of social and economic life, and thus into conformity with capitalist culture and practices. In particular, disadvantage was pathologized and, through a whole variety of government-funded schemes (Educational Priority

Areas, Community Development Projects, etc.), emphasis was laid upon the links between school, family and community participation. This was essentially a *reformist* view of community education, though it is worth noting that, as Jane Thompson has argued with some asperity, many advocates of this perspective on community adopted a wholly uncritical series of assumptions about the proper domestic and familial roles of women. Jean Barr has analysed Scottish schemes in similar terms.[16]

More radical interpretations of community, within this same period, have followed through into lifelong learning. There are two essential characteristics of this approach. First, community is viewed collectively rather than individually. Disadvantaged communities are composed of interlocking collectivities of particular groups, almost always of double disadvantage. That is, such communities are always working class on any criteria; but they are also, variously, unwaged, of minority ethnic origin, women disadvantaged primarily by their single-parent status, elderly and impoverished people, and so on. There is thus a deep structural inequality.[17] Rather than seeing the problem as being the provision of education and learning, in a wider context of community development, for disadvantaged *individuals*, from this perspective the complex of multiple disadvantage is held to reside in collective social and political impoverishment and disempowerment.

This leads directly to the second characteristic. To a greater or lesser extent – and there have been variations between, for example, the approaches of Tom Lovett, Keith Jackson and the Leeds 'Pioneer Work' team – community education is seen as a *political* process, involving education for empowerment and often a direct politicization of the communities to take action to resolve, at least partially, their problems.[18] Whether or not the programmes that were initiated and led by advocates of such perspectives veered too far towards 'politics' rather than 'education' has been a matter of some dispute.[19] This is not directly germane to the discussion here, but it is worth noting that issues of commitment, objectivity and the principles appropriate to higher education pedagogy are central to one key part of the debate over postmodernist approaches.

There have been, finally, several radical commentators and practitioners who have seen the development of concepts of community education in the context of 'New Times' and postmodernism as a welcome break from 'all the crude forms of class analysis that had . . . impoverished [the radical tradition in adult education in terms of both] its theory and practice'.[20] The new emphases upon the plurality of communities, and the disadvantage of many groups other than the traditional (male) manual working class, 'seemed to offer the possibility of reappropriating community as a site of struggle, working with progressive social movements . . . and [respecting] difference and . . . [reconciling] it with solidarity'.[21]

In this context of the appropriate conception of community for radical educators, there is direct ideological conflict between neo-socialist and postmodern perspectives – as there is in many of the other respects of theory and practice discussed in this book. To claim that socialist perspectives reduce disadvantage, and thus community education, to an exclusive concern with manual working-class men, organized in the Labour Movement and working 'at the point of production', is itself reductionist – and, more importantly, is a perspective long since abandoned, to the extent that it was ever widely held. Among many other examples, there is the multiplicity of community adult education provision, with clearly socialist motivations, in the 1970s and 1980s in British post-compulsory education provision. On the other hand, the foregrounding of previously marginalized groups, and the greater sensitivity and understanding of what is clearly a radically changed structure of inequality, is clearly necessary. These changes, though, take place in an international capitalist system of unprecedented power, which in Ian Martin's words has been 're-formed, not transformed'.[22]

Our view, therefore, is that community for radical educators and thus for a progressive policy formulation is located clearly within the re-formed, but deeply unequal and class-structured, context of late capitalism.

Globalization

Globalization has become a key concept in the analysis of, and policy prescriptions for, higher education.[23] The phenomenon of globalization is normally held to have developed from, approximately, the 1970s in the wake of technological, economic and political changes. It is moreover closely linked to other notions central to postmodernist perspectives on late capitalist societies.[24]

However, before entering into this discussion and its relevance for higher education, it is interesting to note that the seeds, at the very least, of the globalization thesis can be traced to an earlier period. David Cesarani, in his masterly biography of Arthur Koestler,[25] notes that as early as 1960 Koestler 'stumbled on the concept years before most sociologists'.[26] Cesarani notes that 'before technology made it possible to sample diverse cultures while remaining stationary, an individual could achieve the same effect by moving rapidly across political and cultural borders'.[27] Koestler's analysis focused on the implications of the new globalization in terms of the development of a mass, homogenized culture, which paradoxically would involve far larger numbers of people in cultural experiences but of a debased form. This, in turn, he foresaw would undermine the high culture of European civilization, which he regarded as a cornerstone of western society.[28]

There is an even more fundamental, and obvious, sense in which globalization is neither a new concept nor a new material reality.

> [From] the sixteenth century, there began the plunder and the genocide which attended the conquest of North and South America, followed by the plunder and subjugation of Africa and most of Asia . . . Ever since then, by far the most important feature of world history has been the merciless exploitation by Western powers of the rest of the world.[29]

This is not the place to enter into the appalling, bloody history of this global capitalist domination, or to debate Leninist and subsequent theories of the supposed causal connections between the growth of imperialism and the inherent economic and social contradictions of capitalism. The point here is, rather, two-fold: first, global factors have been present, and dominant, in the development of capitalist societies from at least the sixteenth and seventeenth centuries; and, secondly, that the contemporary phenomenon of globalization, while clearly of a somewhat different order, is fundamentally a further development of this longstanding characteristic of capitalism. The 'autonomous nation state' was always, largely, a rhetorical creation by national governing classes designed to mask the material realities of the (anarchic) global capitalist system. As the Vice-Chancellor of the University of the West Indies put it in his presentation to the Conference of the International Council for Adult Education in the summer of 2001, globalization is 'essentially a new name for old obscenities'. Nevertheless, notwithstanding all these observations, the development of globalization in the late twentieth and early twenty-first century *is* to an extent novel, because it is so pervasive and dominant, and because technology has facilitated this process in a variety of ways. In the context of higher education, the phenomenon is of real importance.

There is a fundamental difference of view between those, of broadly postmodernist persuasion, who argue that this new globalization marks a sharp qualitative change and those, generally Marxisant, who base their analyses on the sort of arguments noted above. The intention of this part of this chapter is to outline and examine the former position; the latter, to which we adhere, forms a part of the discussion of 'agency' questions in Chapter 9.

The globalization thesis, interpreted in a variety of ways, has become a widely accepted analytical framework in general social science. The phenomenon is held to have several key features: among them, transnational inter-connectedness and the decline of the nation state, the spread of global culture, and the impact of electronic and other technology on 'shrinking' our world.[30] The two leading social scientists in the field in Britain, arguably, have been Anthony Giddens and David Harvey.[31] The global and the local are conflated and there is, in Harvey's words, a 'time–space compression'.[32] Globalization, it is argued, is 'essentially *dialectical* in nature and *unevenly* experienced across time and space'.[33] There are thus many ' "binary oppositions": universalization versus particularization . . . homogenization versus differentiation . . . integration versus fragmentation . . . centralization versus decentralization'. And so on.[34]

In his analysis, which centres more on the ways in which globalization affects specifically higher education, John Urry argues that the new world environment has fatally undermined two longstanding assumptions underlying western capitalism. First, the liberal concept of the individual citizen in relation to the wider but *national* society of which he or she was a member, was linked to 'the belief that human progress should be measured and evaluated in terms of the domination of nature rather than through transforming the relationship between "humans" and "nature".[35] Secondly, and related to this, is the conviction – which became by the nineteenth century an assertion and assumption – that human progress was both natural and virtually inevitable, and that it could be achieved through individual and collective human endeavour and technological advance. This latter perspective characterized most progressive thought and analysis in the nineteenth century, including pre-eminently the work of Karl Marx.

The twentieth century has brought a realization, however, that these beliefs are flawed, to say the least (as was discussed in Chapter 1). The contribution of globalization to this argument, Urry maintains, is the awesome power of global technology and its 'inhuman' potential for destruction (for example, Chernobyl), which both disempowers individuals, political parties and the like, and seriously undermines the sovereignty and overall credibility of the nation state.

The postmodern 'take' on these developments is that this removal of control and rationality from both socio-political structures and the nation state is combined with a reconceptualization of traditional models of social class structures and international relations and diplomacy. The metaphor is now, it is argued, one of complex networks or webs and their 'spread across time and space' through the increasingly widespread use of information technology.[36] There is clearly a growth of 'borderlessness' and thus global networks and processes. Obvious examples of this include: the round-the-clock (and increasingly volatile and chaotic) international finance system facilitated through IT; a whole variety of related technologies – credit cards, satellite TV, computer networks and e-mail, mobile telephones, relatively cheap jet aeroplane travel and the development of the leisure and travel industries; global phenomena such as AIDS, mass (largely American) culture and products such as Coca-Cola, McDonalds, etc.; developments in bio-technology (for example, genetic engineering); and, of course, the phenomenon of global terrorism and the responses to it.

The list could be extended, but the point is made that there is a range of developments – some undeniably positive, some equally clearly negative – associated with global developments. As always, the differences arise in ideological analysis. What postmodernists all too often ignore are the starkly obvious connections between *all* these changes and the now fully global power of international capital. We have drawn attention before to the centrality of huge and increasing inequalities, and the associated miseries and sufferings, created by global capital. Far from the ending of the Cold War resulting in a more rational, equal and civilized world order, the opposite has occurred. The gap between the rich, late capitalist societies and the Third World has grown in terms both of material wealth and poverty and of economic and political power.[37] And this is to say nothing of the resultant and horrific wave of terrorism in the early years of the twenty-first century.

As we noted earlier, contrary to the relentless rhetorical barrage, there is sharply increasing inequality *within* all late capitalist societies, pre-eminently the USA.[38] As far as Britain is concerned, the evidence is unequivocal: inequality has clearly increased. 'In 1979, discrepancy between earnings for non-manual workers (both male and female) and manual workers (both male and female) was 21 per cent; by 1998, this was 55 per cent.'[39] Economically, far from the new globalism producing coherence of production and distribution, the anarchy of capital, roving the globe in irrational and unpredictable exploitation, has never been more marked – nor the human and environmental costs so horrific.[40]

These arguments need restating as a balance to the seeming celebration of globalization by some contemporary commentators on the higher education world – Barnett, Urry and Usher among others – and their emphases on the relative minutiae.[41]

Globalization, though, certainly has had significant impact on higher education. There has been, to begin with, a marked increase in the numbers of international students; in Britain, for example, there was a 127 per cent increase in the enrolment of international students in higher education between 1989–90 and 1995–96 (to a total of 196,346).[42] As Bruch and Barty argue, 'UK institutions want international students for two main reasons: they believe that internationalization adds educational and cultural value to the institution, and they want the cash value accruing from full-fee paying international students.'[43] As governments, in Britain and elsewhere and of all political complexions, have persistently reduced unit cost funding, so the latter motivation has become increasingly dominant: 'Institutions are motivated by a powerful instinct – survival: . . . if the income from international students dried up . . . [s]ome departments or units, particularly at postgraduate level, would be threatened with closure.'[44] The economic impact of international students has certainly been a significant element for the finances of some universities. A 1995 CVCP study 'estimated that international students' tuition fees and associated expenditure in Britain generated in excess of £1 billion a year in invisible exports and helped sustain between 35–50,000 jobs'.[45]

Globalization also has an increasing impact on research and development, particularly in science and technology – and, with English rapidly becoming the *lingua franca* of academic discourse and the growth of IT-based academic communication, universities are being absorbed 'into a distributed knowledge production system'.[46] There are, however, some paradoxes in this seeming homogenization of higher education through global development. Traditional disciplinary boundaries have become blurred and definitions of disciplines themselves and established academic methodologies have come under increasing intellectual and philosophical attack, for reasons that are related only tangentially to the globalization factors discussed here; these issues relating to epistemology and disciplinary definition were discussed in Chapter 3. Inter-disciplinarity and 'relevance' have become the order of the day.[47] Yet, at the same time, 'splintered fractions' of disciplines have become ever more specialized – and self-referential. As Frank Webster has argued, academics increasingly communicate *with each other*, rather than with the outside world.[48] Moreover, academics are often becoming more locked into their own highly specialist research areas, and communicate both orally and in scholarly writing in abstruse, jargon-ridden language. Terry Eagleton makes the point with customary force, in relation to literary studies and the ways in which postgraduate students are now introduced to the research field.[49] The expansion of higher education has occurred not only in the late capitalist world but globally: the number of students in higher education in the world as a whole 'increased from 51 million in 1980 to about 82 million in 1995',[50] an increase of about 61 per cent. This has been combined with an introversion and *inaccessibility*, intellectually.

The final paradox we wish to draw attention to in this context is that, despite this retreat into the abstractions of the academy, higher education has become in reality increasingly dominated by the business culture and its assumptions. At the crudest empirical level, the rapid growth of business studies and associated programmes at undergraduate, but particularly at postgraduate, MBA level, is highly significant. But so, too, is the adoption of business language and concepts noted earlier in the discussion on community, and the involvement of private sector employers and entrepreneurs at senior level in policy bodies. Relevance is equated with uncritical acceptance of private sector market ideology and culture. There is now a plethora of Business School chairs in traditional, research-led universities, in the now seemingly respectable areas of Marketing, Accountancy – even Credit Management. Appointments such as the latter, if not the former, would have been academically and intellectually unthinkable twenty years earlier. At a more general level, the phenomenon of the global, corporate university located entirely within the private sector and usually with a strong emphasis on IT delivery and a virtual existence, is increasingly common, especially in the USA (for example, Motorola University).

The *positive* impact of these global influences upon higher education is notable. The broadening, flexible and more diverse curricular and pedagogic approaches within a multicultural framework have now become more common, if by no means dominant, in most higher education systems in the late capitalist world. Higher education is arguably one significant cultural counter to nationalist and xenophobic, imperialistic perspectives within these societies. These are real achievements and benefits.

The potential, educationally, of the new technologies on a global scale is also a highly significant factor, although it is arguably something of a mixed blessing. On the one hand, the spread of literacy and numeracy and the general global educational awareness now being achieved through the mass media and through IT have enfranchised, at least potentially, huge numbers in the Third World. One example of this is the rapid growth, globally, of higher education, referred to above. However, the pervasive and undeniably baleful influence of media moguls such as Rupert Murdoch and his relentless cultural trivialization and scandal-mongering is a deeply negative phenomenon. (Not for nothing did the British writer Denis Potter proclaim, when terminally ill, that he had named his cancerous tumour Rupert!)

The homogenization of mass culture on a global scale, a process in which higher education plays a major role, has been combined, as Peter Scott and others have observed, with the commodification of culture.[51] This is a part of the hegemony of capital in the new global order. The point need not be laboured, but the overarching reality of the globalization process, within which all other developments must be assessed, is the heightened dominance in all respects of international capital. It is over the interpretation of, and value judgement made on, the phenomenon that postmodernists and socialists disagree, at least in terms of emphasis. As with the other concepts discussed, such debate and analysis is not only an abstract, academic issue; the perspectives and emphases adopted have a direct impact on policy formulation and, subsequently, higher education culture and practice.

Learner autonomy[52]

There are numerous other contested concepts that could be discussed in this chapter, in the context of the lifelong learning policy framework. For example, the much-vaunted notions of 'difference and diversity' are central to both general postmodernist and higher education debates in the early twenty-first century.[53] Are these notions to be celebrated, in the higher education context, as an exemplar of pluralistic flexibility, individual choice, a freeing of the learner to pursue his or her interests and inclinations? Or are they rather a smokescreen and rationalization for a steeply hierarchical and still class-structured higher education system? Is the objective of creating institutions and cultures of higher education that are 'equal but different' a real policy goal, or merely rhetoric and sophistry? These are, again, issues we touch on in the final chapter of this book. Here, for the final contested concept analysed in this chapter, we concentrate on the area of learner autonomy and the contrast between contemporary, individualistic and market-driven assumptions, and the more collective interpretations within the democratic socialist framework.

In most late capitalist societies, considerable emphasis is placed upon the individual learner and his or her interests, and the need for a higher education system that is more responsive to the expressed needs of learners. In Britain, for example, the Secretary of State for Education in the Labour Government, writing in 1999 in the Foreword to the influential policy document on lifelong learning, *The Learning Age*, emphasized the role that learning played in supporting 'active citizenship and democracy, giving men and women the capacity to provide leadership in their communities'.[54]

There is, apparently, consensus about the importance of the principle of 'learner empowerment' and self-directed learning in the new, mass higher education system. Learners should be put centre stage, as active participants in the process of learning, not passive recipients. However, this (often largely rhetorical) commitment masks fundamentally different conceptions: on the one hand, the democratic, egalitarian perspective and, on the other, the more postmodern – and, in Britain, New Labour – view in which learners are contextualized within the dominant market ideology.

A prominent strand in the democratic tradition stems from radical adult education. In a 1968 lecture, E.P. Thompson referred to the symbiotic relationship, in adult education, between the worlds of life experience and work, and the abstract theorization and historical knowledge of the academy.

> All education which is worth the name involves a relationship of mutu-
> ality, a dialectic: and no worthwhile educationalist conceives of his
> material as a class of inert recipients of instruction. But, in liberal adult
> education, no tutor is likely to last out a session – and no class is likely
> to stay the course with him – if he is under the misapprehension that
> the role of the class is passive. What is different about the adult student
> is the experience which he brings to the relationship. This experience
> modifies, sometimes subtly and sometimes more radically, the entire
> education process . . . To strike the balance between intellectual rigour
> and respect for experience is always difficult. But the balance today
> [1968] is seriously awry . . . [I wish to redress it a little] by reminding us
> that Universities engage in adult education not only to teach but also
> to learn.[55]

The learner in this context is not simply an individual recipient of received knowledge and wisdom. This is far from a simple, one-way process of
transmission. When the process works, the learning is a collective as well as
an individual experience. The empowerment, self-confidence and understanding that flow from interaction are just as valuable as the specific knowledge attained. All this applies to settings other than adult education,
although it is more evident here both because of the life experience that
adult learners bring and because of their often low levels of self-confidence
and previously negative experience of the education system.

However, the democratic tradition of learner autonomy and self-directed
learning in adult education is about far more than this. As the quotation
from E.P. Thompson implies, learning in this context has at least three
other key characteristics when operating ideally: first, it values highly the
lived experience of the learners and regards that experience as a key element,
in all its varied forms, in the construction of genuine, socially relevant
knowledge (the 'really useful knowledge' concept); secondly, and following
from this, curriculum content and specific syllabus construction take place
through collective discussion, facilitated by the tutor but always a consensu-
ally agreed, *negotiated* process; and, finally, the learning process is seen
explicitly within a context of social purpose. And this social purpose has
centred on equity, on the socialist priority for creating an egalitarian social
system.

Historically, adult education has been a part of a social movement –
or, rather, a series of interlocking social movements. (The most obvious

examples are the labour movement, linked to trade union day release provision and wider industrial and political education; and the women's movement linked *inter alia* to New Opportunities and Access programmes and Women's Studies as critique.) In the past, this was rooted in the strong belief in the liberatory power of education: 'knowledge is power' and the political centrality in the thinking of a succession of labour movement activists of attaining equality of educational opportunity – from William Lovett and the 'moral force' Chartists through to revisionist social democrats such as Anthony Crosland and Shirley Williams.

All this is to paint a general and rather too rosy picture of the learner empowerment and social purpose perspective as central to the liberal tradition of adult education. There are two large caveats: the complexity and, arguably, inadequacy of the political commitments noted; and the fractured, highly contested nature of the wider liberal tradition. On the first issue of political commitments there is, of course, a whole literature on both the theory and the historical practice of the political movements of the Left. In the British context, radical adult education has been largely aligned to left Labourism (or democratic socialism, as its advocates would prefer). Even this, though, is a huge generalization: and the commitments were often, anyway, more implicit than explicit. Many adult educators and adult learners were aligned to very different perspectives – predominantly, until the 1970s, Marxist or Marxisant in emphasis. While some from this perspective exemplified the very best of democratic practice, including learner empowerment, many were committed to the educational equivalent of democratic centralism, where the emphasis was much more upon the centrality than the democracy. Within the Mainstream Labourist tradition, though, commitment to learner empowerment was at best patchy. The shifting orthodoxy of Labourism was very evident, particularly in the Cold War years from the 1940s onwards.[56] Too often, the learner-centred, social purpose approach was blocked at one level or another because of a conservative insistence on both established bureaucratic practice and ideological orthodoxy.

From the 1970s, radical adult education also reflected the explosion of new social movements, and the challenging of hitherto established orthodoxies, both educational and political. In particular, the women's movement had a profound influence on adult education policy and practice – and this was concerned centrally both with the lived experience of women and its impact upon curriculum and pedagogy, and with the need to establish a democratic process of learning (with, of course, strong social purpose motivations).[57]

The concept of a democratic structure, ensuring learner autonomy and aspiring to self-directed learning, within a radical democratic tradition, has thus characterized radical adult education, but only intermittently. But there *is* a long and continuous history, stretching, as J.F.C. Harrison, for example, has graphically described, from at least the eighteenth century onwards.[58] Others have described, analysed and celebrated more contemporary articulations of this tradition.[59] Education has been a key element of eman-cipation and radicalization, albeit with very different ideological orientations in different periods.

However, radical adult education has been situated in a liberal tradition – a liberal theory and a liberal practice – that is far from wholly democratic and learner-centred. Some analysts have gone so far as to characterize the liberal tradition as quintessentially elitist, conservative and instrumental.[60] Others, such as Jane Thompson,[61] have seen the liberal tradition as patri-archal and exclusive. From the other side, politically, the liberal tradition has been perceived as anachronistic and a brake upon a more vocational professional approach.[62]

The liberal tradition is certainly based upon the assumptions and per-spective of the wider liberal world view. This is centred on individualism, largely *possessive* individualism, and upon the priority that should be given to freedom, socially and economically.[63] At one level, then, this position places the individual learner at the centre of the system: it is his or her educational welfare and development that is the key measure of success (the key performance indicator in today's parlance). However, there is an obvious tension here with the idea of a collective, group approach. Learn-ers are seen, rather, as discrete individuals and the tutor as the arbiter and reconciler of different interests, levels of ability and so on. Add to this the acceptance of a whole series of assumptions about the linearity of know-ledge, education as a one-way transmission process and the sanctity of dis-ciplinary boundaries, and it becomes clear that there is a conservatism in much of the traditional approach to adult learning. To a large extent, this was mirrored too in the traditional mainstream practice of university higher education, as many analysts have recognized.[64] There is also the obvious and predictable empirical fact that the large majority of those involved not only in adult education but also in mainstream higher education are middle- or upper-class, white and relatively well-educated. The liberal tradi-tion is thus both pluralistic and contested.

How, then, does this complex of social purpose and the liberal tradi-tion relate to New Labour perspectives on learner autonomy and self-directed learning? New Labour ideology, as articulated from the later 1990s, is notoriously difficult to tie down. Part of its attraction is its packaging of being 'all things to all people' and its relentless pursuit of the new and fashionable. It is, in some ways, the contemporary articulation of McLuhan's 'the medium is the message'. Nevertheless, certain characteristics are clear, many of them in tension with each other. There is, first, a genuine aspira-tion to humanistic values in education, as in other fields, as reflected in the quotation from David Blunkett cited earlier. Similarly, there are Christian Socialist roots to Tony Blair's perspective, as proclaimed in a variety of interviews and speeches. The old ILP tradition of Labourism, though in so many respects an anathema to New Labour, also drew upon Christian Socialism, and argued for social equity on essentially non-conformist Chris-tian grounds.[65]

More important than these influences, however, have been the directly political legacies of Social Democratic Party (SDP), social democratic ideologies, drawing not only on politicians like Roy Jenkins and Shirley Williams, but on their more weighty ideological precursors, particularly Anthony Crosland and Hugh Gaitskell. The ideological amalgam, stripped of the hype, the spinning and all the rest, is clearly a variant on the 'caring capitalism' theme. As we argued in Chapter 1, this was first articulated in the Cold War environment by revisionist social democrats who argued that ownership and control had become separated, through economic and organizational development, thus rendering redundant traditional Marxist and neo-Marxist class analysis. New Labour politics essentially replicates this social democratic ideology. The 'Third Way', championed by Tony Blair, his 'think-tank' staff and supportive academic advisers, is a cruder, glitzier and modernized version of Crosland's original blueprint.[66]

Of course, by far the most significant change in this context, between the 1950s and 1960s political climate in which Crosland *et al.* were writing and the New Labour period of the 1990s and beyond, has been the collapse of Soviet Communism, the discrediting of Marxism-Leninism and the consequent undermining of the whole socialist project and its accompanying ideology.

How does New Labour ideology impact upon the particular, microcosmic concerns of this discussion? Self-directed learning, within New Labour thinking and practice, is defined primarily, we would argue, in three ways. First, there is a genuine commitment to cultural change in the educational context, so that learners should have a real say in that learning process. Learners are stakeholders and have a right to negotiate and, to an extent, to choose, what, when and how they study. The strong impetus is to make education and learning more relevant to the perceived needs of learners. There is also a principled commitment to enabling far more people to have the opportunity to study and enjoy the arts and to engage in 'citizenship activity'.

These positive attributes are often overlooked; but, having noted these commitments, it has to be emphasized that they are greatly overshadowed by the priority given to skills training and competence-based education. At all levels in the education system (including schools, although this lies beyond the scope of this discussion), the key objective is to enhance the skills base of the workforce to produce a more efficient and thus competitive economy for the United Kingdom. The learner is thus conceptualized largely within this particular version of the economic framework. This reflects the neo-liberal market orientation of New Labour. Within this pervasive market context, then, the learner is seen as a *customer*, a consumer of learning in the marketplace.[67] Self-directed learning is thus seen as a process in which the learner should be able to 'shop around to find the best buy' to meet his or her requirements. Learning is thus commodified; buying learning is no different from buying a car or a packet of cornflakes. Implicitly, the criteria against which the educational experience should be judged are instrumental: what is the most cost-effective level of investment in learning that will yield the greatest return in terms of earning potential? Of course, it is never formulated in quite these terms; but it is hard to interpret the roots of New Labour ideology in any other way.

The third important element in New Labour's definition of self-directed learning complements the second. New Labour's ideology, like that of Labour's social democratic wing, some adherents of which broke away in the 1980s to form the SDP, is fundamentally individualist rather than collective. There are deep historical roots for this stance: the early Labour Party *was* influenced more by Methodism than Marxism, as the old examination question has it. The Liberal (as well as liberal) inheritance of the Labour Party was always dominant, as many analysts have argued convincingly.[68]

The longstanding, individualist perspective has had profound consequences for Labourist social analysis and, in the context of this discussion, for education policy specifically. Moreover, now that Labour's broad church has become virtually a single, centralist creed from which little or no perceived deviation, however mild, is normally tolerated, this individualist focus has become more pronounced. The result, in the context of this discussion, is to exclude consideration of the collective, the group needs. This is no mere abstraction. The policy and its implementation articulate this perspective clearly: the Higher Education Funding Council for England's welcome initiatives in the late 1990s on Widening Participation, for example, are focused almost entirely upon the *individual's* accessibility and progression.[69]

Putting these three elements together, then, produces a version of self-directed learning sharply distinct from that of the democratic tradition; in New Labour's framework, self-directed learning is in part inspired by liberal humanism, but largely by a consumerist, individualistic conception of the learner, operating within the marketplace, and assumed to be motivated by uncritically accepted free market ideology. Again, therefore, the seemingly consensual and straightforward commitment to self-directed learning and learner autonomy within the lifelong learning framework masks deep and important differences of ideological perspective.

As we stated at the beginning of this chapter, the concepts of community, globalization and learner autonomy are three of the areas within the lifeling learning frame of reference that are particularly important and contentious. At another level, though, the lifelong learning that is so characteristic of the developing *mass* system of higher education is part of a change in the nature and orientation of the learning that now takes place in the academy.

Many of the social and economic pressures in late modern societies that have led to the development of mass higher education are connected to the increasingly preponderant emphasis upon professional and vocational education within the academy. This is not merely a matter of intellectual or academic fashion – the equivalent of, say, modern history becoming more popular a subject than political studies; it is rather a response to the perceived role of higher education in the labour market, and the need for universities to reorient themselves to become more 'relevant' to the requirements of employers and professional bodies. The rapid growth of professional and vocational education is again assumed often to be uncontentious – an academically responsible and appropriate response to the expressed desires of the wider community. In our view, however, this phenomenon is in reality similarly contested. It is to a consideration of these issues that we turn in the next chapter.

Notes

1. See, for example, Robin Usher and Richard Edwards (1994) *Postmodernism and Education*. London: Routledge.
2. This is exemplified in the Report for the Committee of Vice-Chancellors and Principals (CVCP) written by John Goddard *et al.* (1994) *Universities and Communities*. London: CVCP.
3. Ibid., Executive Summary, pp. 1–2.
4. See Stuart Hall and Martin Jacques (eds) (1989). *New Times*. London: Lawrence & Wishart.
5. Peter Wilby, the *Observer*, 11 June 2000.
6. Ian Martin (1996) Community education: the dialectics of development, in Roger Fieldhouse and Associates, *A History of Modern British Adult Education*. Leicester: NIACE, p. 140.
7. Robert Dahl (1956) *A Preface to Democratic Political Theory*. Chicago, IL: University of Chicago Press.
8. See, on India, Tom Steele and Richard Taylor (1998) *Learning Independence: A Political Outline of Indian Adult Education*. Leicester: NIACE; Marjorie Mayo (1974) Community development: a radical alternative, in Ron Bailey and Mike Brake (eds) *Radical Social Work*. London: Edward Arnold, pp. 129–43.
9. See Harry Ree (1973) *Educator Extraordinary*. London: Longman; Cyril Poster (1982) *Community Education: Its Development and Management*. London: Heinemann.
10. Martin, op. cit., note 6, p. 111; the quotation is taken from Ree, op. cit., note 9, p. 147.
11. Harry Ree (ed.) (1984) *The Henry Morris Collection*. Cambridge: Cambridge University Press, pp. 38–9; cited in Martin, op. cit., note 6, p. 111.
12. Martin, op. cit., note 6, p. 112.
13. John Wallis and Geoffrey Mee (1983) *Community Schools: Claims and Performance*. Nottingham: University of Nottingham Department of Adult Education, p. 13; cited in Martin, op. cit., note 6, p. 113.
14. Martin, op. cit., note 6, p. 117ff.
15. Ibid., p. 119.
16. Jane Thompson (1983) *Learning Liberation: Women's Responses to Men's Education*. Beckenham: Croom Helm; Jean Barr (1999) *Liberating Knowledge*. Leicester: NIACE.
17. See Kevin Ward and Richard Taylor (eds) (1986) *Adult Education and the Working Class: Education for the Missing Millions*. Beckenham: Croom Helm, Chapter 1.
18. For a general discussion of these variations, see Martin, op. cit., note 6, pp. 126–8. For more detailed explication, see Ward and Taylor, op. cit., note 17; Keith

Jackson (1970) Adult education and community development, *Studies in the Education of Adults*, 2: 165–72; Keith Jackson (1980) Some fallacies in community education and their consequences in working class areas, in Colin Fletcher and Neil Thompson (eds) *Issues in Community Education*. Brighton: Falmer Press, pp. 39–46; Tom Lovett (ed.) (1988) *Radical Approaches to Adult Education*. London: Routledge; Tom Lovett (1975) *Adult Education, Community Development and the Working Class*. London: Ward Lock Education; Tom Lovett *et al.* (1983) *Adult Education and Community Action*. Beckenham: Croom Helm; Richard Taylor and Kevin Ward (1988) Adult education with unemployed people, in Tom Lovett (ed.) *Radical Approaches to Adult Education*. London: Routledge, pp. 242–62.

19. For a discussion of these issues, see Roger Fieldhouse (1985) Objectivity and commitment, in Richard Taylor, Kathleen Rockhill and Roger Fieldhouse, *University Adult Education in England and the USA: A Reappraisal of the Liberal Tradition*. Beckenham: Croom Helm.

20. Martin, op. cit., note 6, p. 139.

21. Ibid.

22. Ibid., p. 140.

23. See, for example, Peter Scott (ed.) (1998) *The Globalization of Higher Education*. Buckingham: SRHE and Open University Press.

24. See, for example, Peter Scott (1995) *The Meanings of Mass Higher Education* Buckingham: SRHE and Open University Press; Ronald Barnett (1990) *The Idea of a University*. Buckingham: SRHE and Open University Press; Usher and Edwards, op. cit., note 1; Robin Usher, Ian Bryant and Rennie Johnston (1997), *Adult Education and the Postmodern Challenge*. London: Routledge.

25. David Cesarani (1998) *Arthur Koestler: The Homeless Mind*. London: Heinemann.

26. Ibid., p. 463.

27. Ibid.

28. Ibid., pp. 463–4.

29. Ralph Miliband (1994) *Socialism for a Sceptical Age*. Cambridge: Polity Press, p. 34.

30. For a good summary of social science analysis of globalization in the late capitalist world, see Anthony McGrew (1992) A global society?, in Stuart Hall, David Held and Tony McGrew (eds) *Modernity and its Futures*. Cambridge: Polity Press in association with the Open University, pp. 61–116.

31. See Anthony Giddens (1991) *Modernity and Self-Identity: Self and Society in the Late Modern Age*. Cambridge: Polity Press; Anthony Giddens (1990) *The Consequences of Modernity*. Cambridge: Polity Press; David Harvey (1989) *The Condition of Postmodernity*. Oxford: Blackwell.

32. Harvey, op. cit., note 32, p. 240; cited in McGrew, op. cit., note 31, p. 67.

33. Harvey, op. cit., note 32, p. 240; cited in McGrew, op. cit., note 31, p. 74.

34. Ibid., pp. 74–5.

35. John Urry (1998) Contemporary transformations of time and space, in Scott (ed.), op. cit., note 23, p. 2.

36. Ibid., p. 3.

37. See, for example, John Pilger (1994) *Hidden Agendas*. London: Vintage; Thomas Byrne Edsall (1984) *The New Politics of Inequality*. New York: W.W. Norton.

38. See Griff Foley (2001) *Strategic Learning: Understanding and Facilitating Organisational Change*. Sydney: Centre for Popular Education, University of Technology; Zygmunt Bauman (1999) *In Search of Politics*. Cambridge: Polity Press, pp. 175ff.

39. Ivan Reid (1998) *Class in Britain*. Cambridge: Polity Press, p. 80.

40. See Pilger, op. cit., note 38; Brian Wynne (1994) Scientific knowledge and the global environment, in Michael Redclift and Ted Benton (eds) *Social Theory and the Global Environment*. London: Routledge; Mark Murphy (2000) Adult education, lifelong learning and the end of political economy, *Studies in the Education of Adults*, 32 (2): 166–80.
41. See, in particular, Peter Scott's argued differentiation between 'globalization' and 'internationalization' in Peter Scott (1998) Massification, internationalization and globalization, in Scott, op. cit., note 23.
42. Higher Education Statistics Agency (HESA) (1997) cited in Tom Bruch and Alison Barty (1998) Internationalizing British higher education: students and institutions, in Scott, op. cit., note 23, p. 19.
43. Ibid., p. 21.
44. Ibid., p. 22.
45. David Elliott (1998) Internationalizing British higher education: policy perspectives, in Scott, op. cit., note 23, p. 41.
46. Michael Gibbons (1998) A Commonwealth perspective on the globalization of higher education, in Scott, op. cit., note 23, p. 73.
47. For discussion of these issues, see Chapters 1, 5 and 9.
48. Frank Webster (1998) The post modern university? The loss of purpose of British universities, paper presented to the SRHE Conference, Lancaster University, December.
49. Terry Eagleton (1996) *The Illusions of Postmodernism*. Oxford: Blackwell.
50. Jan Sadlak (1998) Globalization and concurrent challenges for higher education, in Scott, op. cit., note 23, p. 101.
51. Scott, op. cit., note 24; Bill Williamson (1998) *Lifeworlds and Learning*. Leicester: NIACE.
52. This section draws upon Richard Taylor (2000) Concepts of self-directed learning: re-establishing the democratic tradition, in Jane Thompson (ed.) *Stretching the Academy*. Leicester: NIACE, pp. 68–79.
53. See, for two very different discussions of these issues, Usher and Edwards, op. cit., note 1 and the National Committee of Inquiry into Higher Education (the Dearing Report), 1997.
54. David Blunkett, Secretary of State for Education, Britain, writing in Department for Education and Employment (1999) *The Learning Age: A Renaissance for a New Britain*. London: HMSO.
55. Edward P. Thompson (1968) *Education and experience*, the Fifth Albert Mansbridge Memorial Lecture, University of Leeds.
56. Roger Fieldhouse (1985) *Adult Education and the Cold War*, Leeds Series in Adult Education. Leeds: University of Leeds; Fieldhouse and Associates, op. cit., note 6.
57. Thompson, op. cit., note 16; Barr, op. cit., note 16.
58. J.F.C. Harrison (1961) *Learning and Living*. London: Routledge.
59. For example, Marj Mayo and Jane Thompson (eds) (1995) *Adult Learning, Critical Intelligence and Social Change*. Leicester: NIACE; Rennie Johnston (1997), Adult learning for citizenship, in Usher *et al.* (eds), op. cit., note 24.
60. Usher (1997) in Usher *et al.* (eds), op. cit., note 24, pp. 11–120.
61. Thompson, op. cit., note 16.
62. Gilbert Jessop (1991) *Outcomes: NVQs and the Emerging Model of Education and Training*. Brighton: Falmer Press.
63. Taylor *et al.*, op. cit., note 19; Frank Coffield and Bill Williamson (eds) (1997) *Repositioning Higher Education*. Buckingham: SRHE and Open University Press.

64. For example, Scott, op. cit., note 24; Barnett, op. cit., note 24.
65. See Tom Nairn (1961) The nature of Labourism, in Perry Anderson and Tom Nairn, *Towards Socialism*. London: New Left Books and Fontana; Samuel H. Beer (1959) *Modern British Politics*. London: Allen & Unwin; Colin Pritchard and Richard Taylor (1978) *Social Work: Reform or Revolution?* London: Routledge & Kegan Paul.
66. See, for example, Anthony Giddens (1998) *The Third Way*. Cambridge: Polity Press; Anthony Crosland (1956) *The Future of Socialism*. London: Cape.
67. David Robertson (2000) Students as consumers, in Peter Scott (ed.) *Higher Education Re-formed*. Brighton: Falmer Press.
68. For example, Ralph Miliband (1973) *Parliamentary Socialism*, 2nd edn. London: Merlin Press; David Coates (1974) *The Labour Party and the Struggle for Socialism*. Cambridge: Cambridge University Press.
69. HEFCE, Widening Participation: special funding programme 1998–99, June 1998; HEFCE, Widening Participation in higher education. Invitation to bid for special funds: 1999–2000 to 2001–2002, May 1999. Similar orientations are to be found in policy documents of the Scottish and Welsh Funding Councils.

8

Professionalism and Vocationalism

At the straightforwardly empirical level, one of the most striking and significant elements in the new mass higher education in the United Kingdom has been the very rapid growth of professional and vocational provision. This has profound implications for all aspects of higher education and it results from a variety of pressures both from within the system itself and from the wider society. Similar patterns of development are apparent in most comparable western European societies.[1] In the immediate political context in the United Kingdom, the development of a higher education more oriented to professional and vocational provision has been a prominent theme in New Labour's policy agenda. As David Watson has observed:

> In its combined enthusiasm for 'education, education, education', and 'Lifelong Learning' the government elected in May 1997 has done much to create the circumstances in which professional higher education should flourish.[2]

There is a definitional or historical paradox here. In the contemporary policy arena, 'professional and vocational' are often twinned or paired together: but the usual inference is that the professional has the higher status. The professional label implies that the individual, and the disciplinary programme, has been accepted into an elite or quasi-elite club, whereas the vocational usually refers to lower-status, often applied, occupational training. In effect, therefore, the vocational is often held to be sub-professional. However, historically the academy's central purpose was seen as the proper *vocational* preparation of undergraduates for entry into the most important and prestigious occupations in the wider society: the established church, medicine and the law.

The roots of the expansion and increasing importance of this area of higher education lie much deeper than contemporary political policy imperatives. The relationship between the academy, the professions and vocationalism has been central to each phase of higher education's development – not least in the contemporary period where the unprecedented scale of this phenomenon is argued by some to be a key element in the system's increasing incorporation into a culture of marketization and postmodern theorizing about the nature of the academy in relation to the wider society.

This chapter examines this relationship in the context of the historical evolution of the 'professional ideal', the increasing prominence of professionalism and vocationalism in both higher education and the wider society, and contemporary policy debates about the ideology and practice of higher education. As was noted in both Chapter 1 and Chapter 5, universities have always had a close relationship with the professions and with vocational training; indeed, in one sense their central *raison d'être* has been the social reproduction of appropriately educated and trained professional elites. The fundamental difference in the twentieth century has been the *centrality* of professionalism to the social and economic structure of the whole society and the impact this has had on the nature of the academy. In contrast to earlier societies based upon economic capital, 'professional society is based on human capital created by education and enhanced by strategies of closure, that is, the exclusion of the unqualified'.[3]

The chapter begins with an analysis of this phenomenon, then discusses the ways in which higher education has played a central role in the articulation of this 'professional ideal'. The implications of the recent rapid development of this orientation and culture in higher education are, finally, analysed in the context of our overall discussion of postmodern analyses of higher education policy.

The intellectual middle class – what Perkin terms the 'forgotten middle class'[4] – occupied a pivotal position in nineteenth- and early twentieth-century industrial society. From its inception, it was this group that provided the concepts, terminology and cultural parameters of established society and thus were instrumental in creating bourgeois class consciousness: 'they also mounted a critique of industrial society'.[5] It was the interaction between socio-economic change and development, and ideological structures of thought, which gave rise to the increasing dominance of the professional ideal. Whereas in the early and hectic years of industrial Britain it was entrepreneurial culture that held sway, by the end of the nineteenth century this was being challenged, indeed overtaken, by the professional ideal.

In capitalism the profit motive, the 'bottom line' criterion, is always dominant, by definition. We are not arguing that the increasing dominance of the professional ideal, and the collective bureaucratic organizational structures of which it was a part, *replaced* this motivation. Rather, it is that as capitalism became more complex in structure, the articulation of this motivation became necessarily more complex too.

For the free market capitalist entrepreneur, the role of the state and the restrictions imposed via taxes, legislation and so on should be minimal; for the professional, however, and especially the professional working for the state in the public sector, the state, and the accompanying bureaucratic structures, rapidly became the guarantor and regulator of status and security.

Clergy, doctors and lawyers – and to an extent intellectuals *per se* – had long held high status in the United Kingdom, as elsewhere in western Europe. Other professionals – teachers, for example – occupied a rather more ambivalent social position. As the social and economic structure changed through the later nineteenth century and into the twentieth, so the numbers of people engaged in professional occupations increased rapidly. The whole culture of professionalism was different from the pure, free market and capitalist ethos:

> The history of the professions goes hand in hand with the social process of modernization and rationalization: with professionalization and bureaucratization, with the development of 'school cultures' and the meritocratic system, and with juridification, medicalization and technical and economic progress.[6]

There were, however, connections to an older ideology: that of high Tory, aristocratic *noblesse oblige*. The notion of public service has permeated at least a substantial part of professionalism as it did 'charitable work' by many of the upper classes, particularly upper-class women, in the nineteenth century.

Traditional Conservatism had a genuinely humanitarian strain, at least in its self-perception. While never the dominating factor, it was a persistent part of Conservative ideology over a long period. From Disraeli to Macmillan there was a concern, often carried into positive, legislative action, for social welfare within the very particular frameworks of Conservative thinking. This has been interwoven with the high Tories' commitment to Christianity, or more specifically Anglicanism.[7] This was in effect the Conservatives' 'social contract': wealth and power were rightful privileges of the upper class, but carried with them onerous duties of government and civic duty. The moral imperative was strong. Equally strong, of course, was the strategic grasp of Conservative politicians and thinkers (Edmund Burke, for example): and much of the ideology and legislation of the Conservative Party can be convincingly explained as adaptation to radically changing social, economic and political circumstances to ensure survival.

Be this as it may, the legacy of Tory *noblesse oblige* politics should not be ignored. This is particularly so in the contemporary period. Since the late 1970s and the advent of the 'garagiste' Conservatism of Margaret Thatcher and her successors, such moral imperatives seem distant indeed, although they are still there, albeit very *sotto voce*. The spirit of this culture and its tension with entrepreneurial motivations is well captured in Thomas Hughes's classic *Tom Brown's Schooldays*. In the following passage, Tom Brown is being upbraided by his Rugby tutor:

> You talk of 'working to get your living' and 'doing some real good in the world' in the same breath. Now you may be getting a good living in a profession, and yet not doing any good at all in the world . . . keep the latter before you as a holy object, and you will be right, whether

you make a living or not; but if you dwell on the other, you'll very likely drop into mere money making.[8]

The relevant point here is to note the continuity between this tradition, the better known moral conscience politics of the Liberalism of J.S. Mill and his successors, and the public service ethos of the influential Fabian wing of the Labour coalition.

The Fabian commitment to the professional, public service ethos was central to Labour's conception of the new, planned, rational and efficient society, centred on collective, bureaucratically structured endeavour through the state structure. Such a new social system, it was argued by the Webbs and others,[9] would produce both a far more efficient, productive and fair economy, *and* a more egalitarian and democratic social structure. The engine for achieving this was to be a disinterested, expert (highly educated and trained) elite, working within a predominantly public sector environment and inspired by the public service, professional ethos. Of course, this ideal was never fully achieved, but it acted as a powerful motivating factor over several decades of labour movement development,[10] although it was persistently contested by the radical, democratic left.

One key element of this public service ethos was the commitment to what Michael Young was later to conceptualize as meritocracy.[11] The professional elite would gain their positions, and their status, power and relatively high salaries, through education and training, proven ability and achievement, and hard work. This was the ideology, too, of the expert: the trained, specialist professional would be the key to achieving social and economic progress.

In Perkin's view, 'the increasing complexity and inter-dependence of the modern world automatically generates specialization and organized professions'.[12] This aspect of the professional ethos was quite at odds with the old high Tory idea of the all-round, amateur gentleman – the Renaissance man.[13] Winston Churchill probably spoke for many when he wrote to H.G. Wells in 1902:

> Nothing would be more fatal than for the Government of States to get into the hands of experts. Expert knowledge is limited knowledge: and the unlimited ignorance of the plain man who knows where it hurts is a safer guide than any vigorous direction of a specialized character. Why should you assume that all except doctors, engineers etc. are drones or worse?[14]

But the dominance of the corporate, bureaucratic social structure – and for the major part of the century at any rate, its counterpart of the collective industrial labour movement – was complete. The Conservative Party itself became increasingly absorbed within this corporate culture and indeed became, from the 1920s onwards, primarily the representative political organization for corporate – and particularly *finance* – capital.[15]

The dominance of the professional ethos was not monolithic, however. The professional class was almost from the outset bifurcated. The division has been between

> those who perform a public service, paid for out of taxation or voluntary contributions not derived from their immediate clients, and those employed by private corporations . . . we may call them the public sector and private sector professionals . . .[16]

Ideally, public sector professionals are engaged in providing high-quality social services, in the broadest sense, to society at large; generally, such professionals believe both that their services should be provided on a basis of equality and at low or no cost and that their particular service, and usually the public sector overall, is severely underfunded. Private sector corporate managers, on the other hand, for all the talk of caring capitalism, interactive management and the rest, are essentially serving the interests of capital, which are by definition concerned with the 'bottom line' mentality. As we touched on in Chapter 1 and Chapter 7, analysts since Anthony Crosland, and arguably since James Burnham,[17] have argued that the structure of capitalism has changed and that capital is no longer dominant; but it remains the case that the fundamental commitment has to be, by definition, to the interests of the corporation and thus to capital.

Of course, this is too schematic a picture: many professionals on either side of this divide have espoused the values and perspectives of the 'other side'. Nevertheless, the broad dichotomy holds. Private sector professionals certainly have been meritocratic in spirit – as, indeed, were Margaret Thatcher and her free-market supporters. They believed in social mobility, equality of opportunity and also – maybe – in alleviating 'the patches of real hardship which still exist'.[18] However, while public sector professionals generally held to a service ethic and an objective of social equality, or at least to equality of opportunity, their private sector counterparts emphasized the attainment of economic efficiency and thus greater wealth for all, which could be achieved without interfering, in effect, with hierarchies of income (and by implication social class) – and in general they believed strongly in the entrepreneurial values of the capitalist private sector.

In the world of higher education, the rapid expansion of the system has been characterized to a large extent by the development of both programmes and an overall ethos of vocationalism and professionalism. As noted earlier, there is an implicit distinction in the contemporary context between vocationalism and professionalism. Much of the vocational programme development in the new universities has led to the creation of second division professions, many of them involving a majority of female learners and subsequent employees. (Nursing is the most obvious example here.)

The creation by Anthony Crosland (and his senior civil servants, notably Toby Weaver) of the polytechnics, and their subsequent expansion and incorporation into a unified higher education sector (see Chapter 5), facilitated the bringing together of 'the "academic" values associated with subjects and disciplines and the "professional" values attached to practice and vocation'.[19] This innovation gave explicit recognition by government to the central importance of vocationalism and professionalism in the development of the economy. For many years, governments had been emphasizing the need to increase the supply of appropriately trained personnel for the changing needs of the labour market. In the Labour Governments of 1945 to 1951, for example, the key policy requirement for higher education was to increase the supply of trained technologists and scientists to develop the post-war economy.[20] However, historically universities had retained their autonomy: the professional bodies had their (self-constructed) standards, and recognition of university provision by such bodies – for example, the professional organizations of the various branches of engineering – was occasionally the source of some tension, and has remained so. Essentially, though, universities were jealous of their autonomy and they were thus reluctant to compromise this position by 'negotiated' provision with other interested parties, whether they were employers, professional bodies or indeed students themselves. This was certainly the case in 1945–51, for example, when the majority of the bodies representing universities were opposed to governmental proposals for developing technological and scientific training programmes in the academy.[21]

Crosland's creation of the polytechnics was, in this context, a recognition of two interrelated factors: the imperative need for a substantial higher education sector engaged primarily in vocational and professional training; and, secondly, the acknowledgement by government that universities – or at least their governing stratum – were unwilling to adapt their culture and practice to meet these demands. British universities have been inherently traditionalist in a number of respects, as have their counterparts in similar societies in Europe, not least in their cultural attachment to the superiority of abstract and 'pure' intellectual enquiry compared with the practical and applied.[22] This reflects the prevailing anti-industrial tenor of the British ruling elite through the nineteenth and twentieth centuries.[23] The need to correct this ideological imbalance was the central argument advanced by the advocates of the polytechnics and was central, too, to their perspective on higher education and their successor university institutions. Moreover, as Peter Scott has argued, in the 1980s and 1990s it was the culture and practice of the polytechnic tradition, rather than that of the universities, that has been dominant, as we discussed in Chapter 5.[24] David Watson, for example, has argued that

> British culture and British public life is . . . profoundly hierarchical, and the advocates of this expansion of professional higher education have had to fight many of the same battles as those concerned to improve the status and recognition of vocational qualifications in the compulsory and '16–19' phases of education. There are now, within the context of the Lifelong Learning debate, encouraging signs that the key battles are being won.[25]

Certainly, both the flexibility over modes of study and qualification, and the 'swing towards professionally and vocationally relevant subjects of study',[26] support David Watson's argument – and the empirical evidence confirms these assertions. The rapid and large-scale expansion of higher education has been most dramatic in the vocational and professional areas of study.

In 1997–98, the top five of twenty-one subject groups in terms of student registrations are all in this area, to a greater or lesser extent: business and administrative studies, social studies, creative arts, subjects allied to medicine, and mathematical sciences and informatics.[27] This listing, however, raises fundamental questions about the *nature* of vocational and professional higher education. The most obvious point is that this expansion is not in the traditional, elite professional areas – law, medicine and so on. These are *new* professions, predominantly in the second division professions, which, nevertheless, are central to the new knowledge society. The curriculum involved is concerned very largely, if not exclusively, with the acquisition of specialist skills relevant to subsequent professional employment. Nor is this surprising. As Catherine Watts has noted:

> The notion that a professional has a specialist knowledge base is central to the ideology of professionalism. It is this specialist knowledge base that gives a profession social recognition and forms the basis of the professional skills and expertise that are offered to the client.[28]

However, this raises the issue of the autonomy of the academy and the proper role of higher education itself. Of course, the assertion of traditional university values (see Chapter 5) can be, indeed *has* been, used by universities on occasion for elitist, 'ivory tower', intellectually snobbish and reactionary purposes. But, equally, this jealously guarded autonomy has allowed a crucial space for the exploration and articulation of dissident voices. One of the central themes of our book is the importance – particularly in the contemporary context – of the academy as a *critical* agency, facilitating the symbiosis between academic, theoretical knowledge and practical, lived experience in the 'real world'. (This is one of the issues we discuss further in the concluding chapter of this book.)

Clark Kerr noted as long ago as 1973 that, in the new socio-economic context, 'there is a smaller place for the humanities and arts, while the social sciences are strongly related to the training of the managerial groups and technicians for the enterprise and for government'.[29] (However, he did go on to say that increased leisure time will allow a 'broader public appreciation of the humanities and the arts'.[30]) Peter Jarvis comments that industrialism is no longer, in the twenty-first century, the driving force of change; rather, it is the 'infrastructural forces ... [which] are now global rather than State or country-wide. These forces lie in the control of capital and the utilization of information technology'.[31] We would argue, however, that the ownership and control of the productive processes, and the wealth and power that accompany them, remain the foundation of capitalist power.

The trends noted by Jarvis and others *complement* rather than challenge these power bases.

The expansion of vocational and professional education raises in this context at least two crucial concerns. First, the purposes, the curriculum, the *culture* of such provision are, by definition, uncritical. The whole point of such education and training is to prepare specifically trained graduates for entry into specific parts of the labour market. It is unlikely, to say the least, that business studies programmes will include critical analyses and the positing of alternative systems of thought in relation to capitalist structures, assumptions and theoretical assertions. The same argument applies by extension to virtually all other vocational and professional areas. Of course, it can be argued with good reason that a large part of the university system – in applied science, technology and related subject areas – has *never* seen it relevant to engage in such critical discussion. However, in parenthesis it should be noted that the same cannot be said of at least some of the elite professions – in particular, law with its emphases on jurisprudence, and moral and political philosophy as applied to legal systems. The point, though, is that the new prominence of vocational and professional education is threatening to dominate, if not eliminate, the autonomous, sceptical – essentially the radical liberal – conception of the academy. As Peter Jarvis has observed, 'at the heart of the knowledge society lies positivist and technical knowledge'.[32]

In part cause and in part effect of this whole process has been the development of the idea and the practice of 'stakeholding'. Historically, as noted, universities have regarded themselves, justifiably, as autonomous. Their legal status and their public recognition lay in their Charters, and the consequent rights they had to award degrees and organize their own 'business' – including what we would now term quality assurance procedures. Polytechnics were organized on quite different assumptions and structures. Originally in local authority control, and subject always too to external validation procedures and dependent upon equal relationships with the occupational, professional organizations which related to their programme provision, polytechnics had very *little* autonomy.

The position of higher education in the 1990s changed in part as a result of this polytechnic legacy; but mainly, in our view, because of two other factors. The first was that government, and especially the Treasury, became increasingly concerned with the steep rise in the absolute cost of higher education, resulting from the rapid expansion (the corollary of this, however, was the continuing reduction in the 'unit of resource'; that is, the amount of public financial support to institutions per full-time student). The government thus became increasingly intent on exercising both policy direction and quality control, through audit, to achieve value for money and what it regarded as the implementation of the appropriate policy priorities. The creation of the Higher Education Funding Councils, for example, signalled not only the coming together of the former polytechnics and the longer-established universities, but also the policy control that government was intent upon imposing. This was in sharp contrast to the culture and practice of the old University Grants Committee.[33]

The second factor was the growth in social thinking generally of the belief that higher education was too important an area to leave exclusively to the institutions themselves; moreover, there was an articulation of a particular sort of populist democracy, which emphasized the rights of consumers in any social processes. In this case, the consumers were of course the learners.[34] When the 1997 Labour Government introduced the new funding systems for students, following on from the Dearing Committee's Report (though not implementing its funding proposals), this argument was strengthened considerably.[35] In tune with the spirit of the times, consumers, who were paying in large part for the 'product', should have a major say in the whole enterprise. Increasingly, in all western societies since the last quarter of the twentieth century, 'the recipients of knowledge have been not only elites but also mass publics. With the democratization of knowledge and the opening of higher education to all classes, knowledge has ceased to be the exclusive privilege of the elites'.[36] Thus not only have universities long since ceased to be the exclusive site of knowledge and cultural production, the environment of higher education has become more 'client-centred', in terms of a variety of stakeholders and their perceived interests. Knowledge has ceased, in Gerard Delanty's words, 'to be something standing outside society, a goal to be pursued by a community of scholars dedicated to the truth, but is shaped by many social actors under the conditions of the essential contestability of truth'.[37]

There is, superficially, an ethos of democratization surrounding these processes. A challenging of elite arrogance and exclusivity through the incursions of other stakeholders into both the epistemological and the policy forums of debate; the plurality of voices contesting and formulating knowledge production; the rise of the culture of 'accountability'; the prevalence of the 'Mode 2' knowledge paradigm; and of course the fact of *mass* higher education – all these are in many ways important factors in breaking down traditional hierarchies of cultural and intellectual control. What such arguments so often ignore, however, is that all this has taken place, and continues to take place, within 'the neo-liberal consensus, which today is hegemonic around the globe, [and] demands that marketisation principles and practices permeate the entire social domain', including of course higher education.[38] This has been characterized, accurately in our view, as 'academic capitalism'; that is, as higher education becomes more dependent on income streams other than public funding for teaching and research, so the system becomes inexorably integrated into market capitalism. This applies both at the practical, day-to-day level and at the cultural and ideological level. As Frank Webster has argued, two key elements of this are:

the by now routine insistence from research councils that projects to be funded will be driven, not by intellectual curiosity, but by their contribution to improvements in competitiveness and, secondly, the increasing emphasis in state policy across the western world

> that universities should strive to produce 'human capital' that equips graduates to function effectively in the global commercial world . . . [and to] raise the competitive edge.[39]

Thus, far from opening up higher education to democratic forces, to 'difference' and 'plurality', there is a strong argument for asserting that the system is becoming incorporated, unilinear and more limited. In this context, the growth of vocationalism and professionalism can be seen as the practical articulation of this ethos.

How does this fit with the notion of 'professionalism'? Accord to Michael Eraut, 'the three central features of the ideology of professionalism are a specialist knowledge base, autonomy and service'. However, because of the growth of 'client rights' and the general 'marketization' of public policy, the nature of the professionals' relationship to higher education has changed.[40] The outcome of these processes – plus the fact that 'professionalization' now reaches much further down into the labour market with large numbers of occupational groups now claiming professional status – has been to change the nature not only of the academy but of professionals themselves. Slaughter and Leslie put the point succinctly:

> The *raison d'être* for special treatment for universities, the training ground of professionals, as well as for professional privilege, was undermined, increasing the likelihood that universities, in the future, will be treated more like other organizations and professionals more like other workers.[41]

This development has thus been a contributory factor to the partial deprofessionalization of the 'academic profession'. Academic staff are subject to increasing processes of audit, inspection and bureaucratic regularization. The growth of vocational models of education has reduced the academics' professional autonomy, and severely undermined their critical capacities; and the increasing invasion of mandatory corporate capital perspectives have reduced the academic role, in some contexts, to that of 'passive trainer'. Finally, the combination of the expansion of the profession and the persistent reductions in salary levels and social status, have led not only to demoralization but to a diminution in the academy's positions of influence in the wider society.

These processes are related to the contemporary and prospective roles of public intellectuals in western society, and are also one of the dimensions of the debate over 'agency' – that is, over how radical objectives can be achieved in a persistently conservative and controlled society.

All this may be to paint too gloomy a picture, however. We would agree with Catherine Bargh and her colleagues that the 'professionalization of expert society' and the 'academicization of intellectual culture' are probably irresistible trends.[42] Even more dangerous, in our view, than accepting uncritically the professed democratization thesis in relation to professional and vocational education in the new mass higher education, would be a retreat into ivory tower traditionalism. If we are to promote the reconfiguring of higher education in the directions argued for in this book, we need to address the real world problems of how to promote such a reconfiguration speaking from where we are, as academics and in relation to particular social groups, interests and movements, and according to professed social and ideological commitments.

One of the most positive views of professional development and higher education is that espoused by David Watson and his co-authors in two books on this theme.[43] The academy, on this argument, can broaden, humanize and make more reflective the professionals and their education and training. 'At its best the dialogue contributes constructively to the development of progressive models of professional practice . . . [and to] the development of a genuinely "reflective" and self-aware practitioner'.[44] Moreover, as Aaronowitz has noted, professional knowledge is now not concerned exclusively with specialist training *per se*, but more with a process of experience, reflection, reoriented action followed by reflection; and, of course, the rapid pace of technological and social change necessitates continual updating and reconceptualization of technical and professional knowledge.[45] The process of dialogue can thus be of benefit to both the professional world and to the academy. Clearly, all this applies particularly to public sector professionals; however, as some practitioners have argued, there is an increasing employment sector in the new professions, which are, so to speak, *sui generis* and do not fit easily into the categorization of public or private sectors. For example, programmes in creative arts, art and design, the professions in the health field and various branches of informatics.[46]

Such a perspective lay at the centre of the polytechnics' original mission and underlay several subsequent initiatives in this tradition. Sir Toby Weaver, the former Deputy Secretary in what was then the Department for Education and Science, was instrumental both in the creation of the polytechnics and later in the 'Education for Capability' Committee. The Committee's manifesto referred to an imbalance in education, producing people who were 'able to understand, but not to act'. It added:

> There exists, in its own right, a culture which is concerned with doing, making and organizing, and the creative arts. This culture emphasises the day-to-day management of affairs, the formulation and solution of problems and the design, manufacture and marketing of goods and services.[47]

In our view, these motivations and the developments that have flowed from them reflect pressures and needs in the wider society, and they can be beneficial to the radicalization of both the culture and the practice of the academy. However, we would emphasize several cautionary considerations based on our earlier analysis. First and foremost, the development of professional and vocational higher education (and post-compulsory education generally) has taken place in a global society dominated increasingly by capital and its accompanying free market ideology and increasingly in explicit opposition to *any* of the conceptions of the public service ethos. Professional values and practice are not neutral, in ideological terms. Clearly, this is the case in relation to business studies and related areas, but it also permeates other professional and vocational programmes. The pretence, or still worse the unconscious assumption, that these epistemologies and curricula are somehow detached, consensual and uncontentious has to be confronted directly. As we argued earlier, those who wish to radicalize higher education and reassert the critical, sceptical perspective must confront and where possible resist the 'creeping embrace' of the business studies ethos.

Similarly, the assumption that the contemporary socio-economic context is characterized by a professionalized workforce and by implication a diminution of inequality and hierarchy is profoundly mistaken, as we have argued throughout this book. Many of those who now qualify formally as professionals remain in reality in 'proletarianized' occupations. Indeed, as Elizabeth Wilson has observed, within Britain, academic life itself has declined in status with many lecturers approximating to a *lumpen intelligentsia*.[48] Alongside this and not unrelated to it is another significant and seldom remarked upon change in the 'knowledge class' in recent years: its altered gender and ethnic constitution.[49]

More importantly, the majority of the population in all western societies remain outside this professionalized structure and, of course, inequalities of wealth and power both in the United Kingdom and globally have increased dramatically in recent decades (see Chapters 1, 2, 6 and 9).

Thirdly, there is an assumption in much of the writing and policy development in professional and vocational higher education that professional occupations and the education and training that accompanies them are homogeneous. Yet this is far from the case: the professional environment, as everything else, is situated in an ideological context. Public sector, public service professions are, from a radical perspective, inherently preferable to those informed by a neo-liberal, market perspective – and the academy should be encouraged to support and develop the former and minimize the impact of the latter. At the very least, the reality of this political choice needs to be made explicit in the policy debate, both in national contexts and in the microcosm of policy development and resource allocation in individual institutions.

Finally, we should resist the capture by the dominant neo-liberal ideologues of the commitment to 'relevance', 'involvement with the community' and so on. These are important elements in the radicalization of the academy; but they are *not* co-terminous with the *business* community and free market ideology as we discussed in the broader context in the previous chapter. Rather, we believe, we should give priority to a higher education that relates to the interests and needs of the whole community in all its pluralistic complexity, and especially those who are committed actually or potentially to the caring and progressive areas of the public sector. As we argued earlier, this should also be linked to those social movements and voluntary sector groups that complement those working in such professions.

Within this context, vocational and professional education and training, in higher education as elsewhere, should be welcomed and embraced. But, as the old political slogan used to have it, 'without illusions'; that is, professionalism is not an undiluted good, still less an uncontentious, new paradigm for higher education development, especially when such professionals, at least in elite private sector occupations, are both unaccountable and drawn from restricted backgrounds (in terms of class, gender and ethnic origin). Here, as elsewhere, we must be vigilant to protect the commitments of the academy to 'free inquiry, academic rigour, detachment and disinterestedness'[50] within an ethos that is egalitarian and democratic in spirit, rather than elitist (as we discussed in Chapters 3 and 4). To the extent that the drive towards professionalism and vocationalism is undermining such commitments and replacing them, effectively, with market-driven criteria, we should be 'with the resistors'.[51] However, we should not throw out the baby with the bathwater: properly construed and articulated, the development of professional and vocational programmes in higher education can be an important part of the radicalization process.

Notes

1. See, for example, John Field (1996) Vocational education and training, in Roger Fieldhouse and Associates, *A History of Modern British Adult Education.* Leicester: NIACE; John Field (1998) *European Dimensions: Education, Training and the European Union.* London: Jessica Kingsley.
2. David Watson (2000) Lifelong learning and professional higher education, in Tim Bourner, Tim Katz and David Watson (eds), *New Directions in Professional Higher Education.* Buckingham: SRHE and Open University Press, p. 8.
3. Harold Perkin (1989) *The Rise of Professional Society: England since 1880.* London: Routledge, p. 2.
4. Ibid., p. xii.
5. Ibid.
6. Hannes Siegrist (1994) The professions, state and government in theory and history, in Tony Becher (ed.) *Governments and Professional Education.* Buckingham: SRHE and Open University Press, p. 3.
7. See Samuel H. Beer (1959) *Modern British Politics.* London: Allen & Unwin; R.A. Butler (1971) *The Art of the Possible.* London: Hamish Hamilton; Colin Pritchard and Richard Taylor (1978) *Social Work: Reform or Revolution?* London: Routledge & Kegan Paul, Chapter 3. On the Christian roots of Conservatism, see Quintin Hogg (Lord Hailsham) (1947) *The Case for Conservatism.* London: Penguin; on Conservative ideology, see Noel O'Sullivan (1999) Conservatism, in Roger Eatwell and Anthony Wright (eds) *Contemporary Political Ideologies,* 2nd edn. London: Continuum.
8. Thomas Hughes (1857) *Tom Brown's Schooldays*; cited in Perkin, op. cit., note 3, p. 120.

9. See numerous works by Sidney and Beatrice Webb, in particular (1897) *Industrial Democracy*. London: Longmans; 1920 edition reprinted in 1965 by Kelley, New York. See also Margaret Cole (1961) *The Story of Fabian Socialism*. London: Mercury Books.
10. See Ralph Miliband (1973) *Parliamentary Socialism*, 2nd edn. London: Merlin Press; Pritchard and Taylor, op. cit., note 7, Chapter 4.
11. See Michael Young (1962) *The Rise of the Meritocracy*. London: Penguin.
12. Perkin, op. cit., note 3, pp. 23–4.
13. See Michael Oakeshott (1962) *Rationalism in Politics*. London: Methuen; Beer, op. cit., note 7.
14. Winston Churchill, letter to H.G. Wells, 17 November 1902, *Wells Collection*. Urbana-Champaign, IL: University of Illinois; cited in Perkin, op. cit., note 3, p. 169.
15. For a penetrating analysis of Conservatism, from a Marxist perspective, see Nigel Harris (1972) *Competition and the Corporate Society*. London: Methuen.
16. Perkin, op. cit., note 3, p. 399.
17. Anthony Crosland (1956) *The Future of Socialism*. London: Cape; James Burnham (1942) *The Managerial Revolution*. London: Putnam.
18. Michael Shanks (1961) *The Stagnant Society*. London: Penguin; cited in Perkin, op. cit., note 3, p. 448.
19. David Watson, op. cit., note 2, p. 3.
20. See Jean Bocock and Richard Taylor (in press) The Labour Party and Higher Education, 1945–51, *Higher Education Quarterly*.
21. Ibid.
22. See, for example, Gordon Roderick and Michael Stephens (1982) *Performance, Education and Training in Britain Today*. Brighton: Falmer Press.
23. Martin Wiener (1983) *The Decline of the Industrial Spirit*. Cambridge: Cambridge University Press.
24. Peter Scott (1995) *The Meanings of Mass Higher Education*. Buckingham: SRHE and Open University Press, especially pp. 57–60; see Chapter 5, this volume.
25. Watson, op. cit., note 2, p. 4.
26. Ibid., p. 5.
27. HESA Statistics, 1998, cited in Watson, op. cit., note 2.
28. Catherine Watts (2000) Issues of professionalism in higher education, in Bourner *et al.* (eds), op. cit., note 2, p. 13.
29. Clark Kerr *et al.* (1973) *Industrialism and industrial man*, 2nd edn. London: Penguin, p. 47; cited by Peter Jarvis (2000) The corporate university, in John Field and Mal Leicester (eds) *Lifelong Learning: Education Across the Lifespan*. London: Routledge Falmer, pp. 43–4.
30. Ibid.
31. Jarvis, op. cit., note 29 p. 44.
32. Ibid., p. 46.
33. See Scott, op. cit., note 24, especially pp. 14–20.
34. For a discussion of the changing ideological interpretations of 'learner centred' higher education, see Richard Taylor (2000) Concepts of self-directed learning in higher education: re-establishing the democratic tradition, in Jane Thompson (ed.) *Stretching the Academy: The Politics and Practice of Widening Participation in Higher Education*. Leicester: NIACE, pp. 68–79.
35. See David Watson and Richard Taylor (1998) *Lifelong Learning and the University: A Post-Dearing Agenda*. Brighton: Falmer Press.

36. Gerard Delanty (2001) *Challenging Knowledge: The University in the Knowledge Society*. Buckingham: SRHE and Open University Press, p. 104.
37. Ibid., p. 105.
38. Frank Webster (2000) *Postmodernity and Higher Education: What's the Point: Response to Ron Barnett, Realizing the University in an age of supercomplexity*. (Buckingham: SRHE and Open University Press.
39. Ibid.
40. Michael Eraut (1994) *Developing Professional Knowledge and Competence*. Brighton: Falmer Press, p. 223; cited in Bourner *et al.*, op. cit., note 2, p. 12.
41. Sheila Slaughter and Larry Leslie (1997) *Academic Capitalism: Politics, Policies, and the Entrepreneurial University*. Baltimore, MD: Johns Hopkins University Press, p. 5; cited in Delanty, op. cit., note 36, p. 124.
42. Catherine Bargh, Peter Scott and David Smith (1999) *Governing Universities: Changing the Culture?* Buckingham: SRHE and Open University Press, p. 177.
43. Hazel Bines and David Watson (1992) *Developing Professional Education*. Buckingham: SRHE and Open University Press; Bourner *et al.*, op. cit., note 2.
44. Bines and Watson, op. cit., note 43, p. 4.
45. See Stanley Aaronowitz (1997) The new knowledge, in A.H. Halsey *et al.* (eds), *Education, Culture, Economy and Society*. Oxford: Oxford University Press, pp. 193–206; for further discussion of this aspect of lifelong learning in higher education, see Watson and Taylor, op. cit., note 35.
46. See specific case studies in these areas in Bourner *et al.*, op. cit., note 2.
47. Cited by Tyrell Burgess, Obituary Notice, Sir Toby Weaver, the *Guardian*, 13 June 2001.
48. Elizabeth Wilson (2001) *The Contradictions of Culture: Cities, Culture, Women*. London: Sage, p. 68.
49. Rita Felski (1998) Images of the intellectual: from philosophy to cultural studies, *Continuum: Journal of Media and Cultural Studies*, 12(2): 168.
50. Webster, op. cit., note 38.
51. Ibid.

Part 4

Conclusion

9
Radical Perspectives for the New Higher Education

Introduction

> Is it inevitable that the university will be reduced to the function of
> providing, with increasingly authoritarian efficiency, prepacked intel-
> lectual commodities which meet the requirements of management?
> Or can we, by our efforts, transform it into a centre of free discussion
> and action, tolerating and even encouraging 'subversive' thought and
> activity, for a dynamic renewal of the whole society within which it
> operates?[1]

Hugo Radice, in an article in *Red Pepper* in 2001,[2] recalls these questions of
Edward Thompson, in 1970, in the bitter struggle then taking place at the
University of Warwick, captured in all its intensity in the collectively authored
book *Warwick University Ltd.* There have been massive changes, in higher
education and in the wider society, in the decades since then, but the questions retain their relevance and importance.

In this book, we have tried to analyse these changes from various perspectives but with an underlying commitment to the values and analytical framework of Thompson and similar 'New Left' analysts and, taking as a central
focus, the dangers inherent in much postmodernist analysis and prescription. This final chapter does not attempt to provide a blueprint or scheme
for a radicalized higher education. Rather, we try to draw together some of
the main arguments and focus on several key themes, in particular those
that may provide some positive opportunities for radical advance.

Late capitalist society

One of the foundations of our argument has been the pervasive context of
inequality and capitalist hegemony that characterizes contemporary society
and has exercised so powerful an influence on the higher education system

in both policy formulation and culture, and the actual practice within the sector. In the various themes discussed in this book, we have referred repeatedly to the ways in which the persisting class structures of inequality, and the accompanying systemic discrimination on grounds particularly of gender, are endemic. We make no apology for returning again to these themes at the start of this final chapter. The contemporary articulation of capitalist structures – social, economic, cultural and political – is the crucial contextual factor shaping higher education policy.

The power of the ideology is indicated by widespread assumptions of consensus about the inevitability and desirability of the interrelationship between the academy and the business community. As Thomas Frank has argued, market ideology developed in the 1990s to become, bizarrely, equated with democratization:

> Since it was markets that expressed the will of the people, virtually any criticism of business could be described as an act of elitism arising out of despicable contempt for the common man . . . the elitists were the people on the other side of the equation: the trade unionists and Keynesians who believed that society could be organised in any way other than the market way.[3]

This was post-Thatcherite populism gone mad. As the *Wall Street Journal* put it during the American presidential election campaign in 2001, 'Mr Bush should tell Americans [that] when my opponent attacks big corporations, he's attacking you and me.'[4] As we argued in Chapter 2, this cultural dominance sits alongside demonstrable and marked increases in structures of inequality, both economic and socio-political.

It is beyond dispute that the capitalist system remains the form triumphant of political economy and of the wider society, its institutions, culture and social relationships. It cannot be argued with any credibility that postmodernism – or any other analysis or prescription for an alternative in the real world – has developed either the theory or the practice of a cooperative, egalitarian socio-economic structure. Nor can it be said unequivocally that education has served the interests of 'enlightenment'. Harold Perkin notes that, far from guaranteeing equality of opportunity, Britain is the least meritocratic of the richest states and that it still has 'an education system where privileged education can be bought for cash'.[5]

There is, therefore, as Luhmann has observed, no 'sharp break between a modern and a postmodern society',[6] except for the new centrality of finance capital. It thus needs asserting forcefully that contemporary society and its economy remain capitalist to the core, with a state political system oriented to support for that socio-economic structure and ideology.

Even this should be heavily qualified. It is not only in *contemporary* Western societies that finance capital is dominant. In the United Kingdom, probably the most extreme example for a number of reasons, many of them connected to its unprecedented imperial power in the nineteenth and early twentieth century, finance capital has been dominant over *industrial* capital since at least the 1920s and arguably much earlier. For many years, political scientists characterized the two main British political parties as representing not 'Capital' and 'Labour' but, respectively, *finance* capital and *industrial* capital: hence the Labour Party's strong adherence to Keynesian, public investment economics for most of the twentieth century. What is remarkable, and from a progressive viewpoint deeply negative, is that most Western governments of the (so-called) Left have become absorbed to a greater or lesser extent into an ideology that *assumes* that finance capital and its ideology is now and forever dominant, and naturally and rightly so.

Despite the dominance of market and finance capital, many of the emancipatory elements of the Enlightenment persist. In Western culture, scientific research is as prevalent, although with more reservations publicly expressed about its consequences; and more than ever our lives depend on technologies. Although recent times have seen the resurgence of a concern for history and tradition as a corrective to over-rationalization, there has been no wholesale desire to return to pre-capitalist forms of social and economic organization. Importantly, in our context, we continue to send our children to school (and increasingly to further and higher education subsequently) for the 'best years of their lives', and believe that more education rather than less is the best preparation for the future.

Yet despite all this clear evidence of a persisting modernist culture, something has changed that makes us feel uneasy about that very future for which we feel we have been inadequately prepared (by education among other things). We can no longer see the transformation in the economy taking tangible shape around us. In the nineteenth and for most of the twentieth century, the growth of urbanization, the development of vast manufacturing and engineering empires, railways and road systems, all brought smoke, noise and change to a hitherto predominantly rural society. The twenty-first century remains recognizably the world of 'telegrams and anger' first evoked by E.M. Forster in *Howard's End*; but the telegrams have been replaced by e-mails and the anger by 'e-rage', and change, though pervasive, remains elusive and unpredictable.

Frederic Jameson notes that capitalism has changed precisely in the way Luhmann mentions and that change has been consequential for the cultural forms, modes of perception and 'structures of feeling', to use Raymond Williams's phrase, of what he terms the postmodern period.[7] One major change is that capitalism has now penetrated into all areas of life, including those that we used to think most private – the family, the home and, especially, our fantasies. It seems that little or nothing is now hidden from the gaze and interference of capitalism, which sees in every desire and disease a market that can be exploited and a public that can be created to buy the commodity that will ease it (usually temporarily and superficially), and this on a marauding, global scale.

Capitalism is a socio-economic form that, over the last two hundred and fifty years, has destroyed all oppositional systems, most recently Soviet communism and, in the near future in all probability, its Chinese variant.[8]

For Jameson, the domination of finance capital has introduced a qualitative change in the cultural sphere. While acknowledging that this assertion could be criticized as economic reductionism, in his view the complexities of ideological critique are no longer necessary. Faced with 'Reagan-Kemp and Thatcher utopias of immense investments and increases in production to come, based on the deregulation and privatization and the obligatory opening of markets everywhere, the problems of ideological analysis seem enormously simplified, and the ideologies themselves far more transparent'.[9]

In summary, capitalism is now, as a result primarily of cybernetic innovations, unprecedentedly volatile, energetic and, above all, internationally pervasive. Finance capital is characterized by a concentration upon 'making money out of money'. It has led to 'spectres of value' rather than real 'use' values, competing with each other in 'vast world wide disembodied phantasmagoria'.[10]

Nation states, increasingly in thrall to these lightning capital transfers, find their programmes of political reform or social welfare suddenly traumatized. Of course, in one sense, this has *always* been the case: the chaotic history of capitalism is littered with examples – the Wall Street crash and resulting worldwide depression in the 1930s, for example. Contemporary developments are thus in no fundamental sense new, as we discussed in Chapter 2, but they have significantly exacerbated the chaos and irrationality of capitalism. Nor should it be forgotten that the developed, capitalist world depends for its manufactured goods, raw materials and the rest, on an increasingly exploited and crisis-ridden third world.

There is, though, with cyberspace being given the illusory status of the 'real world', a widespread belief that finance capital seems 'to live on its own internal metabolism without any reference to an older type of content'.[11] This is, of course, nonsense, but it is a powerful postmodernist myth.

Culturally, this is reflected in the belief that discourses themselves are wholly self-referential and need not signify any external reality or material content. According to Jameson, this perception has become so internalized that the real world is suffused by the 'narrativized image fragments of a stereotypical postmodern language' with the result that there appears to be no outside reality at all![12]

This is to exaggerate of course, but it does signify a bizarre and untenable situation and demands intervention, not least from educationalists. The 'public spheres' identified by Habermas and others enable individuals and societies to make conscious choices about their own identities, and social and political trajectories and involvements. Although no public sphere can be entirely independent of the market ideology and political state structures, the inherently contradictory pressures of the system mean that alternative and oppositional forces can and do form discrete spaces of their own.

It is from these oppositional sites that new social forms can and must develop, and this is one area of focus for progressive higher education in terms of the 'agencies for change' discussed below. In particular, we have maintained that feminism – as both an analytical framework and a social movement – continues to have a vital contribution to make to informed practice. Its emphasis on connecting personal and cultural issues to economic and political matters is important. And its insistence on gender analysis is crucial to a Left that is able to take into account complexity as well as conflict in the experiences of both men and women.

Although scepticism about unreconstructed enlightenment universalism is necessary, the opposite tendency of falling into a pluralistic cultural relativism is just as dangerous. We agree with theorists like Bauman and Habermas who advocate the reconstruction of civil society in which a revitalized notion of citizenship is central. Indeed, we discussed the importance and relevance of the notion of the 'educated public' in Chapter 3. And there is plenty of evidence of oppositional movements concerned, for example, with civil liberties, environmentalism and opposition to global, corporate capitalism. Thus, for good or ill, we continue to live in a world irretrievably modern and fashioned by the ideals of enlightenment, and to pretend otherwise is either wishful thinking or covert reaction – or, of course, both.

Questions of 'agency'

The remaining discussion in this chapter takes place in this context, is framed by it, conditioned by it. In that sense we are therefore not free agents, in higher education or anywhere else. Nevertheless, progressive change *is* possible, indeed necessary given both the fundamental contradictions in the system and its irrationality and immorality. Below, we discuss three areas that we consider to be of particular importance: the debate over the role of 'public intellectuals' and the relationship between such intellectuals and the academy; the policy commitment to 'widening participation' in higher education and the potential dangers as well as advantages with this developmental agenda; and, finally, the ways in which elements of a 'radical social purpose' agenda in higher education can be derived from past experience and ideological commitments.

All these issues, however, should themselves be framed within a discussion of 'agency'. That is, by what means or combination of means can significant, progressive change be achieved in fundamentally conservative societies. This has long been a question that has exercised all those on the Left, from the mildly reformist parties and movements of social democracy through to the wilder fringes of Trotskyism and anarchism, and encompassing just about everything in between. 'Education' has been seen consistently by most of those involved as of some importance – from the moral force Chartists through to the zealots of Mao's 'Little Red Book'.

For postmodernists, any notion of progressive change within a socio-political context is, by definition, redundant. All ideological frameworks are, by definition again, grand narratives, shown by bitter experience to be dangerously fallacious. We do not need here to re-enter the debate of earlier chapters and rehearse the reasons for our disagreement with such perspectives. We are, though, in agreement with the postmodernist position, that all such organizational, all-encompassing progressive agencies are to a greater or lesser degree flawed and untenable. We part company with postmodernists in terms of both analysis and prescription, however, in at least two respects. First, to reject the experience of Marxism-Leninism and the Communist Party ideology does not equate with a rejection of Marxism *per se*. As an analytical and explanatory framework, Marxism and its developed variants retain a relevance and dynamism, never more so than now. Secondly, and related to this, we believe that progressive change in society at large, and by extension in our own focus of enquiry, higher education, is not only possible but necessary.

Although there are no 'easy answers', and certainly no single, magic solution, there are many ways in which a radicalized higher education can play its part in developing a more egalitarian, humanistic and cooperative society. Education has transformatory power. This is the case in a number of ways. One reason so many on the Left have been enthused by the potential of education is encapsulated in the slogan 'Knowledge is Power'. That is, the acquisition of knowledge and understanding is a key – some have said *the* key – to empowerment. In pre-industrial society, this was clearly the case: the small elite of literate, educated men held sway over the mass of the population, not least through the ideological control exercised via organized religion. The elite structure of higher education, and its religious and class exclusivity until the twentieth century, perpetuated this role – in Britain as in most other comparable societies. An important element in the overall democratization of modern societies has been the (partial) opening up and expansion of higher education (not least in terms of gender in the last decades of the twentieth century). *Accessibility* as a means of empowerment is thus one important area for progressive development, although there are potential problems as we discuss below.

Involvement in critical, humanistic higher education is a potential means not only of political empowerment but also of personal and cultural growth and enlightenment. The point need not be laboured, but there is an important role for higher education in deepening understanding, in widening cultural and aesthetic horizons, and in overall personal development. Advocates of liberal education from the Greeks through to Newman and more contemporary writers have enthused over these aspects of the 'university experience'.[13] Historically, this had strongly elitist overtones, however. To some extent, these remain in contemporary higher education too, with the elite universities holding to these traditions, as we have argued in preceding chapters. However, the *radical* aspects of this perspective (discussed below) are also under threat from the contemporary orientations towards private sector and crudely vocational performativity criteria.

One of the major themes of our book has been the need for higher education to reconnect with wider communities in pursuit of democratization. In common with the spirit of the times, higher education concentrates predominantly on the *individual* rather than collectivities or communities. Universities, however, are about the public good as well as about individual advancement. At present, in all late capitalist societies, a culture of individualism predominates: those with a genuine commitment to educational values should reassert, as part of democratization, the need to connect with whole communities. At its worst, such individualism leads to the dangers that Michael Young drew attention to in the 1960s.[14] The most able are picked out from the underprivileged and put on the incorporationist escalator, leaving their communities even more impoverished than before.

There is a paradox in the increasing introversion, narrowness and bureaucratization of higher education, compared with its rapid expansion, rhetoric of 'relevance' and its much vaunted role in the new 'knowledge society'. We should emphasize the potential of partnerships with communities and social movements – regionally as well as nationally and internationally – for developing new, symbiotic alliances, new curricular approaches and new forms of pedagogy. Edward Thompson's advocacy in the 1960s of a dynamic dialogue between 'education and experience' remains as relevant today as it was at the time.

These are not idle abstractions. In the latter decades of the twentieth century there are several examples of the productive interplay between the academy and radical strands in the wider society. Tom Steele, for example, has detailed the intimate interaction between adult education practitioners and the development of cultural studies;[15] industrial relations developed as a field of study, in partnership with trade unions, largely as a result of the extensive programmes of joint working with individual industries' unions and employers, and work with the TUC; peace studies and, in particular, women's studies and gender studies in universities developed as a direct result of interaction with social movements. There are new and analogous partnerships to be formed in the contemporary world and these can be of mutual benefit – in the universities' case, this is so not least to help change institutional culture and power structures internally.

We should not claim too much for education. Political advance is essentially about politics not education, whether higher education or education more generally. But 'politics' is not a monolith: education is a part of this change process and, in that sense, one of the many sites of contestation.

The role of public intellectuals

If higher education, then, has a role to play as one of the important agencies of change, one key area is the role played by academics in ideological terms, not only within the academy but also in the wider society. The role of the 'academic' is not necessarily co-terminous with that of the 'public intellectual', either historically or in the contemporary world. To take two very obvious examples from the modern period, neither Darwin nor Marx were academics, in the sense of being employed in or associated with the academy.

Equally, very large numbers of academics could not be described, and would not describe themselves, as intellectuals, public or otherwise.

Zygmunt Bauman believes that the concept of postmodernism tells us less about changes in the world than it does about the changed position of intellectuals in the world.[16] The expansion of higher education and the knowledge and information industries has led to more and more people engaged in creating and processing knowledge, most of them in ever-more bureaucratized and regulated organizations – including most higher education institutions.

There are several negative factors in the contemporary position of intellectuals and academics. First, as far as universities are concerned, there are many other sites for intellectual profile, status and influence. The internet, the proliferation of 'think-tank' groups, the growth of highly proficient research and development sections in major companies – all these are examples of a very different intellectual landscape from that of the 1970s and 1980s.

A second factor is the increasing specialization of academics, turning to ever more detailed sub-areas within their own disciplines and indulging in largely self-referential discourse. All too frequently, academic specialists find it overtaxing, irrelevant to their professional concerns and intellectually uncomfortable to generalize their ideas and findings or communicate them intelligibly to the public, in the manner of Haldane, Hobsbawm or Bernal, for example. There is little, if any, collective identity: in no real sense is there a 'community of scholars' in most universities. Academics discuss and debate very largely with 'their own kind', in terms of disciplinary perspective. The result is over-specialization, fragmentation and, increasingly, esoteric academic discourses, removed from material reality and the myriad of pressing issues that confront humanity. As always, there are major exceptions to this, in virtually all academic fields, but the predominant trends are clear. Added to this are the emphases, as we noted in earlier discussion, on problem-centred, evidence or 'results' based research, and the replacement of 'truth-seeking' criteria with performativity or use value criteria. In a culture increasingly dominated by private sector, free-market assumptions and values, and an academy permeated by the business studies ethos, genuine intellectual activity is frequently at odds with managerial perspectives and funding priorities. Overall, Bauman's claim that intellectuals have become 'interpreters' rather than 'legislators' in academic matters seems accurate enough.

However, the increasing specialization of the intellectual function can be construed more positively. Foucault's notion of the 'specific intellectual' is apposite here. It makes a break with the traditional figure of the universal intellectual as authoritative prophet or legislator, leading society towards enlightenment; it breaks, too, with the notion of the organic intellectual, regarded as a spokesperson for the views of an oppressed social class or group. The notion of the specific intellectual, in contrast with both of these, acknowledges the irrevocable nature of modern processes of specialization and discrete disciplines, seeing intellectual discourse as a 'local intervention within a particular regime of truth'.[17] Thus, the notion of the specific intellectual derives from that of the intellectual as expert, but whereas expertise and professionalism are usually contrasted to politics (by the Left, who condemn this, and by the Right, who endorse it), the concept of the specific intellectual seeks to bridge this divide. In Foucault's words:

> The work of an intellectual is not to shape others' political will; it is, through the analyses that he carries out in his own field, to question over and over again what is postulated as self-evident, to disturb people's mental habits, the way they do and think things, to dissipate what is familiar and accepted, to re-examine rules and institutions, and on the basis of this reproblematisation (in which he carries out his specific task as an intellectual) to participate in the formation of a political will (in which he has his role as citizen to play).[18]

As Felski comments, this has the advantage of allowing intellectuals to acknowledge and theorize the specific work they do *qua* intellectuals, rather than presenting it as either an 'anaemic supplement to authentic political action or as the superior wisdom of a vanguard'.[19]

This reminder of the specific nature of the kind of work done by intellectuals is useful. So, too, is Pierre Bourdieu's reminder that intellectuals have power-vested interests of their own, interests that concern augmenting their cultural capital. As Delanty points out, for Bourdieu, all intellectual creation is an expression of the 'scholastic view' and all scholarly, intellectual work is restricted by the fact that the academic must withdraw from the world in order to study it.[20] But the distancing and separateness from its object of study is also its strength, according to Bourdieu, because it means that knowledge can be reflexively constituted. Disinterestedness is not, however, possible, since the scholastic position is concerned to reproduce itself and its point of view and is, of course, always ideologically and socially constructed, and thus by definition partial.[21] The challenge for intellectuals is to protect their hard-won autonomy as cultural producers, according to Bourdieu, who, in his later writings, relates reflexivity to doubt, believing that intellectuals can only play an emancipatory role in the critique of ideology and power if they acknowledge that this critique cannot itself escape the field of power.

In emphasizing the relationship between cultural production and power, Bourdieu maintains that intellectuals *qua* cultural producers hold a specific kind of symbolic power, which they may put at the service of the dominant or the dominated. The problem in contemporary higher education is that all too frequently, not least because of comfortingly 'apolitical' postmodernist perspectives, university academics in effect and often by default put themselves at the service of the former not the latter. As Frank Webster has argued,[22] the absence of a stratum of left of centre public intellectuals in contemporary societies *is* a real loss. In Britain alone, in the last thirty or forty years of the twentieth century, a more or less random list of such figures could include Isaac Deutscher, Edward Thompson, Raymond Williams, Antoinette Pirie, C.P. Snow, Bertrand Russell, F.R. Leavis, A.J.P. Taylor, Stuart Hall and Jacquetta Hawkes. Elite figures these may have been, in some senses, but they acted as a bridge between the academy and the real world, were hugely influential in popular social movements, and were a *political* as well as an intellectual force in their own right. Those on the Left cannot, and most would not wish, to recreate the context or the style in which such intellectuals operated, but we do need to rekindle an engagement between an open, radical culture, intellectual formulations and debate, *and* the material reality of a deeply irrational and problem-riven world.

One way to approach this issue, in the concrete reality of policy develop-ment in higher education is, following Gerard Delanty, to view universities as using their quasi-autonomy to humanize technology and to recreate new expressions of citizenship.[23] His claim is that universities occupy an import-ant space in the production and communication of knowledge, a space that is growing and not declining as a result of changes in the role of the state as well as in markets and in technology. As the university loses its exclusive role in the production of knowledge, its role could increase in the com-munication of knowledge. He stresses that 'reflexive communication' is not a matter of a one-way transmission of an established body of knowledge to 'users' in the wider society. Rather, it involves 'the inclusion of as many voices as possible in the construction of knowledge'. The thesis is that the role of the university is enhanced, not undermined, in the knowledge society, for 'the university occupies a space in which different discourses interconnect'.[24]

This notion of knowledge seeking and communicating fits in well with our argument throughout this book concerning the democratic role of universities in relation to various communities. Responsiveness to the mar-ket is only one possible reaction to the current climate. Neo-liberalism and the response to it by universities – the 'academic capitalism' referred to earlier – is not the only strategy. There is also the possibility that the increas-ing internationalization of national education systems[25] could promote the 'self-transformation of cultures through a critical engagement with each other'.[26]

As always in all social and organizational processes under capitalism, there are *contradictory* forces shaping the contemporary university. Thus the very pessimistic, postmodern analyses of the university[27] tend to underplay the fact that the university has been a site of social and cultural citizenship for much of the twentieth century and one of the main locations in society where democratic values were developed. The university is not 'in ruins' as Readings maintains; it is more a 'battleground', a site of conflicts, as we have maintained in this book.

There can be no return to the traditional role of the universities as cul-turally defined according to those political and ethical imaginaries critiqued in our study. We cannot, either, look to the market and its instrumentalism for a future role. Nevertheless, in our view, a reconstituted university sector, based on promoting the democratic, radical values in partnership with the wider community has much to contribute to the overall radicalization project. This assertion, essentially *political* in tone, is complementary to Delanty's view that, if universities are to go beyond the two most powerful intellectual trends of contemporary society, relativism and instrumentalism, they need to become serious players in shaping cosmopolitan forms of citizenship. As 'sites of social interconnectivity, universities can contribute to the making of cosmopolitan forms of citizenship which link social, cultural and technological citizenship'.[28] And, echoing the projected orientation argued for in this book, Delanty maintains that, in reality, 'the history of the university can be written as the extension of knowledge beyond the realm of the ivory tower to the social world'.[29] Maybe we are now on the threshhold of a new beginning, the renewal of the cosmopolitan project.

Problems of 'widening participation'

The commitment to 'widening participation' is an important element in the lifelong learning policies of almost all late capitalist societies, and is potentially radical and challenging. In the United Kingdom, widening participation is one of two main focuses of policy attention in the early years of the twenty-first century; the other is developing relationships with the business community through joint partnership activity – clearly, from our point of view, a somewhat less positive policy dimension.

The expansion of higher education is seen, for the first time in mainstream university and higher education policy circles, as not exclusively concerned with 'more of the same', but rather with attracting learners from across wider constituencies in society. Detailed analyses have been undertaken to identify 'currently under-represented groups', as the policy jargon has it.[30] It came as no surprise to those with any knowledge of adult education, or even rudimentary acquaintance with the structures of inequality in all capitalist societies, that by far the most 'under-represented group' is the working class, the C2, D and E groups under the old categorization of the Registrar General in the British system.

Various mild incentive measures have been employed to encourage higher education institutions to broaden their intake of these and other potentially able students, especially those of standard age but from disadvantaged backgrounds. (Other under-represented groups targeted include disabled people and particular minority ethnic communities, such as Afro-Caribbean men and Bangladeshi women.[31])

At first sight these developments seem entirely to the good, albeit modest in scale; and participation has begun to rise moderately, though the imposition of the new fee structures for higher education in England has had negative effects. There are, however, several ideological and policy issues to be raised, which, in our view, make this both an important and contested area of development. There are two preliminary concerns. The first is that the motivations for this policy development on the part of both government and higher education institutions are by no means entirely within the progressive ideological framework advocated here. The primary purposes, for government, are based explicitly on human capital arguments; that is, that the priority is to produce appropriately trained cohorts of graduates for employment in the labour market, which is assumed unproblematically to be within the current neo-liberal capitalist framework. Moreover, the bulk of those so trained (rather than educated) would be destined for the second-tier, lower-status occupations, discussed in Chapter 8. The twin objectives of government policy in this area, maybe too crudely stated, are: to recruit significantly larger numbers of working class 18- to 21-year-olds into vocational degree and sub-degree programmes to train them for appropriate slots in the labour market; and, secondly, to identify more thoroughly than has been the case in the past the potential 'stars' from the state school sector and ensure that they progress to the elite institutions.

As far as higher education institutions are concerned, some – mainly the new universities and certain enthusiasts in the older universities, such as adult educators and some politically radical educators in the arts and social sciences – welcome on genuinely progressive grounds such initiatives. Many more, however, see this as another 'bandwagon' for plugging funding gaps, and also for digging deeper into constituencies of potential recruits to ensure that quotas, and therefore income streams, are secured.

The second preliminary issue, though, is more complicated. The new universities in Britain argue, with some reason, that they are best equipped, by mission, experience, curricular provision, managerial perspective and regional identity, to be the institutions through which the widening participation policy is implemented. Whereas, they argue, the elite institutions – especially Oxford and Cambridge – have a wholly different and inappropriate cultural identity for this policy area. Moreover, whereas the new universities are financially very hard pressed, Oxford and Cambridge in particular are internationally prestigious institutions with enormous amassed wealth.

The policy for widening participation, however, is sector-wide; indeed, there was, for a brief period in the early years of the twenty-first century, a significant element of targeted funding to provide incentives for the older universities to engage with this agenda. And there is a case for this, given the hierarchical structure of British higher education. Such a hierarchy is replicated, with variants, in virtually all comparable late capitalist societies. If the elite parts of the sector are not provided with incentives to participate in this agenda, then there is a strong probability that the hierarchical structure will be exacerbated. The elite institutions will continue to cater for standard age and background students, leaving the (perceived) second-class institutions to cater for the non-traditional learners.

There is, therefore, a political policy dilemma here and, in the real world of higher education prosaic politics, radical educators have to press both for the models of provision advocated here, and for the need for proper and equitable treatment of learners and institutions across the sector.

All this, though, is in one sense a preliminary to the fundamental question, 'what is widening participation *for*?' There is a real danger that, in the prevailing 'apolitical' culture of higher education, widening participation will be seen as an end in itself. To 'open up' the system, to make the student body more heterogeneous and more representative of the wider society are desirable ends. But if higher education is to fulfil a radical, liberating agenda, it does matter what learners learn, which frameworks of analysis and perspectives they adopt. There is a long history of 'incorporation' into the existing culture of relatively small numbers of non-traditional learners into the higher reaches of the established order, and higher education has played a key role in this process.

The contemporary context is rather different. The numbers involved are much larger, the system has expanded way beyond anything known in the past, the social structure is both more complex and more volatile than previously and, most important of all, the perception that we live in a depoliticized reality is widespread. But it is the argument of this book that this latter point at least is dangerous nonsense. The territory of higher education is in reality not based upon a consensual, let alone permanent, agreement on programmes, objectives, curriculum, approaches to research, priorities, epistemology and all the other features of the system. On the contrary, it is all highly contested, reflecting the contestation ideologically in the wider society. It does, therefore, matter profoundly what ends are served by the democratizing processes of widening participation.

To reduce it to the crudest level, it would not be conducive to the ethos and objectives of the radicalized higher education that we have advocated in this book, if virtually all those who benefit individually from widening participation development complete their higher education learning experience as well-trained, but uncritical functionaries. The fundamental purpose of a truly *higher* education learning experience must centre on developing an understanding of the values of democracy and equality in social life, as well as personal development that hones critical expertise, the creative faculties and intellectual rigour.

The widening participation agenda is thus a *political* agenda at every level. For radical educators involved at both the policy level nationally and regionally, and within their own institutions, there are important and 'winnable' battles to be fought.

Renewing radical social purpose

It will be clear from the tenor of the arguments in this book that all three authors come from a left of centre position professionally and politically. It is also the case that all three have, for most of their careers, worked in the field of university adult and continuing education, broadly defined. We conclude this study with a brief discussion of some of the ways in which the radical social purpose practice from this field may be adapted and revitalized to become a relevant aspect of the broader higher education system that has been the subject of our analysis. We concentrate here on three of the central characteristics of a renewed social purpose perspective to give an indication of the 'agenda' we have in mind: work, community and the nature of learning.

Although work and its relationship to education has been a central concern of both adult educators – in terms of working-class, usually trade union based education – and of the mainstream academy, in the ways discussed in Chapter 8, we have not discussed directly as yet this relationship in the contemporary context. In many ways, the foundation of the radical, committed adult education movement of the twentieth century was the relationship between organized, predominantly male, labour in the trade union movement and adult education provision. (This was clearly *not* the case in the mainstream academy!) This is not the place to enter into the complex and contested analysis of that relationship, but it did provide both a rationale for, and an exemplification of, the connection between abstract or theoretical learning and the 'world of work', and it can be argued that it was one means of securing at least partial empowerment, however tinged with ideological compromise, for the leading cohorts of industrial labour.[32]

However, as postmodern and post-Fordist analysts argue (and as we discussed in Chapters 1, 6 and 7), that industrial modernist structure has passed and, although union education remains a powerful and important aspect of provision,[33] the real point is that the conceptualization of work itself is in the process of change.

Andre Gorz argues that the function of work in forming basic identities is now archaic. Contemporary employment practices in late capitalist economies no longer guarantee longevity or seniority, and status related to occupation is now, for the most part, far more volatile than in the past. Previous conceptualizations of the constructive links between 'education' and 'work' in terms of socialization, in as much as they were ever true, now certainly ring hollow. The social solidarity that Durkheim, for example, saw as the outcome of the educational system has not been realized. Without a critical, humanistic framework in higher education, the system tends to produce technically competent but socially, morally and politically disengaged, and thus, in the 'public' sense, amoral graduates. Education has, therefore, to lose its association with the kind of socialization that merely prepares people for social functions like work and return to the problem of autonomy. Gorz maintains that education that is conflated with socialization, training and conditioning is unlikely to bring out in individuals the autonomous capacity to take charge of themselves and to relate to the world and others. Subordination to the new work ethic, symptomatic of governments of all capitalist societies and of all shades in recent times, only distorts education and those to whom it is administered:

Socialization will continue to produce frustrated, ill-adapted, mutilated, disorientated individuals so long as it persists in emphasizing 'social integration through employment', to the exclusion of all else, and investing all its efforts into a 'society of workers', in which all activities are considered as 'ways of earning a living'.[34]

The new form of radical social purpose education, we argue, has therefore to attend to the kind of education that facilitates the development and growth of individuals capable of leading fulfilling and responsible lives and who have a reflexive grasp of what is in the best interests of themselves, their families, their communities and their society. The question of work skills will arise out of this priority rather than being subordinate to it.

In terms of 'community', we need only in effect to summarize and reiterate the arguments made throughout this book. We do, however, think these are crucial for the perspectives we advocate. First, we believe that the ideologically constructed equation of 'community' with '*business* community' needs to be countered, and that the academy must reach out in dialogue and partnership with the wider community. Related to this, as we have argued, symbiotic partnerships need to be forged with social movements that can provide dynamism, radicalism and relevance to the provision of the academy, and strengthen its connections with the socially vital parts of the wider society.

At present, 'business' in all its many guises has a strong involvement in both the governance and the cultural definition of higher education. Ever since the neo-liberal heyday of Reagan and Thatcher in the 1980s, the governments of the major capitalist nations have sought to involve business and its perspectives in all aspects of public life. Higher education – and education more generally – is no exception. Radical educators should widen community representation and involvement so that the *whole* community is involved and feels itself to be involved in the life, and thus the culture, of institutions.

Such involvement spills over again into curriculum issues. Many programmes in the current context are devised in specific partnership with business, or with a 'business market' in mind. This can be countered, and to a limited extent has been, by provision planned and implemented in conjunction with public sector bodies, or deriving from social movements as we discussed earlier.

The language and conceptual universe of the business culture also predominates at present. We cited in an earlier chapter examples from the work of Frank Coffield and Bill Williamson, who draw attention to the pervasiveness of business terms in higher education discourse and, more importantly, to the associated prevalence of the 'bottom-line' financial criteria as priority, and the growth of the audit culture. Redressing this balance by introducing different perspectives into the discourse would be a modest, although useful, contribution to the radicalization process.

This brief discussion of community links, finally, to our concluding comments on the nature of the learning experience. We certainly reject the old elitist model of the university as consisting of knowledge transmission from the *cognoscenti* to the uninitiated, and thereby the socialization of new generations into elite culture. And we also support strongly the involvement of *learners* in the process of knowledge construction (although with the caveats that were expressed about the contemporary articulations of this policy; see Chapter 7).

However, we see the fundamental heart of this process as one of dialogue, of symbiotic relationships between varied communities of learners and the academy. Thus, a wide spectrum of learners and a wide spectrum of communities has to be brought into real, constructive, academic and intellectual partnership with the academy.

This may appear overly rhetorical and general. But the historical experience of university adult education, located though much of it is in times past and permeated though much of it was by values and assumptions that we would reject, has much to offer here. Education should, after all, be about opening intellectual doors, extending horizons, challenging assumptions and cultural and ideological beliefs; and about instilling both the spirit of rigorous intellectual enquiry and the humanistic and sceptical mindset.

Such a perspective offers, in other words, the possibility of engaging the university with the whole community, and with the material reality of a deeply troubled world, bringing to bear rigorous intellectual enquiry into the whole range of areas of importance to human kind. This is, in our view, not only a *proper* role for the academy, it is a vital role for the wider society. If this is held to be a call for a return to radicalized Enlightenment perspectives, then so be it.

Notes

1. Edward Thompson (1971) Afterword, in *Warwick University Ltd.* Harmondsworth: Penguin; cited in Hugo Radice (2001) From Warwick University Ltd to British Universities plc, *Red Pepper*, March, pp. 18–21.
2. Ibid.
3. Thomas Frank, the *Guardian*, 6 January 2001.
4. Cited in Frank, op. cit., note 3.
5. Harold Perkin (1996) *Third Revolution: Professional Elites in the Modern World.* London: Routledge, p. 179.
6. Niklas Luhmann (1995) Why does society describe itself as postmodern?, *Cultural Critique*, Spring, p. 179.
7. Frederic Jameson (1998) *The Cultural Turn: Selected Writings on the Postmodern, 1983–1998.* London: Verso.
8. Although this has been characterized by Trotskyist analysts, not without reason, as essentially another form of capitalism, namely 'state capitalism'.
9. Jameson, op. cit., note 7, p. 137.
10. Ibid., p. 142. Tessa Brennan also points out that 'production under capitalism *is* consumption; it gobbles that which is already there, gives nothing back but waste'. Tessa Brennan (2000) *Exhausting Modernity: Grounds for a New Economy.*

London: Routledge; cited in Christopher Arthur's (2001) review, *Radical Philosophy*, 108: 43–5.

11. Jameson, op. cit., note 9, p. 161.
12. Ibid.
13. For example, see Cardinal Newman, *The Idea of the University*, numerous editions; Harold Wiltshire (1956) The great tradition in university adult education, *Adult Education*, 29: 88–97; Alan Ryan (1999) *Liberal Anxieties and Liberal Education*. London: Profile Books; Martha Nussbaum (1997) *Cultivating Humanity: A Classical Defence of Reform in Liberal Education*. Cambridge, MA: Harvard University Press; Richard Taylor (1996) Preserving the Liberal tradition in 'New Times', in John Wallis (ed.) *Liberal Adult Education: The End of an Era?* Nottingham: University of Nottingham Continuing Education Press, pp. 61–75; Roger Fieldhouse and Associates (1996) *A History of Modern British Adult Education*. Leicester: NIACE.
14. Michael Young (1962) *The Rise of the Meritocracy*. Harmondsworth: Penguin Books.
15. Tom Steele (1997) *The Emergence of Cultural Studies 1945 to 1965*. London: Lawrence & Wishart.
16. Zygmunt Bauman (1987) *Legislators and Interpreters: On Modernity, Post-modernity and Intellectuals*. Cambridge: Polity Press.
17. Rita Felski (1998) Images of the intellectual: from philosophy to cultural studies, *Continuum: Journal of Media and Cultural Studies*, 12(2): 166.
18. Michel Foucault (1988) The concern for truth, in Lawrence Kritzman (ed.) *Michel Foucault: Politics, Philosophy, Culture*. New York: Routledge, p. 265.
19. Felski, op. cit., note 7, p. 167.
20. Pierre Bourdieu (1998) The scholastic point of view, in *Practical Reason*. Cambridge: Polity Press.
21. See Gerard Delanty (2001) *Challenging Knowledge: The University in the Knowledge Society*. Buckingham: SRHE and Open University Press; Richard Taylor, Kathleen Rockhill and Roger Fieldhouse (1985) *University Adult Education in England and the USA: A Reappraisal of the Liberal Tradition*. Beckenham: Croom Helm, Chapter 2.
22. Frank Webster (1998) The postmodern university? The loss of purpose of British universities, paper presented to the SRHE Conference, Lancaster University, December.
23. Delanty, op. cit., note 21.
24. Ibid., p. 154.
25. See Hans Schuetze and Maria Slowey (eds) (2000) *Higher Education and Lifelong Learners: International Perspectives on Change*. London: Routledge Falmer.
26. Delanty, op. cit., note 21, p. 128.
27. For example, Bill Readings (1996) *The University in Ruins*. Cambridge, MA: Harvard University Press.
28. Delanty, op. cit., note 21, p. 158.
29. See the National Committee of Inquiry into Higher Education (1997) *Higher Education and the Learning Society* (Dearing Report). London: HMSO.
30. See Higher Education Funding Council for England (HEFCE) policy papers: *Widening participation in higher education: funding proposals*, Consultation paper 98/39, HEFCE, 1998; *Widening participation: special funding programme 1998–99, Outcome of bids*, Report paper 99/07, HEFCE, 1999a; *Widening participation in higher education: funding decisions*, Report paper 99/24, HEFCE, 1999; *Widening participation in higher education: request for initial statements of plans – invitation to bid for special funds: 1999–2000 to 2001–02; Widening participation: special funding programme 1999–2000 to 2001–02*, Report paper 00/35, HEFCE, 2000.

31. Ibid.
32. See John Holford (1993) *Union Education in Britain: A TUC Activity.* Nottingham: University of Nottingham Press; John McIlroy (1985) Adult education and the role of the client – the TUC education scheme 1929–1980, *Studies in the Education of Adults*, 16(2): 33–58; John McIlroy (1988) Storm and stress: the Trades Union Congress and university adult education 1964–1974, *Studies in the Education of Adults*, 20(1): 60–73.
33. For example, at the Universities of Leeds and Surrey, see Annual Reports of the School of Continuing Education, University of Leeds, and School of Educational Studies, University of Surrey, throughout the 1980s and 1990s.
34. Andre Gorz (1999) *Reclaiming Work Beyond the Wage-based Society.* Cambridge: Polity Press, p. 69.

Bibliography

Aaronowitz, S. (1993) Is a democracy possible?, in B. Robbins (ed.) *The Phantom Public Sphere*. Minneapolis, MN: University of Minnesota Press.

Aaronowitz, S. (1997) The new knowledge, in A.H. Halsey *et al.* (eds) *Education, Culture, Economy and Society*. Oxford: Oxford University Press.

Addams, J. (1964) *Democracy and Social Ethics*. Cambridge, MA: Berknap Press of Harvard University Press.

Alcoff, L. and Potter, E. (eds) (1993) *Feminist Epistemologies*. London: Routledge.

Alexander, J.C. (1995) Modern, anti, post, neo, *New Left Review*, 290: March/April, 63–101.

Allen, T. (1992) Post-industrialism and post-Fordism, in S. Hall, D. Held and A. McGrew (eds) *Modernity and its Futures*. Cambridge: Polity Press and Open University Press.

Anderson, P. (1961) The origins of the present crisis, in P. Anderson and T. Nairn (eds) *Towards Socialism*. London: Fontana and New Left Books.

Anderson, P. (1976) *Considerations on Western Marxism*. London: Verso and New Left Books.

Anderson, P. (1998) *The Origins of Postmodernity*. London: Verso.

Anderson, P. (2000) Renewals, *New Left Review*, N.S., 1(1): 5–24.

Anderson, P. and Nairn, T. (eds) (1961) *Towards Socialism*. London: Fontana and New Left Books.

Arendt, H. (1968) *Men in Dark Times*. New York: Harcourt Brace Jovanovich.

Arendt, H. (1997) *Between Past and Future*. New York: Penguin.

Arendt, H. (1998) *The Human Condition*, 2nd edn. Chicago, IL: University of Chicago Press.

Assiter, A. (1999) Citizenship re-visited, in N. Yuval-Davis and P. Werbner (eds) *Women, Citizenship and Difference*. London: Zed Books.

Bagnall, R. (2000) Lifelong learning and the limitations of economic determinism, *International Journal of Lifelong Education*, 19(1): 20–5.

Bailey, R. and Brake, M. (eds) (1974) *Radical Social Work*. London: Edward Arnold.

Bargh, C., Scott, P. and Smith, D. (1999) *Governing Universities: Changing the Culture?* Buckingham: SRHE and Open University Press.

Barnett, R. (1990) *The Idea of a University*. Buckingham: SRHE and Open University Press.

Barnett, R. (1997) *Higher Education – A Critical Business*. Buckingham: SRHE and Open University Press.

Barnett, R. (2000a) *Realizing the University in an age of supercomplexity*. Buckingham: SRHE and Open University Press.

Barnett, R. (2000b) Reconfiguring the university, in P. Scott (ed.) *Higher Education Re-formed*. Brighton: Falmer Press.

Barnett, R. and Griffin, A. (1997) *The End of Knowledge in Higher Education*. London: Cassell.

Barr, J. (1999) *Liberating Knowledge*. Leicester: NIACE.

Barr, J. (2000) Engaging educational research, *Discourse*, 21(3): 311–21.

Barrett, M. (1992) Words and things: materialism and method in contemporary feminist analysis, in M. Barrett and A. Phillips (eds) *Destablilizing Theory: Contemporary Feminist Debates*. Cambridge: Polity Press.

Barrett, M. and Phillips, A. (eds) (1992) *Destabilizing Theory: Contemporary Feminist Debates*. Cambridge: Polity Press.

Battersby, C. (1998) *The Phenomenal Woman: Feminist Metaphysics and Patterns of Identity*. Cambridge: Polity Press.

Baudrillard, J. (1983) *In the Shadow of the Silent Majorities*. New York: Semiotax.

Bauman, Z. (1987) *Legislators and Interpreters: On Modernity, Post-modernity and Intellectuals*. Cambridge: Polity Press.

Bauman, Z. (1991) *Intimations of Postmodernity*. London: Routledge.

Bauman, Z. (1995) *Life in Fragments*. Oxford: Blackwell.

Bauman, Z. (1997) Universities: old, new and different, in A. Smith and F. Webster (eds) *The Postmodern University? Contested Visions of Higher Education in Society*. Buckingham: SRHE and Open University Press.

Bauman, Z. (1999) *In Search of Politics*. Cambridge: Polity Press.

Bauman, Z. (2001) Community, in *Seeking Safety in an Insecure World*. Cambridge: Polity Press.

Becher, T. (ed.) (1994) *Governments and Professional Education*. Buckingham: SRHE and Open University Press.

Beer, S.H. (1959) *Modern British Politics*, 2nd edn. London: Faber & Faber.

Bell, D. (1973) *The Coming of Post-Industrial Society*. New York: Basic Books.

Bell, D. (1976) *The Cultural Contradictions of Capitalism*. New York: Basic Books.

Bell, D. (1980) The social framework of the information society, in T. Forrester (ed.) *The Microelectronics Revolution*. Oxford: Blackwell.

Benhabib, S. (ed.) (1986) *Critique, Norm and Utopia*. New York: Columbia University Press.

Benhabib, S. and Cornell, D. (eds) (1987) *Feminism as Critique*. Minneapolis, MN: University of Minnesota Press.

Berdahl, R. (1959) *British Universities and the State*. Berkeley, CA: University of California Press.

Bernal, M. (1987) *Black Athena: The Afroasiatic Roots of Classical Civilization*. London: Free Association Books.

Bernstein, B. (1972) *Class Codes and Control*. Vol. 1. London: Routledge & Kegan Paul.

Bhaskar, R. (1979) *Philosophy and the Human Sciences*. Brighton: Harvester Press.

Bhaskar, R. (1989) *Reclaiming Reality*. London: Verso.

Bhaskar, R. (1991) *Philosophy and the Idea of Freedom*. Oxford: Blackwell.

Bines, H. and Watson, D. (1992) *Developing Professional Education*. Buckingham: SRHE and Open University Press.

Blake, R. (1976) *The Conservative Party from Peel to Churchill.* London: Fontana (subsequent editions update to Margaret Thatcher's period of office as Leader of the Party and Prime Minister).

Bocock, J. and Taylor, R. (in press) *The Labour Party and Higher Education, 1945–51,* Higher Education Quarterly.

Bordo, S. (1990) Feminism, postmodernism and gender scepticism, in L. Nicholson (ed.) *Feminism and Postmodernism.* London: Routledge.

Bordo, S. (1993) *Unbearable Weight: Feminism, Western Culture and the Body.* Berkeley, CA: University of California Press.

Bordo, S. (1998) The feminist as other, in J. Kourany (ed.) *Philosophy as a Feminist Voice.* Princeton, NJ: Princeton University Press.

Bottomore, T. and Rubel, M. (1963) *Karl Marx: Selected Writings in Sociology and Social Philosophy.* Harmondsworth: Pelican (first edition 1956).

Bourdieu, P. (1973) Cultural reproduction and social reproduction, in R. Brown (ed.) *Knowledge, Education and Social Change.* London: Tavistock.

Bourdieu, P. (1993) *Sociology in Question.* London: Sage.

Bourdieu, P. (1998) The scholastic point of view, in *Practical Reason.* Cambridge: Polity Press.

Bourdieu, P. and Wacquant, L. (2001) New Liberal speak: notes on the new planetary vulgate, *Radical Philosophy,* 105: 2–5.

Bourner, J., Katz, T. and Watson, D. (2000) *New Directions in Professional Higher Education.* Buckingham: SRHE and Open University Press.

Bowen, J. (1981) *A History of Western Education, The Modern West, Europe and the New World,* Vol. 3. London: Methuen.

Bowles, S. and Gintis, H. (1976) *Schooling in Capitalist America.* London: Routledge & Kegan Paul.

Brecht, B. (1963) *The Life of Galileo* (translated by D.I. Vesey). London: Faber.

Brennan, T. (2000) *Exhausting Modernity: Grounds for a New Economy.* London: Routledge.

Brine, J. (1999) *underEducating Women: Globalizing Inequality.* Buckingham: Open University Press.

Bruch, T. and Barty, A. (1998) Internationalizing British higher education: students and institutions, in P. Scott (ed.) *The Globalization of Higher Education.* Buckingham: SRHE and Open University Press.

Burnham, J. (1942) *The Managerial Revolution.* London: Putnam.

Butler, G. (1957) *The Tory Tradition.* London: Conservative Political Centre.

Butler, R.A. (1971) *The Art of the Possible.* London: Hamish Hamilton.

Callinicos, A. (1989) *Against Postmodernism: A Marxist Critique.* Cambridge: Polity Press.

Callinicos, A. (1991) *The Revenge of History: Marxism and the East European Revolutions.* Cambridge: Polity Press.

Callinicos, A. (2000) Impossible anti-capitalism?, *New Left Review,* N.S., Vol. 2, March/April, pp. 117–24.

Castells, M. (1989) *The Informational City.* Oxford: Blackwell.

Castoriadis, C. (1997) *World in Fragments: Writings on Politics, Society, Psychoanalysis, and the Imagination.* Stanford, CA: Stanford University Press.

Cesarani, D. (1998) *Arthur Koestler: The Homeless Mind.* London: Heinemann.

Coates, D. (1974) *The Labour Party and the Struggle for Socialism.* Cambridge: Cambridge University Press.

Coates, D. and Hillard, J. (1986) *The Economic Decline of Modern Britain.* Brighton: Wheatsheaf.

Cockburn, C. (1999) *The Space Between Us.* London: Zed Books.
Code, L. (1989) Experience, knowledge and responsibility, in A. Garry and M. Pearsall (eds) *Women, Knowledge and Reality.* London: Unwin Hyman.
Code, L. (1995) *Rhetorical Spaces.* New York: Routledge.
Coffield, F. (1997) Can the UK become a learning society?, Fourth Annual Education Lecture, King's College, London.
Coffield, F. (1999a) *Why is the Beer Always Stronger Up North?,* Studies of Lifelong Learning in Europe. London: Policy Press.
Coffield, F. (1999b) Breaking the consensus: lifelong learning as social control. Inaugural Lecture, University of Newcastle, 2 February.
Coffield, F. and Williamson, B. (1997) The challenges facing higher education, in F. Coffield and B. Williamson (eds) *Repositioning Higher Education.* Buckingham: Open University Press.
Cole, M. (1961) *The Story of Fabian Socialism.* London: Mercury Books.
Coole, D. (1990) Habermas and the question of alterity, in M. Passerin d'Entreves and S. Benhabib (eds) *Habermas and the Unfinished Project of Modernity.* Cambridge: Polity Press.
Coward, R. (1989) *The Whole Truth.* London: Faber & Faber.
Crompton, R. (1998) *Class and Stratification: An Introduction to Current Debates.* Cambridge: Polity Press.
Crosland, A. (1956) *The Future of Socialism.* London: Cape.
Crossman, R. (ed.) (1950) *The God that Failed: Six Studies in Communism.* London: Hamilton.
Dahl, R. (1956) *A Preface to Democratic Political Theory.* Chicago, IL: University of Chicago Press.
Dale, R. (1989) *The State and Education Policy.* Buckingham: Open University Press.
Davie, G.E. (1964) *The Democratic Intellect.* Edinburgh: Edinburgh University Press.
Dearing Report (1997) *Report of the National Committee of Inquiry into Higher Education.* London: HMSO.
Delanty, G. (2001) *Challenging Knowledge: The University in the Knowledge Society.* Buckingham: SRHE and Open University Press.
Department for Education and Employment (1997) *Excellence in Schools,* Cm. 3681. London: HMSO.
Deutsche, R. (1996) *Evictions: Art and Spatial Politics.* Cambridge, MA: MIT Press.
Disch, L.J. (1996) *Hannah Arendt and the Limits of Philosophy.* Ithaca, NY: Cornell University Press.
Doyal, L. and Gough, I. (1991) *A Theory of Human Need.* London: Macmillan.
Dupuy, J. (1980) Myths of the information society, in K. Woodward (ed.) *The Myths of Information: Technology and Post-industrial Culture.* London: Routledge & Kegan Paul.
Eagleton, T. (1996) *The Illusions of Postmodernism.* Oxford: Blackwell.
Edsall, T.B. (1984) *The New Politics of Inequality.* New York: W.W. Norton.
Edwards, R. (1997) *Changing places? Flexibility, Lifelong Learning and a Learning Society.* London: Routledge.
Ehrenreich, B. and English, D. (1979) *For Her Own Good: 150 Years of the Experts' Advice to Women.* New York: Anchor Press.
Elliott, D. (1998) Internationalizing British higher education: policy perspectives, in P. Scott (ed.) *The Globalization of Higher Education.* Buckingham: SRHE and Open University Press.

Eraut, M. (1994) *Developing Professional Knowledge and Competence.* Brighton: Falmer Press.

Featherstone, M. (1988) In pursuit of the postmodern: introduction, *Theory, Culture and Society,* 5(2/3): 195–216.

Felski, R. (1998) Images of the intellectual: from philosophy to cultural studies, *Continuum: Journal of Media and Cultural Studies,* 12(2): 157–77.

Ferguson, A. (1993) Does reason have a gender?, in R. Gottlieb (ed.) *Radical Philosophy: Tradition, Counter-Tradition, Politics.* Philadelphia, PA: Temple University Press.

Field, J. (1996) Vocational education and training, in R. Fieldhouse and Associates, *A History of Modern British Adult Education.* Leicester: NIACE.

Field, J. (1998) *European Dimensions: Education, Training and the European Union.* London: Jessica Kingsley.

Field, J. (2000) *Lifelong Learning and the New Educational Order.* London: Trentham Books.

Field, J. (2001) Lifelong education, *International Journal of Lifelong Education,* 20 (1/2): 3–15.

Field, J. and Leicester, M. (eds) (2000) *Lifelong Learning: Education Across the Lifespan.* London: Routledge Falmer.

Fieldhouse, R. (1977) *The Workers' Educational Association: Aims and Achievements, 1903–1977.* New York: Syracuse University Press.

Fieldhouse, R. (1985) *Adult Education and the Cold War,* Leeds Series in Adult Education. Leeds: University of Leeds.

Fieldhouse, R. and Associates (1996) *A History of Modern British Adult Education.* Leicester: NIACE.

Fletcher, C. and Thompson, N. (1980) *Issues in Community Education.* Brighton: Falmer Press.

Foley, G. (1999) Back to basics: a political economy of workplace change and learning, *Studies in the Education of Adults,* 31(2): 181–96.

Foley, G. (2001) *Strategic Learning: Understanding and Facilitating Organizational Change.* Sydney: Centre for Popular Education, University of Technology.

Forrester, K., Payne, J. and Ross, C. (in press) *The Politics of Inclusion: Globalization and Adult Learning.* Leicester: NIACE.

Foucault, M. (1979) *Discipline and Punish.* New York: Vintage Books.

Foucault, M. (1980) *Power/Knowledge: Selected Interviews and Other Writings, 1972–77* (edited by C. Gordon). New York: Pantheon Press.

Foucault, M. (1986) What is enlightenment?, in P. Rabinow (ed.) *The Foucault Reader.* Harmondsworth: Peregrine Books.

Foucault, M. (1988) The concern for truth, in L. Kritzman (ed.) *Michel Foucault: Politics, Philosophy, Culture.* New York: Routledge.

Fraser, N. (1993) Re-thinking the public sphere, in B. Robbins (ed.) *The Phantom Public Sphere.* Minneapolis, MN: University of Minnesota Press.

Fraser, N. (2000a) Rethinking recognition, *New Left Review,* Vol. 3, May/June, pp. 107–20.

Fraser, N. (2000b) Recognition without ethics?, in M. Garber, B. Hanssen and R. Walkowitz (eds) *The Turn to Ethics.* New York: Routledge.

Friedan, B. (1963) *The Feminine Mystique.* Harmondsworth: Penguin.

Frost, N. and Taylor, R. (2001) Patterns of change in the university: the impact of 'lifelong learning' and the 'world of work', *Studies in the Education of Adults,* 33(1): 49–59.

Gavron, H. (1968) *The Captive Wife: Conflicts of Housebound Mothers*. Harmondsworth: Penguin.

Gibbons, M. (1998) A Commonwealth perspective on the globalization of higher education, in P. Scott (ed.) *The Globalization of Higher Education*. Buckingham: SRHE and Open University Press.

Giddens, A. (1990) *The Consequences of Modernity*. Cambridge: Polity Press.

Giddens, A. (1991) *Modernity and Self-identity: Self and Society in the Late Modern Age*. Cambridge: Polity Press.

Giddens, A. (1998) *The Third Way*. Cambridge: Polity Press.

Ginzburg, C. (1980) Morelli, Freud, and Sherlock Holmes: clues and scientific method, *History Workshop Journal*, 9: 5–36.

Goddard, J. *et al.* (1994) *Universities and their Communities*. London: CVCP.

Gorz, A. (1999) *Reclaiming Work Beyond the Wage-based Society*. Cambridge: Polity Press.

Gottlieb, R. (ed.) (1993) *Radical Philosophy: Tradition, Counter-Tradition, Politics*. Philadelphia, PA: Temple University Press.

Grimshaw, J. (1986) *Philosophy and Feminist Thinking*. Brighton: Wheatsheaf.

Grimshaw, J. (1996) Philosophy, feminism and universalism, *Radical Philosophy*, 76: 19–28.

Guha, R. and Spivak, G. (1988) *Selected Subaltern Studies*. Oxford: Oxford University Press.

Habermas, J. (1987) *The Philosophical Discourse of Modernity*. Cambridge: Polity Press.

Habermas, J. (1989) *The Structural Transformation of the Public Sphere* (translated by T. Burger with F. Lawrence). Cambridge, MA: MIT Press.

Hall, S. (1988) Brave new world, *Marxism Today*, October.

Hall, S. and Jacques, M. (eds) (1989) *New Times*. London: Lawrence & Wishart.

Hall, S. (1996) Cultural studies and its theoretical legacies, in D. Morley and K-H. Chen (eds) *Stuart Hall: Critical Dialogues in Cultural Studies*. London: Routledge.

Hall, S., Held, D. and McGrew, T. (1992) *Modernity and its Futures*. Cambridge: Polity Press and Open University Press.

Halsey, A.H. *et al.* (eds) (1997) *Education, Culture, Economy and Society*. Oxford: Oxford University Press.

Hamilton, R. (1995) The educational vision of Jane Addams: the formative years. Unpublished master's thesis, University of Glasgow.

Hampshire, S. (1999) *Justice is Conflict*. London: Duckworth.

Haraway, D. (1991) Situated knowledges, in *Simians, Cyborgs and Women: The Reinvention of Nature*. London: Routledge.

Harding, S. (1986) *The Science Question in Feminism*. Milton Keynes: Open University Press.

Harding, S. (1991) *Whose Science? Whose Knowledge?* Milton Keynes: Open University Press.

Hargraves, G. (1998) The origins of the National Vocational Qualification, with special reference to the Manpower Services Commission, 1974–1986, and to the review of Vocational Qualifications, 1985–1986. Unpublished doctoral dissertation, University of Leeds.

Harris, N. (1972) *Competition and the Corporate Society*. London: Methuen.

Harrison, J.F.C. (1961) *Learning and Living*. London: Routledge.

Harvey, D. (1990) *The Condition of Postmodernity*. Oxford: Basic Blackwell.

Harvey, L. (1990) *Critical Social Science Research*. London: Unwin Hyman.

Hennessy, R. and Ingraham, C. (1997) *Materialist Feminism: A Reader in Class, Difference and Women's Lives*. London: Routledge & Kegan Paul.

Higher Education Funding Council for England (1998) *Widening Participation in Higher Education: Funding Proposals*, consultation paper 98/39. London: HEFCE.

Higher Education Funding Council for England (1999a) *Widening Participation: Special Funding Programme 1998–99, Outcome of Bids*, Report paper 99/07. London: HEFCE.

Higher Education Funding Council for England (1999b) *Widening Participation in Higher Education: Funding Decisions*, Report paper 99/24. London: HEFCE.

Higher Education Funding Council for England (2000) *Widening Participation in Higher Education: Request for Initial Statement of Plans – Invitation to Bid for Special Funds: 1999–2000 to 2001–02: Special Funding Programme 1999–2000 to 2001–02*, Report paper 00/35. London: HEFCE.

Hill, C. (1965) *The Intellectual Origins of the English Revolution*. Oxford: Oxford University Press.

Hoare, Q. and Smith, N. (eds) (1971) *Gramsci: Selections from the Prison Notebooks*. London: Lawrence & Wishart.

Hobsbawm, E. (1994) *The Age of Extremes, The Short Twentieth Century, 1914–1991*. London: Michael Joseph.

Hodgkin, T. (1950/51) Objectivity, ideologies and the present political situation, *The Highway*, XLII.

Hogg, Q. (Lord Hailsham) (1947) *The Case for Conservatism*. Harmondsworth: Penguin.

Holford, J. (1993) *Union Education in Britain*. Nottingham: University of Nottingham.

Honderich, T. (1980) *Conservatism*. London: Hamish Hamilton.

Isaac, J.C. (2000) Intellectuals, Marxism and politics, *New Left Review*, N.S., 2: 111–15.

Jackson, K. (1970) Adult education and community development, *Studies in the Education of Adults*, 2: 165–72.

Jackson, K. (1980) Some fallacies in community education and their consequences in working class areas, in C. Fletcher, C. and N. Thompson (eds) *Issues in Community Education*. Brighton: Falmer Press.

Jaggar, A. and Young, I.M. (eds) (1998) *Companion to Feminist Philosophy*. Oxford: Blackwell.

Jameson, F. (1984) Postmodernism – the cultural logic of late capitalism, *New Left Review*, 146.

Jameson, F. (1991) *Postmodernism or the Cultural Logic of Late Capitalism*. London: Verso.

Jameson, F. (1998) *The Cultural Turn – Selected Writings on the Postmodern, 1983–1998*. London: Verso.

Jarvis, P. (2000) The corporate university, in J. Field and M. Leicester (eds) *Lifelong Learning: Education Across the Lifespan*. London: Routledge Falmer.

Jencks, C. (1986) *What is Postmodernism?* London: Academy Editions.

Jenkins, K. (ed.) (1997) *The Postmodern History Reader*. London: Routledge.

Jepson, N. (1973) *The Beginnings of English University Adult Education*. London: Michael Joseph.

Jessop, G. (1991) *Outcomes: NVQs and the Emerging Model of Education and Training*. Brighton: Falmer Press.

Johnson, P. (1993) Feminism and the enlightenment, *Radical Philosophy*, 63: 3–12.

Johnson, R. (1988) Really useful knowledge, in T. Lovett (ed.) *Radical Approaches to Adult Education*. London: Routledge.

Johnston, R. (1997) Adult learning for citizenship, in R. Usher, I. Bryant and R. Johnston, *Adult Education and the Postmodern Challenge: Learning Beyond the Limits*. London: Routledge.

Keller, E.F. (1985) *Reflections on Gender and Science.* New Haven, CT: Yale University Press.

Kellogg, P. (1987) Goodbye to the working class?, *International Socialism,* 2(36): 108–10.

Kenway, J. *et al.* (1997) Marketing education in the postmodern age, *Journal of Education Policy,* 8(2): 105–22.

Kernan, A. (1999) *In Plato's Cave.* New Haven, CT: Yale University Press.

Kerr, C. *et al.* (1973) *Industrialism and Industrial Man,* 2nd edn. Harmondsworth: Penguin.

Klein, N. (2000) *No Logo.* London: Flamingo.

Kourany, J.A. (ed.) (1998) *Philosophy in a Feminist Voice.* Princeton, NJ: Princeton University Press.

Kuhn, A. and Wolpe, A-M. (1978) *Feminism and Materialism: Women and Modes of Production.* London: Routledge & Kegan Paul.

Kumar, V. (1993) *Poverty and Inequality in the UK and the Effects on Children.* London: National Children's Bureau.

HMSO (1999) *The Learning Age: a Renaissance for a New Britain* (Green Paper). London: HMSO.

Le Doeuff, M. (1989) *The Philosophical Imaginary* (translated by C. Gordon). London: Athlone Press.

Le Doeuff, M. (1991) *Hipparchia's Choice: An Essay Concerning Women, Philosophy, etc.* Oxford: Blackwell.

Lloyd, G. (1984) *The Man of Reason.* London: Methuen.

Lloyd, G. (1998) Rationality, in A. Jaggar and I.M. Young (eds) *The Companion to Feminist Philosophy.* Oxford: Blackwell.

Lovett, T. (1983) *Adult Education, Community Development and the Working Class.* Beckenham: Croom Helm.

Lovett, T. (ed.) (1988) *Radical Approaches to Adult Education: A Reader.* London: Routledge.

Lovett, T. *et al.* (1975) *Adult Education and Community Action.* Beckenham: Croom Helm.

Luhmann, N. (1995) Why does society describe itself as postmodern?, *Cultural Critique,* Spring, pp. 171–186.

Luhmann, N. (1998) *Observations on Modernity.* Stanford, CA: Stanford University Press.

Lukacs, G. (1971) *History and Class Consciousness.* London: Merlin.

Lyotard, J.F. (1984) *The Postmodern Condition: A Report on Knowledge,* 2nd edn. Manchester: Manchester University Press.

MacIntyre, A. (1987) The idea of an educated public, in P. Hirst (ed.) *Education and Values,* The Richard Peters Lectures. London: Institute of Education, University of London.

MacIntyre, A. (1988) *Whose Justice? Which Rationality?* London: Duckworth.

Malcolm, J. and Zukas, M. (2000) Becoming an educator: communities of practice in higher education, in I. McNay (ed.) *Higher Education and its Communities.* Buckingham: SRHE and Open University Press.

Mandel, E. (1975) International capitalism and 'supranationality', in H. Radice (ed.) *International Firms and Modern Imperialism.* Harmondsworth: Penguin.

Mansbridge, J. (1990) Feminism and democracy, *The American Prospect,* 1: 127.

Marcuse, H. (1958) *Soviet Marxism.* London: Routledge & Kegan Paul.

Marcuse, H. (1969) *An Essay on Liberation.* London: Allen Lane.

Marcuse, H. (1974) *Eros and Civilization.* Boston, MA: Beacon Press.

Marcuse, H. (1979) *The Aesthetic Dimension: Toward a Critique of Marxist Aesthetics.* London: Macmillan.

Martin, I. (1996) Community education: the dialectics of development, in R. Fieldhouse and Associates, *A History of Modern British Adult Education.* Leicester: NIACE.

Martin, J. (2000) *Coming of Age in Academe.* New York: Routledge.

Marx, K. (1844) *Economic and Philosophical Manuscripts,* in L. Colletti (ed.) (1974) *Marx's Early Writings.* Harmondsworth: Pelican Marx Library.

Marx, K. ([1846]1968) (with Engels F.) *The German Ideology.* Moscow: CPSU.

Marx, K. ([1846]1968) *Capital, Vol. 1* (translated by B. Fowkes, introduction by E. Mandel).

Marx, K. and Engels, F. ([1848]1969) *The Manifesto of the Communist Party.* A.J.P. Taylor (ed.), Harmondsworth: Penguin Books.

Marx, K. and Engels, F. (1935) *Marx and Engels Selected Works,* Vol. 1. Moscow: CPSU.

Massey, D. (2001) Blurring the boundaries: high-tech in Cambridge, in C. Paechter, M. Preedy, D. Scott and J. Soler (eds) *Knowledge, Power and Learning.* London and Milton Keynes: Paul Chapman in association with Open University Press.

Mayo, M. (1974) Community development: a radical alternative, in R. Bailey and M. Brake (eds) *Radical Social Work.* London: Edward Arnold.

Mayo, M. and Thompson, J. (1995) *Adult Learning, Critical Intelligence and Social Change.* Leicester: NIACE.

McGrew, A. (1992) A global society?, in S. Hall, D. Held and A. McGrew (eds) *Modernity and its Futures.* Cambridge: Polity Press and Open University Press.

McIlroy, J. (1985) Adult education and the role of the client – the TUC education scheme 1929–1980, *Studies in the Education of Adults,* 16(2): 33–58.

McIlroy, J. (1988) Storm and stress: the Trades Union Congress and university adult education 1964–1974, *Studies in the Education of Adults,* 20(1): 60–73.

McLellan, D. (1971) *The Thought of Karl Marx.* London: Macmillan.

McLennan, G. (1992) The Enlightenment Project revisited, in S. Hall, D. Held and A. McGrew (eds) *Modernity and its Futures.* Cambridge: Polity Press and Open University Press.

McNay, I. (ed.) (2000) *Higher Education and its Communities.* Buckingham: SRHE and Open University Press.

Megill, A. (1985) *Prophets of Extremity: Nietzsche, Heidegger, Foucault, Derrida.* Berkeley, CA: University of California Press.

Midgley, M. (1994) *The Ethical Primate: Humans, Freedom and Morality.* London: Routledge.

Midgley, M. (1997) Visions of embattled science, in R. Barnett and A. Griffin (eds) *The End of Knowledge in Higher Education.* London: Cassell.

Miliband, R. (1969) *The State in Capitalist Society.* London: Weidenfeld & Nicolson.

Miliband, R. (1973) *Parliamentary Socialism,* 2nd edn. London: Merlin Press.

Miliband, R. (1977) *Marxism and Politics.* Oxford: Oxford University Press.

Miliband, R. (1994) *Socialism for a Sceptical Age.* Cambridge: Polity Press.

Minnich, E. (1989) *Transferring Knowledge.* Philadelphia, PA: Temple University Press.

Mitchell, J. (1966) The longest revolution, *New Left Review,* 40: 11–37.

Monbiot, G. (2000) *Captive State: The Corporate Takeover of Britain.* Oxford: Macmillan.

Morley, D. and Chen, K-H. (eds) (1996) *Stuart Hall: Critical Dialogues in Cultural Studies.* London: Routledge.

Murphy, M. (2000) Adult education, lifelong learning and the end of political economy, *Studies in the Education of Adults,* 32(2): 166–80.

Nairn, T. (1961) The nature of Labourism, in P. Anderson and T. Nairn (eds) *Towards Socialism.* London: Fontana and New Left Books.

National Committee of Inquiry into Higher Education (Dearing Report) 1997. London: HMSO.

Nelson, L.H. (1990) *Who Knows: From Quine to Feminist Empiricism.* Philadelphia, PA: Temple University Press.

Nelson, L.H. (1993) Epistemological communities, in L. Alcoff and E. Potter (eds) *Feminist Epistemologies.* London: Routledge.

Newman, Cardinal (1976) *The Idea of a University.* Oxford: Clarendon Press.

Nicolson, L. (ed.) (1990) *Feminism and Postmodernism.* London: Routledge.

Noble, D. (1992) *A World Without Women: The Christian Clerical Culture of Western Science.* New York: Oxford University Press.

Nussbaum, M. (1986) *The Fragility of Goodness.* Cambridge: Cambridge University Press.

Nussbaum, M. (1997) *Cultivating Humanity: A Classical Defence of Reform in Liberal Education.* Cambridge, MA: Harvard University Press.

Nussbaum, M. (1999) *Sex and Social Justice.* New York: Oxford University Press.

Nussbaum, M. (2000) *Women and Human Development: The Capabilities Approach.* Cambridge: Cambridge University Press.

Nussbaum, M. and Glover, J. (eds) (1995) *Women, Culture and Development.* Oxford: Oxford University Press.

Nussbaum, M. and Oksenberg, R.A. (eds) (1992) *Essays on Aristotle's De anima.* Oxford: Oxford University Press.

Oakeshott, M. (1962) *Rationalism in Politics.* London: Methuen.

O'Sullivan, N. (1999) Conservatism, in R. Eatwell and A. Wright (eds) *Contemporary Political Ideologies.* London: Continuum.

Paechter, C., Preedy, M., Scott, D. and Soler, J. (2001) *Knowledge, Power and Learning.* London and Milton Keynes: Paul Chapman in association with the Open University.

Parry, G. (1995) England, Wales and Northern Ireland, in P. Davies (ed.) *Adults in Higher Education: International Perspectives in Access and Participation.* London: Jessica Kingsley.

Perkin, H. (1989) *The Rise of Professional Society: England since 1880.* London: Routledge.

Perkin, H. (1996) *Third Revolution: Professional Elites in the Modern World.* Brighton: Routledge.

Perkins, T. (2000) Who (and what) is it for?, in C. Gledhill and L. Williams (eds) *Reinventing Film Studies.* London: Arnold.

Peters, M. and Marginson, S. (1999) Introduction, *Access: Critical Perspectives on Cultural Policy Studies in Education,* 18(2):

Pickering, M. (1993) *August Comte, an Intellectual Biography,* Vol. 1. Cambridge: Cambridge University Press.

Pilger, J. (1998) *Hidden Agendas.* London: Vintage.

Poster, C. (1982) *Community Education: Its Development and Management.* London: Heinemann.

Pritchard, C. and Taylor, R. (1978) *Social Work: Reform or Revolution?* London: Routledge & Kegan Paul.

Rabinow, P. (ed.) (1986) *The Foucault Reader.* Harmondsworth: Peregrine Books.

Radice, H. (ed.) (1975) *International Firms and Modern Imperialism.* Harmondsworth: Penguin.

Radice, H. (2001) From Warwick University Ltd to British Universities plc, *Red Pepper,* March, pp. 18–21.

Ray, L. (1999) Social differentiation, transgression and the politics of irony, in L. Ray and A. Sayer, *Culture and Economy: After the Cultural Turn*. London: Sage.

Ray, L. and Sayer, A. (eds) (1999) *Culture and Economy: After the Cultural Turn*. London: Sage.

Readings, B. (1996) *The University in Ruins*. Cambridge, MA: Harvard University Press.

Redclift, M. and Benton, T. (1994) *Social Theory and the Global Environment*. London: Routledge.

Ree, H. (1973) *Educator Extraordinary*. London: Longman.

Ree, H. (ed.) (1984) *The Henry Morris Collection*. Cambridge: Cambridge University Press.

Reid, I. (1998) *Class in Britain*. Cambridge: Polity Press.

Robbins, B. (1993a) *Secular Vocations: Intellectuals, Professionalism, Culture*. London: Verso.

Robbins, B. (1993b) The public as phantom, in B. Robbins (ed.) *The Phantom Public Sphere*. Minneapolis, MN: University of Minnesota Press.

Robbins Report (1963) *Report of the Committee on Higher Education*. London: HMSO.

Robertson, D. (2000) Students as consumers, in P. Scott (ed.) *Higher Education Reformed*. Brighton: Falmer Press.

Roderick, G. and Stephens, M. (eds) (1982) *Performance, Education and Training in Britain Today*. Brighton: Falmer Press.

Rodriguez, R. (1982) *Hunger of Memory*. Boston, MA: David R. Godine.

Rowbotham, S. (1973) *Woman's Consciousness, Man's World*. Harmondsworth: Penguin.

Rowbotham, S. (1983) *Dreams and Dilemmas: Collected Writings*. London: Virago.

Rowbotham, S. (1999) *Threads Through Time: Writings on History and Autobiography*. Harmondsworth: Penguin.

Ryan, A. (1999) *Liberal Anxieties and Liberal Education*. London: Profile Books.

Sadlak, J. (1998) Globalization and concurrent challenges for higher education, in P. Scott (ed.) *The Globalization of Higher Education*. Buckingham: SRHE and Open University Press.

Said, E. (1991) *Musical Elaborations*. New York: Columbia University Press.

Sanders, K. and Le Doeuff, M. (1993) Reconsidering rationality, *Australian Journal of Philosophy*, 71(4): 426–34.

Sayer, A. (1999) Valuing culture and economy, in L. Ray and A. Sayer (eds) *Culture and Economy: After the Cultural Turn*. London: Sage.

Sayer, A. (2000) *Realism and Social Science*. London: Sage.

Schiebinger, L. (1989) *The Mind Has No Sex?* Cambridge, MA: Harvard University Press.

Schuetze, H. and Slowey, M. (eds) (2000) *Higher Education and Lifelong Learners: International Perspectives on Change*. London: Routledge Falmer.

Scott, P. (1995) *The Meanings of Mass Higher Education*. Buckingham: SRHE and Open University Press.

Scott, P. (1997) The postmodern university?, in A. Smith and F. Webster (eds) *The Postmodern University? Contested Visions of Higher Education in Society*. Buckingham: SRHE and Open University Press.

Scott, P. (1998a) *The Globalization of Higher Education*. Buckingham: SRHE and Open University Press.

Scott, P. (1998b) Massification, internationalization and globalization, in P. Scott (ed.) *The Globalization of Higher Education*. Buckingham: SRHE and Open University Press.

Scott, P. (ed.) (2000) *Higher Education Re-formed*. Brighton: Falmer Press.

Seigfried, C. (1998) Pragmatism, in A. Jagger and I.M. Young (eds) *Companion to Feminist Philosophy*. Oxford: Blackwell.

Segal, L. (1999) *Why Feminism?* Cambridge: Polity Press.

Seller, A. (1997) Whose knowledge? Whose postmodernism?, in R. Barnett and A. Griffin (eds) *The End of Knowledge in Higher Education*. London: Cassell.

Sen, A. (1990) Gender and cooperative conflicts, in I. Tinker (ed.) *Persistent Inequalities: Women and World Development*. New York: Oxford University Press.

Shanks, M. (1961) *The Stagnant Society*. Harmondsworth: Penguin.

Siegrist, H. (1994) The professions, state and government in theory and history, in T. Becher (ed.) *Governments and Professional Education*. Buckingham: SRHE and Open University Press.

Simon, B. (1960) *Studies in the History of Education, 1780–1870*. London: Lawrence & Wishart.

Simon, B. (1965) *Education and the Labour Movement 1870–1920*. London: Lawrence & Wishart.

Slaughter, S. and Leslie, L. (1997) *Academic Capitalism: Politics, Policies and the Entrepreneurial University*. Baltimore, MD: Johns Hopkins University Press.

Smith, A. (2000) Review of Ronald Barnett, 'Realizing the university in an age of supercomplexity', *Times Higher Education Supplement*, 21 April.

Smith, A. and Webster, F. (eds) (1997) *The Postmodern University? Contested Visions of Higher Education in Society*. Buckingham: SRHE and Open University Press.

Soper, K. (1990) *Troubled Pleasures*. London: Verso.

Soper, K. (1997) Realism, postmodernism and cultural values, in R. Barnett and A. Griffin (eds) *The End of Knowledge in Higher Education*. London: Cassell.

Spelman, E. (1988) *Inessential Woman: Problems of Exclusion in Feminist Thought*. Boston, MA: Beacon.

Stabile, C. (1997) Feminism and the ends of postmodernism, in R. Hennessy and C. Ingraham (eds) *Materialist Feminism: A Reader in Class, Difference and Women's Lives*. London: Routledge & Kegan Paul.

Steele, T. (1997) *The Emergence of Cultural Studies 1945 to 1965*. London: Lawrence & Wishart.

Steele, T. (2000) Common goods: beyond the world of work to the universe of the imagination, in J. Thompson (ed.) *Stretching the Academy: The Politics and Practice of Widening Participation in Higher Education*. Leicester: NIACE.

Steele, T. and Taylor, R. (1998) *Learning Independence: A Political Outline of Indian Adult Education*. Leicester: NIACE.

Stewart, W.A.C. (1989) *Higher Education in Postwar Britain*. Basingstoke: Macmillan.

Tallis, R. (1997) *Enemies of Hope, A Critique of Contemporary Pessimism*. New York: St. Martin's Press.

Taylor, R. (1983) The British Nuclear Disarmament Movement of 1958 to 1965 and its legacy to the Left. Unpublished doctoral dissertation, University of Leeds.

Taylor, R. (1993/94) Continuing education and the accessible university, Inaugural Lecture, 26 April 1993, published in *University of Leeds Review*, 36: 314–15.

Taylor, R. (1996) Preserving the Liberal tradition in 'New Times', in J. Wallis (ed.) *Liberal Adult Education: The End of an Era?* Nottingham: University of Nottingham Continuing Education Press.

Taylor, R. (1998) Lifelong learning in the 'Liberal tradition', *Journal of Moral Education*, 27(3): 301–12.

Taylor, R. (2000) Concepts of self-directed learning in higher education: re-establishing the democratic tradition, in J. Thompson (ed.) *Stretching the Academy: The Politics and Practice of Widening Participation in Higher Education.* Leicester: NIACE.

Taylor, R. (2001) Lifelong learning in higher education in Western Europe: myth or reality?, *Adult Education and Development Journal* (DVV, Germany), 56.

Taylor, R. and Ward, K. (1988) Adult education with unemployed people, in T. Lovett (ed.) *Radical Approaches to Adult Education: A Reader.* London: Routledge.

Taylor, R., Rockhill, K. and Fieldhouse, R. (1985) *University Adult Education in England and the USA: A Reappraisal of the Liberal Tradition.* Beckenham: Croom Helm.

Thompson, E.P. (ed.) (1960) *Out of Apathy.* London: A.&C. Black.

Thompson, E.P. (1968) Education and experience, Fifth Albert Mansbridge Memorial Lecture, University of Leeds.

Thompson, E.P. (1971) *Warwick University Ltd.* Harmondsworth: Penguin.

Thompson, E.P. (1978) *The Poverty of Theory and Other Essays.* London: Merlin Press.

Thompson, J. (1983) *Learning Liberation: Women's Response to Men's Education.* Beckenham: Croom Helm.

Thompson, J. (ed.) (2000) *Stretching the Academy: The Politics and Practice of Widening Participation in Higher Education.* Leicester: NIACE.

Thompson, K. (1992) Social pluralism and postmodernity, in S. Hall, D. Held and A. McGrew (eds) *Modernity and its Futures.* Cambridge: Polity Press and Open University Press.

Thrift, N. (1999) Capitalism's cultural turn, in L. Ray and A. Sayer (eds) *Culture and Economy: After the Cultural Turn.* London: Sage.

Touraine, A. (1971) *The Post-Industrial Society.* New York: Random House.

Townsend, P. (1979) *Poverty in the UK.* Harmondsworth: Penguin.

UNESCO (1972) *Learning to Be: The World of Education Today and Tomorrow* (the Faure Report). Paris: UNESCO.

Urry, J. (1998) Contemporary transformations of time and space, in P. Scott (ed.) *The Globalization of Higher Education.* Buckingham: SRHE and Open University Press.

Urry, J. and Wakeford, J. (eds) (1973) *Power in Britain.* London: Heinemann.

Usher, R. and Edwards, R. (1994) *Postmodernism and Education.* London: Routledge.

Usher, R., Bryant, I. and Johnston, R. (1997) *Adult Education and the Postmodern Challenge: Learning Beyond the Limits.* London: Routledge.

Wain, K. (2000) The learning society: postmodern politics, *International Journal of Lifelong Education,* 19(1):

Walkerdine, V. and Girls and Mathematics Unit (1989) *Counting Girls Out.* London: Virago.

Wallis, J. and Mee, G. (1983) *Community Schools: Claims and Performance.* Nottingham: University of Nottingham, Department of Adult Education.

Ward, K. and Taylor, R. (1986) *Adult Education and the Working Class: Education for the Missing Millions.* Beckenham: Croom Helm.

Watson, D. (2000a) The Two Worlds of Ron Barnett: a pragmatic critique, paper presented to the SRHE and Open University Press Symposium on the work of Ron Barnett, 20 January.

Watson, D. (2000b) Lifelong learning and professional higher education, in T. Bourner, T. Katz and D. Watson (eds) *New Directions in Professional Higher Education.* Buckingham: SRHE and Open University Press.

Watson, D. and Taylor, R. (1998) *Lifelong Learning and the University: A Post-Dearing Agenda*. Brighton: Falmer Press.

Watts, C. (2000) Issues of professionalism in higher education, in T. Bourner, T. Katz and D. Watson (eds) *New Directions in Professional Higher Education*. Buckingham: SRHE and Open University Press.

Webb, S. and Webb, B. ([1897] 1920) *Industrial Democracy*. London: Longman.

Webster, F. (1998) The postmodern university? The loss of purpose of British universities, paper presented to the Annual Conference of the Society for Research into Higher Education (SRHE), Lancaster University, December.

Webster, F. (2000) Postmodernity and higher education: what's the point: response to Ron Barnett, *Realizing the University in an age of supercomplexity*, University of Birmingham, December 1999/January 2000.

Wiener, M. (1983) *The Decline of the Industrial Spirit*. Cambridge: Cambridge University Press.

Williams, R. (1980) *Problems in Materialism and Culture*. London: Verso.

Williamson, B. (1998) *Lifeworlds and Learning*. Leicester: NIACE.

Wilson, E. (2001) *The Contradictions of Culture: Cities, Culture, Women*. London: Sage.

Wiltshire, H. (1956) The great tradition in university adult education, *Adult Education*, 29: 88–97.

Wood, N. (1959) *Communism and British Intellectuals*. London: Gollanz.

Woodward, K. (1980) *The Myths of Information: Technology and Post-industrial Culture*. London: Routledge & Kegan Paul.

Wright, E.O. (1997) *Class Counts: Comparative Studies in Class Analysis*. Cambridge: Cambridge University Press.

Wynne, B. (1994) Scientific knowledge and the global environment, in M. Redclift and T. Benton (eds) *Social Theory and the Global Environment*. London: Routledge.

Young, I.M. (1987) Impartiality and the civic public: some implications of feminist critiques of moral and political theory, in S. Benhabib and D. Cornell (eds) *Feminism as Critique*. Minneapolis, MN: University of Minnesota Press.

Young, I.M. (2000) *Inclusion and Democracy*. New York: Oxford University Press.

Young, M. (1962) *The Rise of the Meritocracy*. Harmondworth: Penguin.

Index

The Society for Research into Higher Education

The Society for Research into Higher Education (SRHE) exists to stimulate and coordinate research into all aspects of higher education. It aims to improve the quality of higher education through the encouragement of debate and publication on issues of policy, on the organization and management of higher education institutions, and on the curriculum, teaching and learning methods.

The Society is entirely independent and receives no subsidies, although individual events often receive sponsorship from business or industry. The Society is financed through corporate and individual subscriptions and has members from many parts of the world.

Under the imprint *SRHE & Open University Press*, the Society is a specialist publisher of research, having over 80 titles in print. In addition to *SRHE News*, the Society's newsletter, the Society publishes three journals: *Studies in Higher Education* (three issues a year), *Higher Education Quarterly* and *Research into Higher Education Abstracts* (three issues a year).

The Society runs frequent conferences, consultations, seminars and other events. The annual conference in December is organized at and with a higher education institution. There are a growing number of networks which focus on particular areas of interest, including:

Access	Learning Environment
Assessment	Legal Education
Consultants	Managing Innovation
Curriculum Development	New Technology for Learning
Eastern European	Postgraduate Issues
Educational Development Research	Quantitative Studies
FE/HE	Student Development
Funding	Vocation at Qualification
Graduate Employment	

Benefits to members

Individual

- The opportunity to participate in the Society's networks

- Reduced rates for the annual conferences
- Free copies of *Research into Higher Education Abstracts*
- Reduced rates for *Studies in Higher Education*
- Reduced rates for *Higher Education Quarterly*
- Free copy of *Register of Members' Research Interests* – includes valuable reference material on research being pursued by the Society's members
- Free copy of occasional in-house publications, e.g. *The Thirtieth Anniversary Seminars Presented by the Vice-Presidents*
- Free copies of *SRHE News* which informs members of the Society's activities and provides a calendar of events, with additional material provided in regular mailings
- A 35 per cent discount on all SRHE/Open University Press books
- Access to HESA statistics for student members
- The opportunity for you to apply for the annual research grants
- Inclusion of your research in the *Register of Members' Research Interests*

Corporate

- Reduced rates for the annual conferences
- The opportunity for members of the Institution to attend SRHE's network events at reduced rates
- Free copies of *Research into Higher Education Abstracts*
- Free copies of *Studies in Higher Education*
- Free copies of *Register of Members' Research Interests* – includes valuable reference material on research being pursued by the Society's members
- Free copy of occasional in-house publications
- Free copies of *SRHE News*
- A 35 per cent discount on all SRHE/Open University Press books
- Access to HESA statistics for research for students of the Institution
- The opportunity for members of the Institution to submit applications for the Society's research grants
- The opportunity to work with the Society and co-host conferences
- The opportunity to include in the *Register of Members' Research Interests* your Institution's research into aspects of higher education

Membership details: SRHE, 76 Portland Place, London
W1B INT, UK Tel: 020 7637 2766. Fax: 020 7637 2781.
email: srhe@mailbox.ulcc.ac.uk
world wide web: http://www.srhe.ac.uk./srhe/
Catalogue: SRHE & Open University Press, Celtic Court,
22 Ballmoor, Buckingham MK18 1XW. Tel: 01280 823388.
Fax: 01280 823233. email: enquiries@openup.co.uk